On the Cover: Stills from *The Wolf House* [*Las Casa Lobo*], © 2018 courtesy KimStim

Cover design by Irene E. O'Leary, © 2020

366 Weird Movies Yearbook 2020

By 366 Weird Movies Staff * Edited by Gregory J. Smalley * Copy editing by Giles Edwards * Contributors: Giles Edwards, Jake Fredel, El Rob Hubbard, Simon Hyslop, Gregory J. Smalley, Shane Wilson

Text copyright ©2020, 366 Weird Movies, all rights reserved. All images and promotional materials used with permission, copyrights remain with the original copyright holders.

Text copyright ©2020, 366 Weird Movies, ALL RIGHTS RESERVED. DO NOT REPRINT WITHOUT PERMISSION; except that, if accompanied by a citation to the original, short excerpts may be quoted for purposes of criticism, comment, news reporting, teaching, scholarship, or research.

On the Cover: Stills from *The Wolf House [Las Casa Lobo]*, © 2018 courtesy KimStim

Cover design by Irene E. O'Leary, © 2020

Interior image credits:

The Antenna, photo credit Dark Star Pictures

Butt Boy, Sleepless Beauty, The Wave courtesy Epic Pictures

Chained for Life, courtesy Kino-Lorber

Color out of Space, an RLJE Films release, photo courtesy of Gustavo Figueiredo

Deerskin, courtesy Greenwich Entertainment

Disappearance at Clifton Hill, courtesy IFC Films

Fried Barry, Labyrinth of Cinema, Shakespeare's Shitstorm courtesy Fantasia International Film Festival

Horse Girl, I Lost My Body, I'm Thinking of Ending Things, "The Midnight Gospel," *The Platform,* "What Did Jack Do?", courtesy Netflix

In Fabric poster © A24

Jesus Shows You the Way to the Highway, © 2019 Lanzadera Films

Photograph of Miguel Llansó on set of *Jesus Shows You the Way to the Highway*, courtesy Michal Babinec

Possessor, She Dies Tomorrow poster courtesy Neon

Redoubt, Production still © 2018 Matthew Barney, courtesy Gladstone Gallery, New York and Brussels, and Sadie Coles HQ, London. Photo: Hugo Glendinning

She's Allergic to Cats, © 2019, still courtesy Michael Reich

Spindrift's Haunted West courtesy Indican Pictures

Synchronic, courtesy Well Go USA

Time Warp: The Greatest Cult Films of All Time poster courtesy Quiver Distribution

The Twentieth Century, VHYes, We Are Little Zombies courtesy Oscilloscope Laboratories

Welcome to the Circle courtesy Artsploitation Pictures

Why Don't You Just Die?, © 2018 Arrow Video

The Wolf House, © 2018, images courtesy KimStim

All images belong to their original copyright holders.

INTRODUCTION TO THE 2020 EDITION

Ah, 2020! Friend to no man (or woman). You brought us chaos, plagues, protestors in the streets, and toilet paper shortages. You closed movie theaters and canceled film festivals. You forced Hollywood to postpone all of its summer blockbusters and did what Thanos could not: you killed off the entire Marvel Cinematic Universe (for a year, at least).

But you could not kill weird movies, as this volume attests. 2020 still brought us a fairy tale about a South American Aryan cult refugee who adopts piglets, a gonzo flick about a hunchbacked dwarf CIA agent sucked into an alternate history version of Facebook, and so much more. Even if we had to watch the majority of it online, the weirdness poured in, beamed directly to our quarantined home TV screens.

If you're into "weird" movies—the umbrella term we coined to cover everything from Surrealist classics like *Discreet Charm of the Bourgeoisie* to midnight movies like *Rocky Horror Picture Show* to oddities like Ed Wood's 1953 pro-transvestite documentary *Glen or Glenda?*—then you already know about 366weirdmovies.com, the world's most complete source of information about weird movies. If not, we hope you'll find you're in for a treat, and discover some... *unusual* films.

We originally started 366 Weird Movies to determine the 366 Weirdest Movies ever made (that's one for every day of the year, with a spare for leap years). With that goal completed (and available for you to peruse at the back of this volume), we've continued to focus on new releases, presenting you with what we believe to be the 10 weirdest movies of the year, along with exclusive interviews, listings of the year's other strange cinema competitors, newly discovered re-releases, heads-ups on odd television shows, our film festival diary (altered this year by Covid-19), an extensive supplementary catalog of films we couldn't get to, and an availability grid. That's a lot of movie info packed into just over 100 pages.

For Yearbook purposes, our calendar year runs from November to November, so that we can get this out in early December, in time for the Christmas buying season. So, be sure to buy an extra one to gift to that weirdo friend with the "Un Chien Andalou" eyeball-slitting t-shirt! (We mean it; we need the beer money.)

Also new in 2020: you can now join us for curated movie watching experiences (well, bull session movie watching experiences, really) through our bi-monthly Weird Watch Parties. You might see anything from *Willy Wonka and the Chocolate Factory* to *The Texas Chainsaw Massacre 2*, depending on *your* vote. Check 366weirdmovies.com for details.

And, we should also mention that we are working behind the scenes on a print reference version of the entire 366 Weird Movies canon. The text of that volume should be completed in 2021, though that doesn't mean you'll see it in print immediately. But the more copies of this volume that you buy for your oddball friends, the more sales figures we'll have to show potential publishers when we shop the project. Just another reason to buy a copy of this book for everyone on your dorm room floor.

And now, our program begins! Enjoy the oddness as we count down our top 10 weird movies of 2020. The only good things that happened this year.—*Gregory J. Smalley, editor-in-chief*

THE 10 BEST WEIRD MOVIES OF 2020

1. *The Wolf House [La casa lobo]*

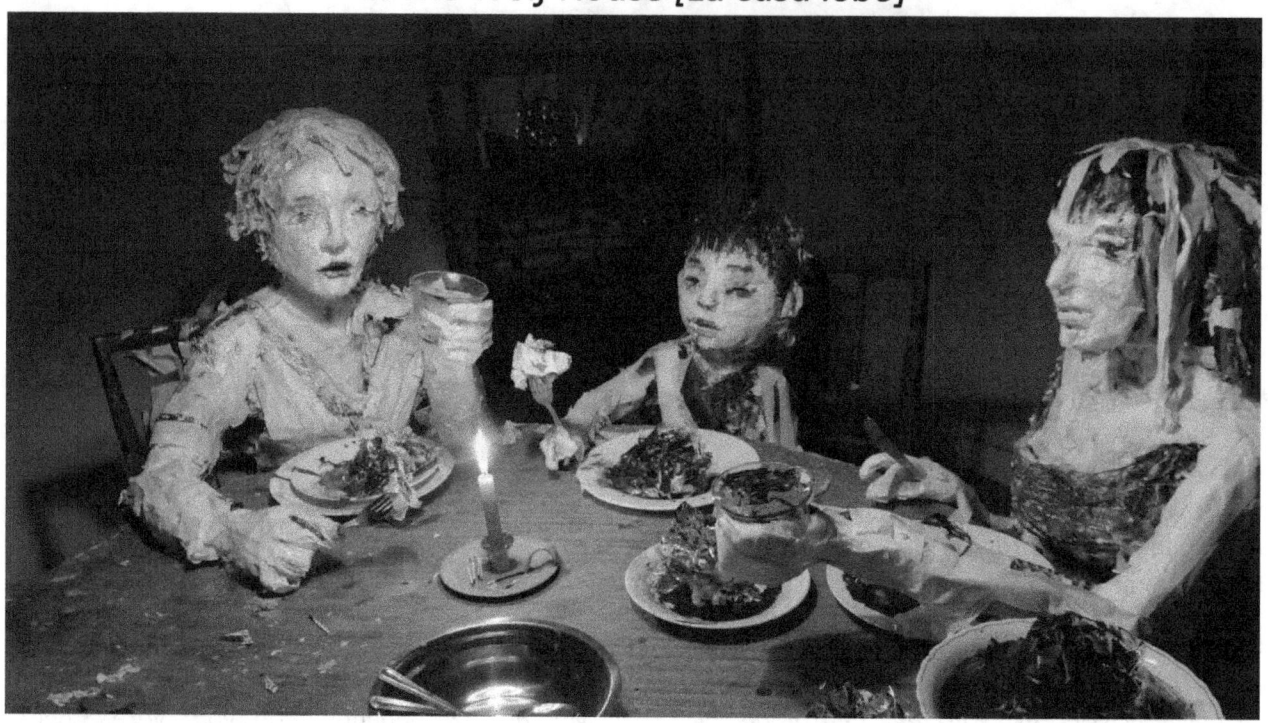

DIRECTED BY: Joaquín Cociña, Cristóbal León

FEATURING: Voices of Amalia Kassai, Rainer Krause

PLOT: Maria flees her community to avoid punishment and finds an abandoned house; fearing the wolf outside, she sequesters herself with two pigs which she raises as her children.

COMMENTS: Everyone knows that idle hands are the Devil's workshop; Joaquín Cociña's and Cristóbal León's are, on the other hand, a two-man workshop revealing the Devil's evil. Stop-motion is undoubtedly the most time-consuming filmmaking method; but sometimes, as in *The Wolf House*, it is the most appropriate. Lacking both real-time film's quick capture of reality and the infinite malleability of "pure" animation's ink and lines, stop-motion is a demanding mistress, but one that allows for the uncanniest uncanny valleys and the most "other" other-worldliness. Cociña and León hand-assemble, hand-craft, and hand-paint a dark fairy tale amalgam that itself masks a far darker period in history.

After World War II, a number of prominent German officials fled Europe and cropped up in various points South American. One of those places was the "Colonia Dignidad," a religious cult compound in Chile. For years, tales of hardship and child abuse drifted through its fortified walls, and the framing of *The Wolf House* is taken from this period. Presented as a counter-propaganda piece to dispel rumors of a "horrible secret" about this truly "isolated and pure" colony of agrarians, *The Wolf House* informs the viewer that the film they are about to see was found in the society's vaults (lovingly "restored" by none other than Cociña and León). The story it tells, in its morphing and cryptic way, concerns a young woman fleeing a harsh punishment meted out by her village's elders, but eventually learning that the parents know best.

The framing "documentary" is creepily reassuring, easing tonally into the movie proper. *The Wolf House* harnesses a variety of stop-motion techniques. Beyond the simplest form (move figure, shoot camera), there's also "live-painting" animation. A young woman, Maria, seeks shelter in an abandoned house. Upon entering, the walls form in front of the camera, and decorations—bookshelves, clocks, framed pictures—appear and move toward their designated positions as Maria looks around. A woman's figure eventually appears in a doorway (or mirror?) before branching from the walls in the form of a papier mâché figurine, who eventually finds two pigs—which, through a game she narrates, eventually morph into human children.

The Wolf House is only seventy-five minutes, about ten of which are credits, with ten more being the "documentary" bookends. But it contains countless chilling allusions. As a paneled window is painted on the wall, it ever so briefly appears as a swastika before the rest of the lines are filled in. There's a mystical honey that causes children who consume it to change from mestizos into blonde Teutonic ideals (the surrounding documentary advertises the German commune's prized honey). Maria's fairy tale within the fairy tale concerns animals fleeing into the ground to escape "the wolf", and a magical tree thanking her for leading them there; in reality, this alludes to the mass graves on the Colonia Dignidad's grounds.

The sinister storytelling framework, sociopolitical overtones, and the fact that you watch its settings and inhabitants literally being built up and broken down right before your eyes as its story unfolds, all make *The Wolf House* a worthy candidate for the weirdest movie of 2020. With stop-motion, Cociña and León find that perfect abutment between reality and nightmare; with *The Wolf House*, they find the perfect abutment between parable and horror.—Giles Edwards

2. *Jesus Shows You the Way to the Highway*

DIRECTED BY: Miguel Llansó

FEATURING: Daniel Tadesse, Agustín Mateo, Gerda-Annette Allikas, Guillermo Llansó

PLOT: Seriously? I'm going to pinch this straight from the IMDb description, because I've got nothing. "CIA Agents Palmer and Gagano are tasked with the mission of destroying a computer virus called 'Soviet Union.' They enter the system using VR but the mission turns into a trap."

COMMENTS: Merriam-Webster defines "gonzo" as, "outlandishly unconventional, outrageous, or extreme"; and so it is with *Jesus Shows You the Way to the Highway*. Stop-motion VR missions to thwart a computer virus called "Soviet Union," a pizza restaurant of your dreams, a second (and third?) coming of the messiah, and a transvestite super-agent are all here. What more could you want? (Don't worry: there is much, much more.)

I'm generally the "king of caveats", but here it goes: you haven't ever seen a movie like this one. Miguel Llansó, an affable Madrid-born professor, has assembled a casserole of '80s-'90s nostalgia, '80s-'90s satire, cyber-dystopia, messianic lampoons, kung-fu fighting, Stalin/Redford/Pryor avatars, giant death-ray bugs, and a "PsychoBook" program (not to be confused at all with a more famous "Book" social media site), all under a banner title that is both long-winded and apt: by the end of the movie, Jesus shows you the way to the highway.

Ah, but what happens before that gratifying finale? Strapping on their VR visors and headphones, intrepid CIA agents D.T. Gagano (Daniel Tadesse) and Palmer Eldritch (Agustín Mateo) enter PsychoBook, an AI/VR intelligence network being held hostage by a computer virus that manifests as a Nike-shoe-clad avatar in a Stalin mask. It wants to make a deal with the agents to start selling "the Substance," a green-goo byproduct of the environment (don't worry, Eldritch stands firm: "I don't make deals with computer viruses!") Meanwhile, Gegano wants to quit the CIA and help his BBW German sweetie Malin start a kickboxing academy. Lurking in the background is the President of Ethiopia (Solomon Tashe), dressed up as the superhero-villain "Batfro". Something goes wrong, and Gegano gets trapped in PsychoBook. Will Jesus' help be enough to allow his escape?

Now you can see what I'm working with here. And that's just one layer of what's going on. Stylistically, it's about as madcap as you can get. The stop-motion forays into PsychoBook, when the agents hunt Stalin, are the stuff of comic nightmares (and apparently took up most of the shooting days). As for the other aesthetic choices, suffice to say it's clear that Llansó grew up in the '80s, as beautiful old computers appear left, right, and center, and heavily influenced the mind-blowing/seizure-inducing credit sequences.

Any fan of the clunky sci-fi joking of "Garth Marenghi's Darkplace" will want to catch this. Anyone wanting to see the Matrix done with no money and maximum humor will want to catch this. Anyone who wants to check out a contender for 2020's weirdest release will want to catch this. Turn on, tune in, and just say, "Fuck you, Stalin!"

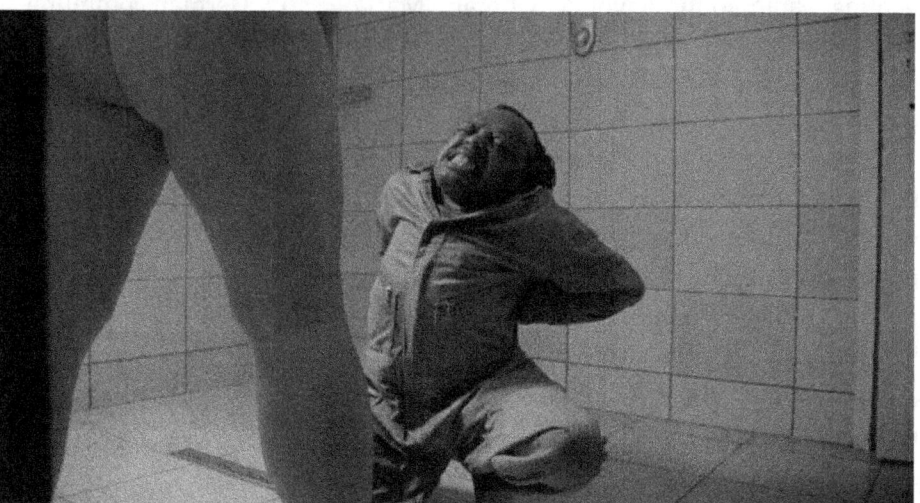

Those who have seen the light will have already purchased Arrow's "2-disc Limited Edition" Blu-ray, which not only has the full complement of extras for the main feature, but also an entire extra movie: Llansó's directorial debut, *Crumbs*. Set in a post-apocalyptic Ethiopia, *Crumbs* explores consumer culture, post-consumer culture, and the fate of mankind by means of a hero's quest, cast-off-toys-cum-relics, and Santa Clause in a bowling alley ball-return.

Meanwhile, back on the main disc, *Jesus Shows You the Way to the Highway* is explained in commentary by two academics, explained in interview by the director, explained in a video essay by *another* academic, and given some context with two of Llansó's early short films. Of the big mixed-bag of goodies, "From Tallinn With Love" is the fastest way to understand just what is going on in *JSYTWTTH*, as Will Webb thoroughly—but succinctly—dissects everything from PsychoBook to cinematic style. Saints be praised, the good people at Arrow have done it again.—Giles Edwards

Miguel Llansó shows you the way

We talked to Miguel Llansó after a screening of *Jesus Shows You the Way to the Highway* at the Fantasia Film Festival in 2019. Audio of the entire interview can be heard on our YouTube channel (www.youtube.com/user/366weirdmovies/); a lightly edited transcript appears below.

366: We seek the world and seek the history of film for the best weird movies, and I hope you take it as a compliment that I was very impressed with your film in the context of what I'm looking for when I come to this festival.

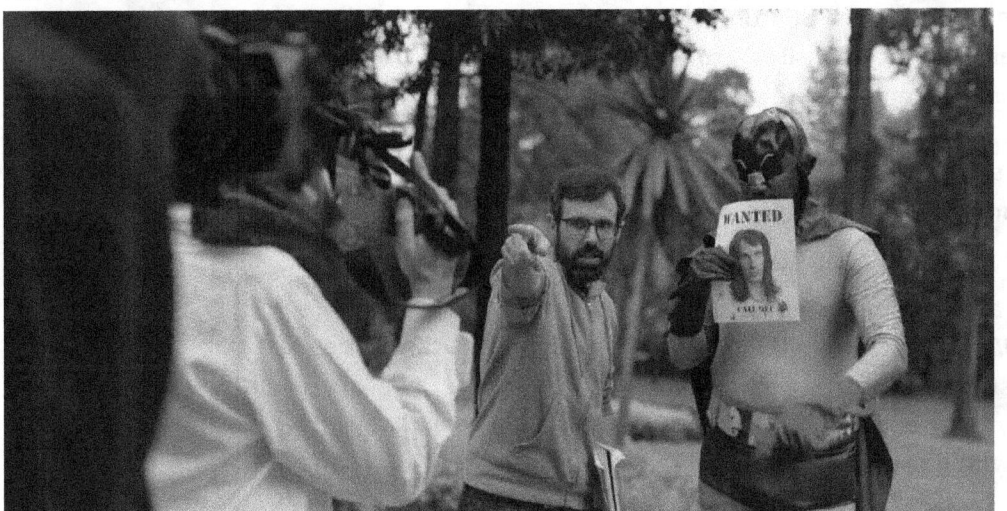

Miguel Llansó on set of" Jesus Shows You the Way to the Highway," photo courtesy Michal Babinec

ML: Thank you!

366: You are primarily a professor? What is it you teach?

ML: Yeah. I teach screenwriting and directing to poor students.

366: So, still keeping in touch with film with your day job. Now, I know you previously did a feature-length film, *Crumbs*, with the same actor in the lead as *JSYTWTTH*. Would you care to explain a little about the inception of the "Jesus" project?

ML: Basically the film is like a "lasagna", right? So I cannot find a point of inception, but more like a collection of ideas. So it's basically me reflecting on: where is globalization going? If you've seen the highest spheres of power, I can mention of course Donald Trump, but also this guy in Saudi Arabia, the king, who is cutting people in pieces, or Putin, riding the horse half-naked—a very powerful gay image, but at the same time very scary—so I discovered that I was making a social drama. [laughs] But this is fear of power, how it's becoming more and more like a comic, like Hitler, eccentric, so we don't understand very much what's going on. I think this fear of power is kind of like managing the masses in a very strong way through a social network.

There is something that clicks in our brain when these people talk, or the way it's managed through social media, through newspapers and everything, that put us in a very strange mode of mass control. That's the film's philosophical reflection, but actually then in this world of comics, of villains, of these very bad, mocking scenarios.

366: You mentioned villains. I suppose the villains in the Jesus piece would be the "Stalin" avatar—"Soviet Union" is his character name. And "Batfro" who seems one of those demagogue eccentric types. He's the president of Ethiopia in the film.

ML: To pick on "the African dictator."

366: Yes, and I think you handled that well, particularly with the likes of Idi Amin and more contemporary groups who I will very politely describe as "eccentric figures" who have run African countries.

ML: I love *Idi Amin Dada*--I love him! I mean, no, not literally; but as a character. I don't know if you've seen that movie, but it was super funny. But at the same time...

366: Yeah, if he had not been in charge and killing people, it would have been a great public personality, but...

ML: But yeah, he was throwing people to crocodiles.

366: So a lot of the characters are based on, if not real people, then real "composites" of people. There's the CIA element... There's one character in particular, I wasn't sure who he was: "Mr. Sophistication" shows up as an Italian power-broker; is that anything you perhaps have some words on?

ML: Yes, the inspiration comes from the Cassavetes film *The Killing of a Chinese Bookie*. There is a "Mr. Sophistication" in that film. He is never in power, he's second in line, kind of a mafia guy. The actor who played the role[1] was a very interesting guy, he was fighting with the mujahedeen in the '70s against the Soviet Union. He got caught and put in a Soviet concentration camp, and the captain there said, "You know, when you beat me in chess, I will liberate you... I will set you free." The actor explained, "For fucking three years I was playing chess and I never won a single game."

So finally there was the end of that war and he got released and came back to Italy. Then he starts some business in Africa... a very interesting guy. He started taking people in a super big truck--a Russian truck--on adventure trips in Africa, but he said nothing was happening, there was no adventure, so he started creating the adventures: suddenly the truck... got stuck and he's like, "Oh no!", and made the tourists push the truck. And that act was fake, but when [the tourists] come back home, they could brag, "Yeah, you know, and the truck got stuck! And we all had to push it out!"

So it's this type of character who I adapted a little bit of the screen-play to his own kind of slow way of understanding things... a very "acid" guy, but very smart at the same time.

366: You mentioned at the question-and-answer session after the opening screening that this was made with, and stars, friends of yours. In particular, I'm curious as to how you came to know this Italian who was in a gulag and then did bogus safari adventures.

ML: I went to the Italian club in Addis Ababa in Ethiopia, "Club Juventus". There are a lot of incredible elements there. People who don't belong to Italy any more, some of them born in Ethiopia. So they meet in a club and they play cards and... [laughs] I could choose *him*, or I could choose *whoever*, because the collection is astonishing.

366: What brought you to Ethiopia in the first place? You were born in Madrid, Spain, and obviously that's not far, but Ethiopia isn't a typical place to move to.

ML: I was doing nothing in Spain, it was a crisis. The Ethiopians gave me a job. It's the opposite now... I started working film in Spain, but I did a lot of work, film jobs, in Ethiopia, and I met a lot of people...

366: Another thing that was obviously an inspiration to you--I'm a little younger than you, but of a certain age that I recognized all those

---

[1] Carlo Pironti.

beautiful computers that sprang up throughout the movie. I imagine you've had a life-long interest in that kind of technology, if you'd care to elaborate that imagery, along with the "Cold War" throw-back feel to the film.

ML: My first computer was a Spectrum ZX3. It was a computer you had to insert a tape, and then you clicked "play", and then it loads forever, like five minutes you're waiting. And then it normally crashes, and you're like "Fuck! No!" It's like BRRRNGGG, and then...

So yeah. It was green screen, then I moved to a Spectrum Sinclair that was color. The Russians, they had their own kind of computers. For the film it was very interesting: we went to a museum of computers in Estonia and they had a lot of Soviet computers. For the film we chose the first Apple computers. For me these computers of the '90s, it was the seed of the capacity, that was developed later...

366: "PsychoBook"?

ML: Yeah, "PsychoBook"... Analysis of human behavior, right? It's a very powerful tool for mass control. You know what the people do, know what the people think. Because what the people do and what the people think is very different. So these computers now are able to analyze millions of data points, millions of things that are happening.

366: I feel compelled to ask: do you have a "Facebook" account?

ML: I do, I have a Facebook. Fuck. Yeah, I'm not paranoid--I'm not saying that nobody spies on me. Me, in particular. Maybe the Russians, since I live in Estonia. But it's more that I like to analyze the trend. Some people understand, criticism confused with paranoia. "They're spying on me!" They're not spying on *you*, they're spying on *everyone*.

They aspire to get certain patterns, to get certain "curves of behavior", so they can click our "mass mode"... like the iPhones, they have different "modes", like "Airplane Mode", so our brains, I think, they work in "modes." So you can click pornographic mode, and we all have our pornographic modes, our fame mode, our intellectual mode. So it depends on what you click, for instance these machines are to analyze our modes. They know that after you read *The New York Times*, you're going to go to "YouPorn"; and you can be reading super-interesting international news, but then you're needing your YouPorn, and these machines know it.

366: Speaking of the news cycle, sometime in the past week, I think it was, Elon Musk (of Tesla) unveiled plans, or a promise, of a device that would allow one to control one's devices by thought. The sensors are outside the brain, but it's kept up close. But he's obviously going for that next step to "make things easier" for everybody.

ML: I think we're living in a world that in fifty years we're not going to recognize, because now we produce real objects, but with augmented reality--once we start interfering with our own biology, not like a "cyborg", but working with DNA--we're going to transform the world, absolutely.

366: I guess that leads me to the question, are you optimistic about where things are going?

ML: Nooo. I'm very skeptical. Especially because all this power is in the hands of capitalism, which is a virus. Everything is profit and power. You see that people want to make films, to sell the films. Just power! They want to be famous. You see in Madrid, in the main street, there no cinemas any more. There are H&Ms...

The industry of cinema, and it's the same. Netflix... everything is a monopoly, a strong monopoly. So the power is working within that

monopoly, and of course there's a counterbalance, but I'm not so optimistic.

366: To close out the interview, can you recommend a hometown restaurant you enjoy? Where you live in Ethiopia, or where you come from, Madrid, a restaurant you think that those in that area might want to check out.

ML: In Ethiopia, I think you should go to the Juventus Italian club, even though it's not Ethiopian. In Estonia, man, I think it's difficult; there's a lot of things, but there's no Estonian cuisine. And I don't know, I'm from Spain, so it's really... there's really good food in Madrid.

366: Thank you very much for your time, it was fascinating to chat with you.

ML: Thank you!

3. *Deerskin* [*Le daim*]

DIRECTED BY: Quentin Dupieux

FEATURING: Jean Dujardin, Adèle Haenel

PLOT: A middle-aged man becomes obsessed with his new deerskin jacket.

COMMENTS: "Sorry, but isn't your movie weird?"

One suspects Quentin Dupieux lifted that line verbatim from his own life experiences for this screenplay. It's one of many self-references in *Deerskin*, whose main character is a delusional fraud[2] posing as an independent filmmaker while undergoing a midlife crisis.

Never fear, *Deerskin*—a movie about a man, a leather jacket, and the destructive pledge that binds the two together—is indeed a weird movie. But considering the manic maximalism of Dupieux's last major outing—2014's *Reality*, which seemed like it had about fifteen interweaving subplots in a dreams-inside-of-dreams structure—*Deerskin* is relatively restrained, focused on only two major characters and a single absurd conceit. It's almost Buñuelian. Indeed, aside from the odd opening (which will be explained later) and a scene of Jean Dujardin flushing his corduroy jacket down a public toilet, nothing beyond the moderately quirky occurs in the film's first fifteen minutes. Dujardin's character is clearly not all there, and occasional horror movie violin strikes suggest looming disaster, but it's not until his deerskin jacket starts talking back to him that Dupieux leans into the scenario's inherent eccentricity. The idea that we see the film from Dujardin's insane perspective "explains" his strange activities for the rest of the movie, and perhaps makes it more palatable for general audiences not accustomed to the dream-logic universes Dupieux typically creates.

Dupieux likely slows down his typical craziness in order to take advantage of Dujardin's presence. The stately actor is *Deerskin*'s biggest asset, and the movie is almost Dupieux's take on a character study. We suspect that the idea of an abstract, arty study of a man in the midst of an existential crisis is what attracted the French star to the project. Ruggedly handsome, if growing a bit paunchy, with a distinguished touch of grey in his beard, Dujardin creates a character who is deeply insecure and ridiculous—because he's both vain and a bit dim. Unmoored and wandering, fleeing a relationship for reasons unstated, Dujardin gives his withered self-confidence a coat of luster with the deerskin jacket, which he believes gives him a "killer style" that everyone envies and talks about. But, in his

---

[2] Neither I nor, I believe, Quentin Dupieux believe that Quentin Dupieux is a delusional fraud—the

metaphor instead plays out like a meta-joke at the expense of artistic self-doubt.

mind, it's not enough that he own the world's *coolest* jacket—wouldn't it be better if he owned the world's *only* jacket?

The jacket concurs.

I'm not sure if *Deerskin*'s subdued style really fits Dupieux's talents. He's always been an over-the-top auteur with a unique voice, and his lack of restraint and focus has always been a key part of that voice. I wonder whether maturity and self-reflection fits him any better than Dujardin's too-tight jacket fits his character. Although *Deerskin* may be a bit easier for the neophyte to buy into than Dupieux's previous larks, I'd still recommend the novice start off by jumping into the deep end with the slasher spoof *Rubber*, where the director sets out his bold manifesto of "no reason." You can circle back to *Deerskin* later and see if you think the director is aging gracefully. I wouldn't object if he went through a truly wild midlife crisis of his own to remind him of his youth.

Deerskin is a victim of 2020's pandemic, unable to receive even the usual limited release in theaters. Distributor Greenwich Entertainment released it online, and it hit home video in late June.—Gregory J. Smalley

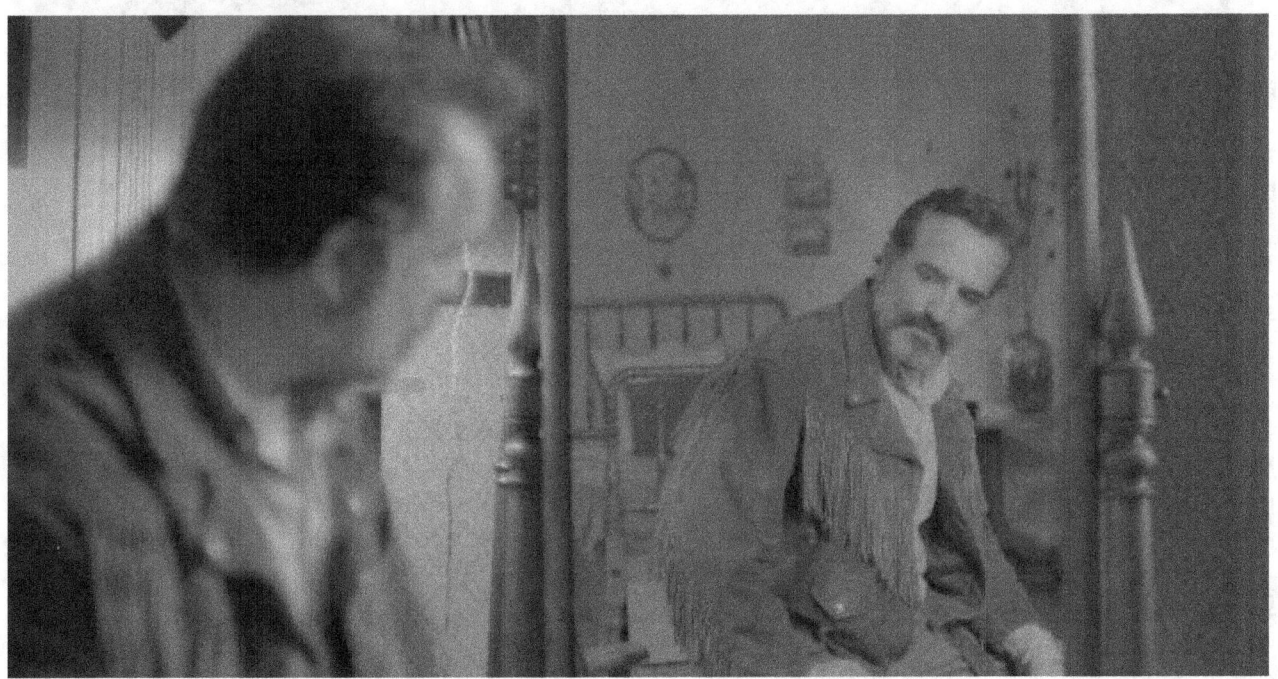

4. I'm Thinking of Ending Things

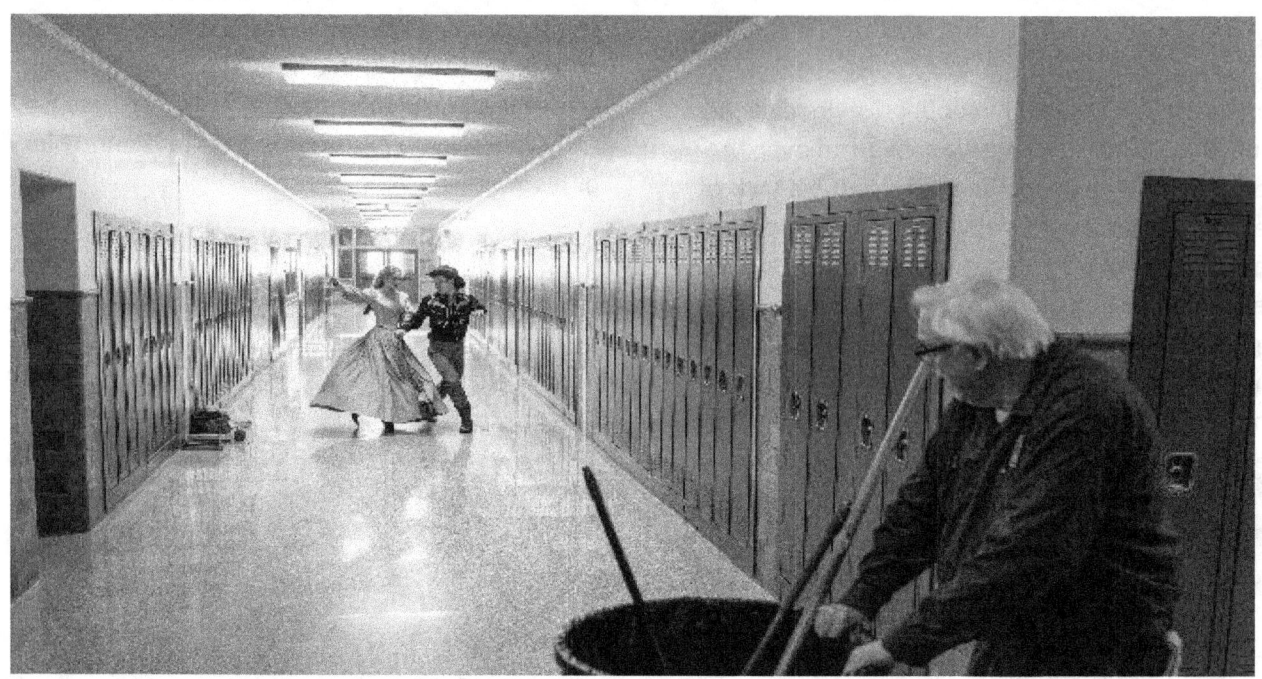

Guy Boyd as Janitor in "I'm Thinking of Ending Things." Cr. Mary Cybulski/NETFLIX © 2020

DIRECTED BY: Charlie Kaufman

FEATURING: Jessie Buckley, Jesse Plemons, Toni Collette, David Thewlis, Guy Boyd

PLOT: A young woman goes on a trip to meet her new boyfriend's parents at their farmhouse on a night when a blizzard is brewing.

COMMENTS: The first inkling that something is not quite right in *I'm Thinking of Ending Things* comes when the young woman (who is first introduced as "Lucy," although it turns out that may not be her real name) thinks to herself, "I'm thinking of ending things." "Huh?" says Jake (that is his real name), from the driver's seat. Can he hear her thoughts? She denies speaking. "Weird," says Jake. "Yeah," she answers.

Things will get weirder. By the time the pig shows up at Jake's old high school, it becomes apparent that this maze of awkward interactions, faulty memories, and uncertain identities may just be Charlie Kaufman's most surreal film. At first, the woman is unsure why she wants to break up with Jake. Her backstory doesn't add up. And she's getting a *lot* of phone calls, which she's not answering. When the couple arrive to meet Jake's parents at their remote farmhouse, things get stranger. As it turns out, Jake's parents would creep out Henry Spencer's in-laws. Dinner is uncomfortable, full of small talk that often sounds like hidden accusations, and—once more—competing, contradictory backstories. Nothing explicitly supernatural or menacing happens, but the creaky farmhouse emanates a horror movie vibe, intensified by Jake's passive-aggressive insistence that his girlfriend stay out of the basement. Then, Jake's parents age precipitously… Meanwhile, Lucy—or whatever her name is—anxiously suggests that Jake take her home before the coming blizzard snows them in and traps her there.

Charlie Kaufman's latest mind-massager is another intensely subjective and literate tour of the lonely corridors of the mind, where nothing is as it seems. It's one of his strangest offerings—particularly when it reaches an irrational finale that departs from the source novel—but perhaps what distinguishes it the most is the exceptional ensemble acting, best seen in the four-way sparring at the dinner table. Their expressions are priceless: Collette smiling to herself at private jokes only she can hear, Thewlis aggressively incredulous at the idea that a landscape could appear sad, Plemons understandably embarrassed by his parent's odd behavior, and trying to coax his girlfriend into revealing the correct details about how they met. We expect accomplished performances from those three celebrated actors, but relative newcomer Jessie Buckley is a revelation. She mutates throughout the film, portraying everything from a nervous recalcitrant girlfriend to an angry feminist to an apparent victim of very early-onset Alzheimer's. She even slips into a Pauline Kael impression. Remarkable.

As with all the best trips, it's the journey that's most memorable, not the destination. There is a reveal at the end, but the twist, while satisfying, is hardly the point. Each scene is structured as an individually confounding moment: on the long ride there and back, Jake and his girlfriend discuss everything from the human experience of time, bad movies as viruses and musical theater (familiarity with "Oklahoma!" will enrich your experience), with citations to Wordsworth, David Foster Wallace, Guy Debord along the way. Jake says he like road trips because "it's good to remind yourself that the world's larger than the inside of your own head"—but does the movie believe this thesis? As they travel, the couple learn less about each other, and more about the slipperiness of human memory, fantasy, and identity. It's Kaufman's favorite theme: the loneliness of our inherent interiority. The paradox is that our inescapable subjectivity is the one thing we all share and bond over.

I'm Thinking of Ending Things was released exclusively on Netflix and remains there exclusively, for the time being.—Gregory J. Smalley

5. *The Twentieth Century*

DIRECTED BY: Matthew Rankin

FEATURING: Dan Beirne, Sarianne Cormier, Seán Cullen, Louis Negin

PLOT: William Lyon Mackenzie King modestly rises to the plateau of Canadian supremacy to become Prime Minister.

COMMENTS: During my first visit to Montreal's Fantasia Film Festival in 2017, I made the acquaintance of several Canadian college students. I had the opportunity to talk politics with one of them—a hot topic at the time. One young man, in particular, was full of passion and ideals, like many college students. But he was very Canadian about it. No fan of Trudeau ("too centrist"), he was also skeptical of the recently elected French president Emmanuel Macron. Despite the fervor I knew burned within him, the most damning criticism of the French prez he dared speak was: "too centrist." He limited his body language to a slightly uncomfortable sidelong glance.

Canada's subdued idealism is captured flawlessly in Rankin's directorial feature debut, *The Twentieth Century*. Structured as a 1940s melodrama and styled as a 1920s Expressionist nightmare, its tone fits squarely (and appropriately) in the realm of a 1930s screwball comedy of manners. Our hero (though he would be loath to designate himself so loftily) is the ever well-intentioned and deferential William Lyon Mackenzie King (Dan Beirne, reminiscent of also-Canadian comedian Martin Short). Ages ago, King's mother had a vision of her son becoming Prime Minister, and though his path to success is long and trying—nigh thwarted at times by a sinister doctor, an embarrassing shoe fetish, and a fascistic Governor General—King ultimately defeats the love-cult Quebecois separatist candidate to become the most foremost (foremostest?) among Canadian equals.

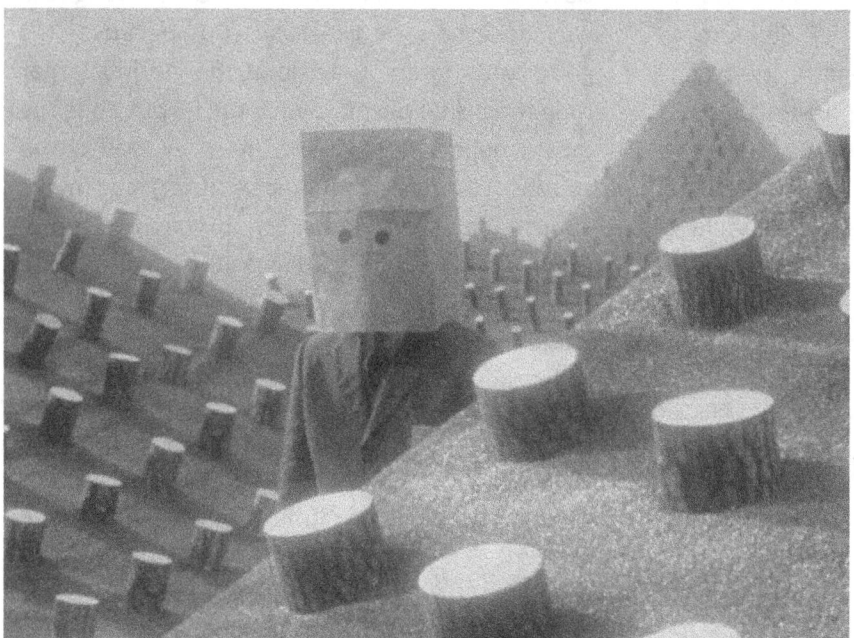

As a comedy, *The Twentieth Century* is pure gold. I ultimately gave up writing down amusing quotes as Rankin & Co. continued to hammer home just how incredibly quaint, civil, and bizarre they and their fellow citizens were and continue to be. (One recurring mantra stands out that sums up the Canadian experience: "...as certain as a winter's day in springtime.") All the sets and special effects are Maddin-esque, to the point that I think the Guy's gone mainstream (in Canada, anyway). The villains are all cartoonishly evil, the heroes are all cartoonishly mild-mannered, and Winnipeg is dismissed as the home of "heroin, bare naked ladies, and reasonably-priced furniture".

Quite a lot of weird goings-on do go on (ejaculating cactus metaphor, blind-folded-ice-floe marriage ceremony, and PM Bert Harper impaled by narwhal, among them). But ultimately it feels like the film is trying too hard, drawing too much attention to the oddities instead of letting them play on the fringes. At the heart of my qualms are the handful of cross-gender casting choices. Only two actually work, yet like other "weird" choices made, they're made without considering their stylistic or narrative merit. The poster crows, "...men play women and women play men!" So what? *The Twentieth Century* succeeds brilliantly in being funny, however, and that's something to actually crow aboot.

Gregory J. Smalley adds: I think we can now officially say that Guy Maddin isn't an auteur; he's a genre. *The Twentieth Century* proves that Guy Maddin movies need not be made by Guy Maddin[3]. Rankin isn't even trying to hide Guy's influence; as a humble and patriotic Canadian, he's embracing his national heritage. But it works, totally. If you're a director making a film noir, you include shadowy lighting, a femme fatale, and a hard-drinking gumshoe. If you're a director making a Guy Maddin movie, you include Expressionist landscapes, a timid hero plagued by sexual fetishes, and Louis Negin in drag.

The Twentieth Century also has an ejaculating cactus. That should automatically make it a candidate as one of the weirdest films of the

---

[3] John Paizs' *Crime Wave* (1985) proved this maxim was true even before there were Guy Maddin movies to emulate.

year. We don't have to overthink this kind of thing.

I know little about William Lyon Mackenzie King, Canada's three-time Prime Minister and FDR contemporary, but I think this biopic may not be completely accurate. Per Wikipedia, King secretly believed in spiritualism and used a medium to speak to his dead mother, historical trivia that may illuminate Negin's role in the film. On the other hand, I highly doubt that King was a proud champion seal-clubber. In America, when we want to make a comedy about a revered leader, we cast Abe Lincoln as a vampire hunter—a take so ridiculous that it can't be possibly seen as impolite or belittling. Canadians, on the other hand, happily depict a national hero as a schmo consumed by repressed ambition and an obsession with boot-sniffing. Superficially polite, actually subversive; that's Canada for ya.

The Twentieth Century debuted in virtual theaters (and possibly a few live venues) on November 20, just beating our 2020 deadline. It may or may not be widely available on home video or streaming options by the time you read this; if not, keep an eye out for it in 2021.— Gregory J. Smalley

6. *VHYEs*

DIRECTED BY: Jack Henry Robbins

FEATURING: Mason McNulty, Christian Drerup, Jake Head, Rahm Braslaw

PLOT: We see the results when 12-year-old Ralph tapes late night 1987 cable television shows, and his own adolescent antics, over his parent's old wedding tape.

COMMENTS: *VHYes* had me at the moment when, after brushing in some happy snowcaps for the mountains she's been crafting, the somnolently friendly Bob Ross-style PBS painting instructor announces "now, let's get back to the spaceship." She's just one of the demented characters you meet as young Ralph experiments in preserving his short attention span channel-surfing for posterity: a kindly cowboy full of inappropriate advice; a couple of shopping-channel salesfolk who banter passive-aggressively; an "Antiques Roadshow"-inspired host who appraises some *unusual* artifacts; the shy hostess of a punk rock public access show (and her supportive parents); and a prescient cultural philosopher who describes the phenomenon of "tape narcissism" and warns that "one day the world will exist only to be filmed." Naturally, there are also a slew of vintage commercial and infomercial parodies. This smorgasbord of ersatz crapola plays like a found footage 1980s version of *The Groove Tube*, except that it periodically returns to check in on the adventures of Ralph, his best friend Josh, and his mom and dad. Some bits are silly and overdone (there's a bit more splattered blood than you'd normally see in an alarm company commercial). Others are subtle and absurd. The big finale is reminiscent of the kind of short that might play on "Adult Swim" post-midnight: Ralph finds himself surreally transported into a jumbled reality where the layers of the tape all bleed together.

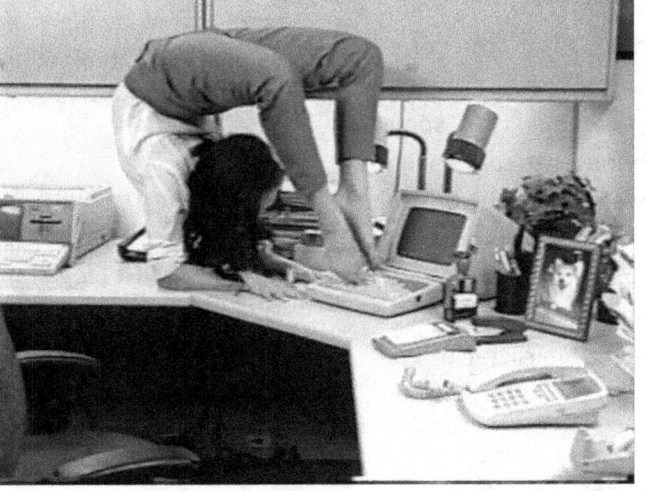

VHYes is a breezy compendium of skewed nostalgia, sometimes hilarious, sometimes weird, and, unexpectedly, sometimes touching. The most substantial complaint to raise against it, in fact, is that it's too short. There must have been plenty of unused tape, and I would have loved to see even more backstory on young Ralph. His scenes are more than just the gimmick that explains the existence of the artifact we're watching; his story of coping with childhood fears and disappointments offer a meaningful counterbalance to the goofy comedy sketches, like the commercial for an ointment that grants cubicle workers "freakish flexibility." On the other hand, maybe it's best to consider *VHYes*' zippy 70-minute runtime an asset rather than a liability. It's a "little" film, but in the best sense: short, punchy, homemade, thoughtful in its unassuming way, and—like the ongoing saga of *Hot Winter*, an ecologically-aware 80s porno with the lesbian orgies edited out—innocent at its heart.

VHYes was shot entirely on vintage VHS and Betacam cameras. The bits with the spooky painter (starring Kerry Kenney, of "Reno 911" fame) are spliced in from Robbins' 2017 Sundance short "Painting with Joan"; the edited porno scenes from "Hot Winter" were also a standalone short. Director Jack Henry Robbins is the son of Tim Robbins and Susan Sarandon, who executive produced and have eye-blink cameos. *VHYes* was released in simpler, more innocent times: January, 2020.—Gregory J. Smalley

7. *Chained for Life*

DIRECTED BY: Aaron Schimberg

FEATURING: Jess Weixler, Adam Pearson, Stephen Plunkett, Charlie Korsmo

PLOT: While starring in a low budget period horror film, Mabel makes the acquaintance of some affable "freaks" brought on set for authenticity; while the main cast and crew's away, the freaks pass the time making their own movie vignettes.

COMMENTS: I found something very odd about my viewing experience of *Chained for Life*, and it wasn't the subject matter. After the brief introduction by the soft-spoken director at a live screening, I was feeling nervous, for some reason. Having thought about it—and having now seen the movie—it was the wider critical interpretation that I'd read beforehand that made me apprehensive, and afterwards made me confused. I'll talk about what other critics saw later; me, I saw a charming, character-driven comedy.

When a busload of disabled people show up at the shoot for a period horror film, there is a hiccup of apprehension on the part of the "normals" already present. The leading lady, Mabel (Jess Weixler), plays the movie's movie's leading lady, a woman blinded by some unexplained accident who is promised to be cured through radical surgery. However, *Chained for Life* focuses primarily on the actors and crew involved, in particular on the blossoming friendship between the physically self-conscious Mabel and the physically self-accepting Rosenthal (Adam Pearson). While primary filming progresses by day, the "freaks" lodge in the hospital by night, eventually deciding to play around with filmmaking themselves. One twist leads to a cute reveal, but the story is pretty simple.

That's not to say it isn't well done. By using the pretentious "art-house" nonsense being filmed by a hyper-Herzog stand-in (billed only as "Herr Director") as a counterpoint to the day-to-day scenes of people interacting with people, Aaron Schimberg crumples up any fear of "the Other" by focusing on the lighter side of the banality everyone faces. There are also moments of considerable hilarity scattered throughout. At one point, Herr Director demands Rosenthal "emerge from the shadows". When asked the simple question, "What am I doing in the shadows?," Herr Director goes off on a lengthy, increasingly impassioned tangent concerning *The Muppet Movie*, the Muppets' epic quest, and the big reveal of Orson Welles. This handily reveals the director's obsessions without providing Rosenthal with any good reason why his character would just be kicking around in the dark, while also nicely linking the two phenomena together: as Schimberg remarked in an interview, whenever there's a big reveal (chair swivel, shadow emergence), it's either a celebrity or a "freak".

But what of those other critics? One used the term "black comedy," and the only interpretation I can make of that is that any comedy involving these kinds of people must be subversive somehow. Another's mind was blown by a modest twist found in the final act; it was as if he watched a far more complicated movie than I had. But despite the unsettling undercurrents discovered by other reviews, I found *Chained for Life* to be as pleasing as it is witty. As the credits appear, they spool over one long take on the bus of the variously disabled actors after the in-movie movie shoot. After so deftly undermining preconceptions about disfigured people, this stunt pays off handsomely. What do we see when we watch them on the bus? Totally normal people being totally, normal, bored. It was an excellent flourish and a perfect way to underline the film's thesis.

Chained for Life was completed in 2018 and did not receive a theatrical release. It debuted on Blu-ray and DVD in January 2020.—Giles Edwards

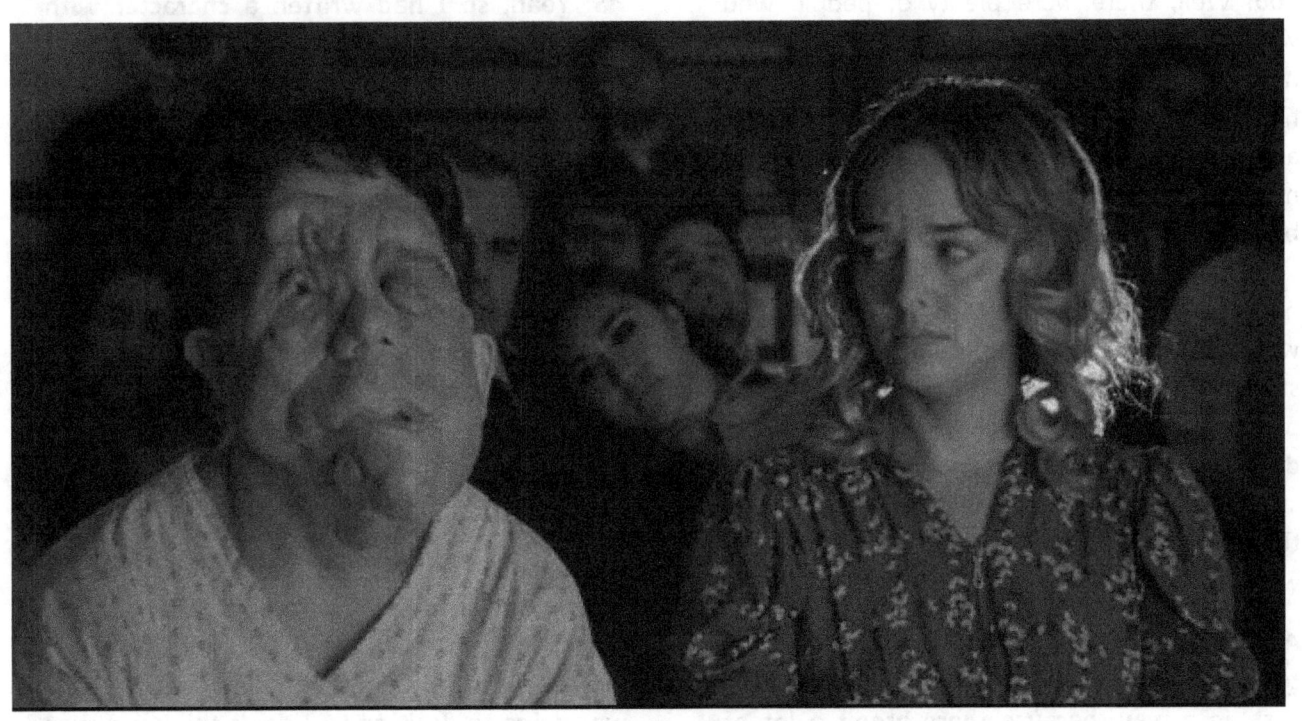

Aaron Schimberg: Keeping It Normal

On Thursday, July 19, 2018, I had the pleasure of meeting with director Aaron Schimberg, whose new movie Chained for Life *had its International Premier the night before. Nestled in a back room in the SGWU, we had a quick chat.*

366: This is Giles Edwards sitting down with Aaron Schimberg who directed *Chained to Life* … Pardon? Oh, *Chained for Life*. Terrible start. It played to a full house, and I also noticed when I was out in line that the press line was as long as the ticket-holder line, so that will hopefully get the word out on this great feature. You probably saw the reaction of the house a lot of clapping and laughing.

AS: I only paid attention to the people who weren't clapping and laughing.

366: Well, there were plenty of people who were. Now, *Chained for Life* is kind of a "meta-movie" about making a period hospital-horror film while mostly focusing the actors' world. We actually recently did a long-form review of the movie *Freaks*, and one of the things remarked on by the reviewer was that that was the kind of film you really couldn't make anymore. But you, obviously, have put together something that, while different in tone, is comparable in structure, with a band of "normal" actors and production people and individuals with different disabilities. So it looks like that kind of thing is still possible. Did you have difficulty corralling the groups together or starting this project in any way?

AS: The film is in many ways a response to *Freaks* and an update of it. It was hard to cast, in a way, because there aren't a lot of advocacy groups for people with disabilities, but not everyone in the film was an "actor." Because it's a low budget film, it's difficult to cast anyway, so I had to cast sort of by any means necessary: either pick people out from the street, or go through casting agents, or friends, or people that we'd seen in other movies. Everyone seemed to me—if you're asking about actors with disabilities—seemed to relate to the script and seemed fully on board. It was almost like a summer camp atmosphere, a very positive environment. It's hard to get a film off the ground, but once we were up and running it was a pretty smooth process.

366: I like how you said "summer camp atmosphere," because that was definitely captured—certainly in the scenes at night at the hospital with just the "freak" part of the cast there, hanging out.

How did you get in touch with your leading man, Adam Pearson?

AS: Yeah, so I had written a character with neurofibromatosis, who was British. I don't know why. I was probably thinking of the "Elephant Man," who had neurofibromatosis—possibly, there's a debate about what disease he had—so I was thinking of that. A soft-spoken person, like Joseph Merrick was. And then, about twenty pages into writing the screenplay, I saw *Under the Skin*, and there was an actor, with neurofibromatosis, who was British, and he was upstaging Scarlett Johansson, and I thought this seems like a good sign, maybe I can get this guy.

I don't write roles for people ever because it's a low budget film and you can get disappointed when people don't want to do it when there's not a lot of money involved. In my first film I wrote a part for Mike Tyson, and I was sure he was going to do it and… I don't think we ever even got it to him; to this day it's a great disappointment to me, I still regret it, so to this day I don't do it. Nevertheless, after I'd seen Adam Pearson I started to write with a little bit of him in mind and hoped for the best. So we

just sent it to him and a couple of days later Adam said he loved the script, and we Skyped, and were on the same page.

And he really loved it and he gives an amazing performance. I think people assume that he's kind of playing himself, but he's actually one of the biggest extroverts I've ever met: very much the life of the party, everybody loves him. He could be a cult leader if he wanted to. But in the film he's a very shy person, and in *Under the Skin* he was similar, so I think people assume that about him.

366: It certainly comes across as very natural, so I guess that speaks to his acting ability.

AS: Yeah, he's great. I think people always think he's playing a variation of himself, but in fact he's got a very wide range. And you see in the film, he has a couple scenes where he's extremely angry, screaming. That's also *not* him... not that I've seen.

366: You mentioned this first movie of yours, that was *Go Down Death*; from my understanding that got a limited release.

AS: "Limited," yeah, that's a polite term. It got distribution, but not much of a theatrical release. You can get it on iTunes, places like that.

366: Since I imagine not many people are going to know about it, what is it about? And what drew you to the subject matter?

AS: *Go Down Death* is a little more experimental. It's about a town that's threatened by an unseen force. Kind of a bunch of vignettes that are slightly related to each other, and it deals with some of the same issues as *Chained for Life*: disability and disfigurement, that's part of the film, but it's very anti-narrative. I wanted to play with narrative... This film, *Chained for Life*, also plays with narrative, it changes course, but it's a lot *more* narrative, more accessible in that way. And I think a lot of the lessons I learned in *Go Down Death*, as my first film, I applied to *Chained for Life*.

366: There was one scene that definitely got a lot of laughs: the German director's "Muppet" tirade. What was it that gave you that idea? Because it was nothing short of amazing.

AS: I was thinking and have observed, the only characters in a film who are introduced as a sort of surprise fashion—emerging from the shadows, turning around in a big chair, something like that—they are either people who are disfigured, hidden in the shadows and revealed at a certain point, or extremely famous kind of cameo actors, like Orson Welles. That sort of surprise element. And the film plays in general with comparing famous, beautiful people with disfigurement, and how in some ways they can relate to each other in terms of always being observed and exposed. And of course, Orson Welles did that a few times, like in *The Third Man* when he emerges from the shadows.

So that scene's the sort of logical conclusion of that observation. After I'd written about thirty pages of the script I noticed that Orson Welles kept popping up in various ways; I don't think it was intentional, but there are several references to him. I could guess, or have some theories about why that is, why my subconscious kept going to him, but it was really unintentional. But it certainly culminated in that scene.

366: Another scene that I think really tied up what I think you were trying to do with the movie was during the closing credits with the single shot of the "freak" characters sitting on the bus. I thought it was a perfect touch: "Oh, that looks so normal and tedious. These are *just* people and should be regarded as such."

AS: Oh yeah.

366: I've got one last question I like to pose to all my interviewees: your home town: where is it? And do you have a recommendation for a restaurant there?

AS: **My original hometown is Minneapolis. I live in New York now, but "Al's Breakfast" in Minneapolis.**

366: Well thank you for that recommendation and sharing your time. I wish you the best of luck with distribution and sharing that film with as many people as possible.

AS: **Thank you.**

8. *She Dies Tomorrow*

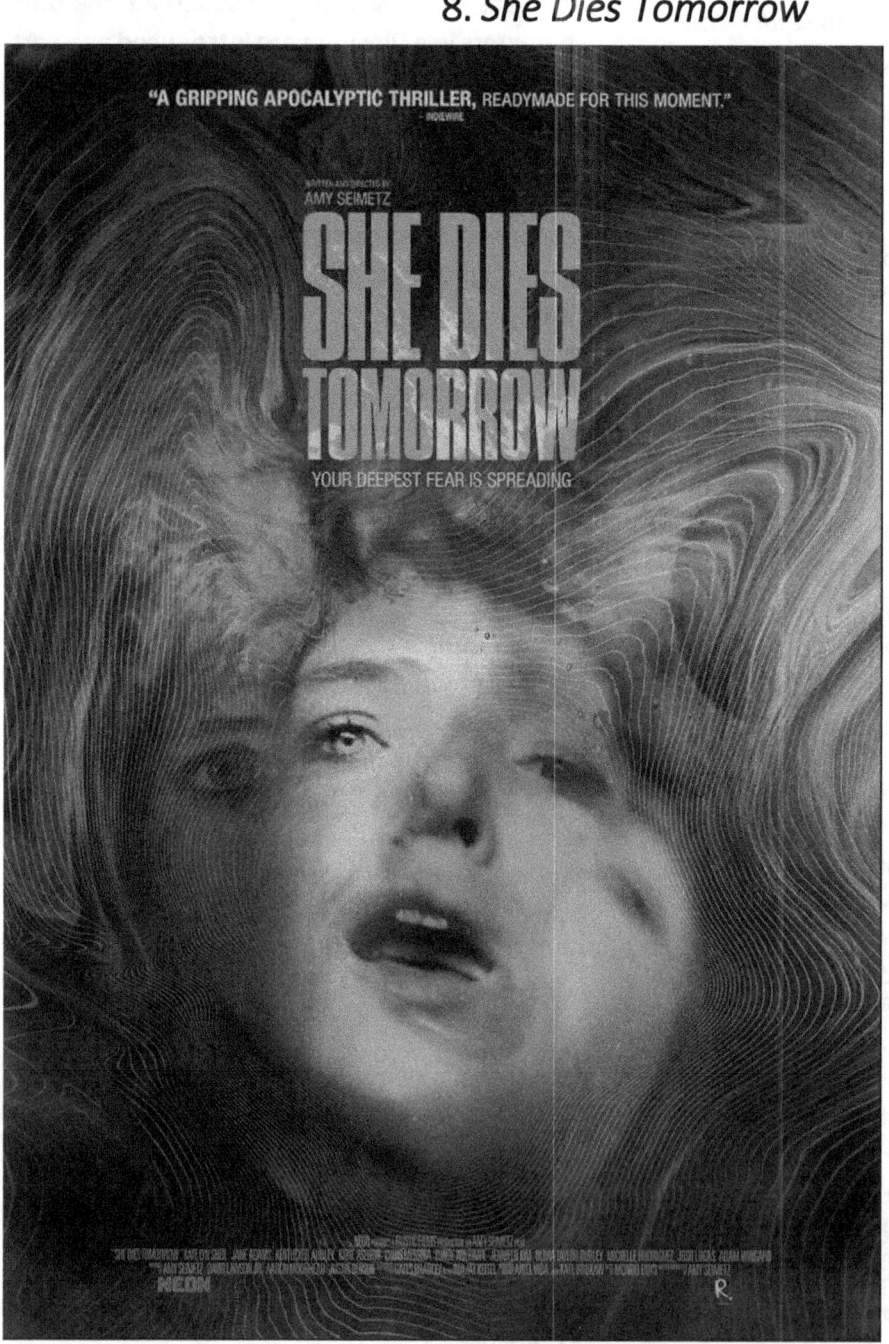

DIRECTED BY: Amy Seimetz

FEATURING: Kate Lyn Sheil, Jane Adams, Kentucker Audley

PLOT: Amy is convinced that she will die tomorrow.

COMMENTS: Amy plays an LP of Mozart's "Lacrimosa" over and over. She calls her friend Jane, who can't come over because she has to go to a birthday party, but sounds worried about her. Amy drinks a bottle of wine, slithers into a cocktail dress, and climbs up on the neighbor's wall with a leaf-blower—never a sign of good mental health. Jane finally arrives, and Amy tells her that she's going to die tomorrow, and asks if Jane will ensure that her body is made into a leather jacket after she's gone.

Kate Lyn Sheil carries the opening act of the film, mostly alone and silent, conveying a despair that builds to resigned madness. The opening features a lot of extreme close-ups of tear-filled eyes, a half-full wine glass, microscope slides with red blood cells; shots that suggest both loneliness, and an uncomfortable intimacy. This solitary mood is sustained about as long as it can be before Jane (Jane Adams) shows up to introduce a more dynamic note. Jane, an artist, dismisses Amy's premonition of death as a self-pitying drunken ramble; but when she leaves, she begins thinking about mortality... and convinces herself that she, too, will die tomorrow. Jane then hauls herself to the birthday party, with predictably dire results.

If I were to assign a genre to *She Dies Tomorrow*, it would be "macabre drama." Writer/director Amy Seimetz takes a simple irrational conceit—what if we were inalterably convinced that we would die tomorrow?—then it fully explores the dramatic ramifications through multiple characters. It's the sort of idea that Luis Buñuel would have turned into a satire, but the tone here is forlorn. There is humor, to be sure—a conversation about dolphin sex, Jane's panicky visit to an emergency room physician, Amy's desire to be turned into post-mortem apparel—but black comedy is not the predominant mood.

Neither is it a science fictional, "Twilight Zone" conceit; there are no firm answers given to why Amy is struck with a paralyzing consciousness of death. Scenes of rainbow-colored flashing strobe lights accompanied by the sound of garbled radio transmissions only confuse matters. The crucial fact that Amy's morbid thinking is contagious converges with 2020's pandemic, creating a layer of accidental relevance to contemporary times—one that you may find too relevant for comfort. A crowd-pleaser, *She Dies Tomorrow* is not; a worthwhile challenge for the brave and introspective, it is.

With its crushing sadness and lack of answers—much less solace—*She Dies Tomorrow* will frustrate the hell out of some viewers, which is a compliment. Seimetz is onto something desperately human here, a truth we'd rather avoid. We like to imagine that if we knew the date of our own deaths, we'd be freed to truly live life, not worrying about next month's rent, pursuing our bucket list, renting a dune buggy. But Seimetz's characters are instead paralyzed by knowledge of their impermanence, unable to enjoy their last moments on Earth or appreciate the simple beauty of a sunrise. The movie is an elegy for us all. True to its own despair, *She Dies Tomorrow* offers not a ray of hope.

Our readers will remember Amy Seimetz best for her performance in front of the camera in *Upstream Color*. This is only her second feature film as director, and it's a great leap forward from 2012's promising *Sun Don't Shine* (which also featured Sheil as lead). Seimetz continues to act and direct TV projects, but she's paid her dues, and let's hope she doesn't have to wait another eight years between features. She might die tomorrow, and that would be a great loss to the film world.—Gregory J. Smalley

9. *We Are Little Zombies* [*Wî â Ritoru Zonbîzu*]

DIRECTED BY: Makoto Nagahisa

FEATURING: Keita Ninomiya, Sena Nakajima, Satoshi Mizuno, Mondo Okumura

PLOT: After meeting at a funeral parlor, four emotionless, orphaned children run away and form a pop band.

COMMENTS: Carnivalesque pop-psychedelics enliven Nagahisa's genre-bending tale of four emotion-deprived orphans wending their way through modern Japan. The final act, which sees the quartet piloting a stolen garbage truck into a black and white ocean of giant amoebas and pulsating anemones before emerging for a (posthumous?) coda, gave it the final push it needed to make our list of the weirdest releases of 2020.

We Are Little Zombies takes its aesthetic inspiration from Nintendo video game systems: a chiptune-based theme song, 8-bit credits and bumpers. It's structured as a series of challenges, with four orphans collecting four quest items (in four flashbacks), and with grief as the final boss. It wrings a surprising amount of depth from its short attention span style, and a surprising amount of empathy from its tale of children whose defining characteristic is that they have no emotions.

Little Zombies bursts with energy and ideas that vibrantly contrast with the enervated performances of its living-dead heroes. Surreal touches sprout through the early reels, including a giant goldfish swimming outside an apartment window, a hobo orchestra, and a talk show hosted by a lime green centaur and co-hosted by an enthusiastic eyeball. The film features multiple, mostly upbeat musical numbers: not just the "Little Zombies" performances, but also improvised drunken karaoke lyrics about the comparative intellectual capacities of an octopus and a three-year-old. The luminous images and digressive fantasies imply a sense of wonder about life—one that the children are incapable of seeing and appreciating, even as it envelops them.

There is an open question of whether the kids are really emotional zombies, or whether they're just temporarily numbed as a way to cope with tragedy. Before being accidentally emancipated, main character Hikari was a "hōchigo," literally, a "left-alone child," the Japanese analog to America's "latchkey kid." From his perspective, mom and dad were more concerned with their careers and affairs than with raising their offspring. Brash kleptomaniac Ikuko was physically abused by his father and brother. Overweight Takemura, whose parents owned a restaurant, comes from a relatively normal background. Ishi, the only female in the quartet, has the most complex backstory: her mother calls her a femme fatale, and she draws creepy attention from older men. There doesn't appear to be much of a common thread generating the zombies' juvenile anomie; and yet, it feels like Nagahisa is on to a real social issue, something he can diagnose but not cure. The only prescription he can offer is this rebellious declaration: "despair is uncool."

We Are Little Zombies was a success at Sundance in 2019, and arrived in select theaters (given circumstances, mostly online theaters) on July 10, 2020. It appeared on video-on-demand and physical media in November.—Gregory J. Smalley

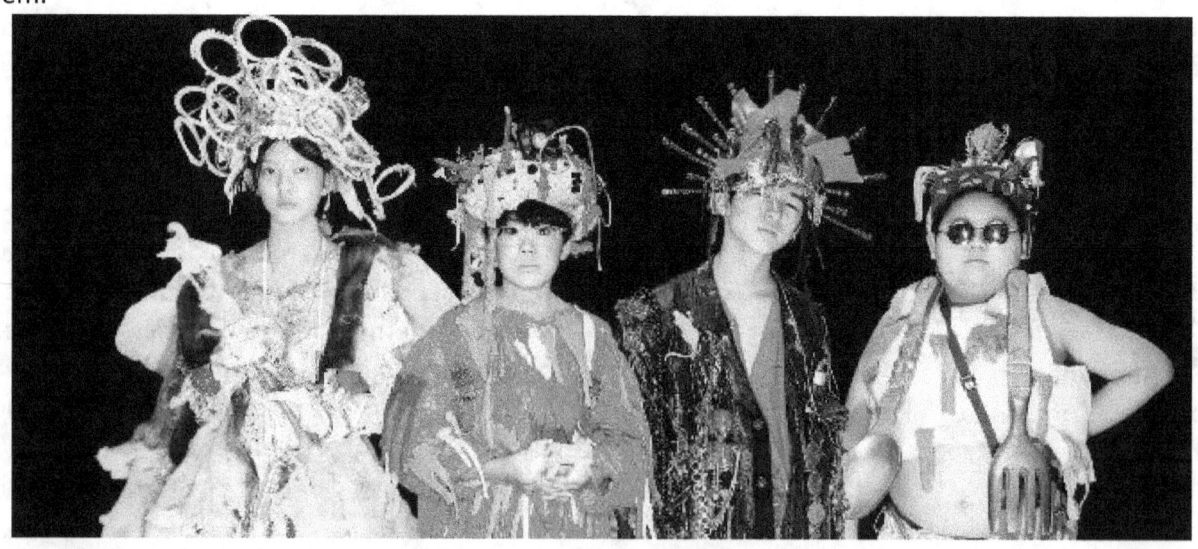

10. In Fabric

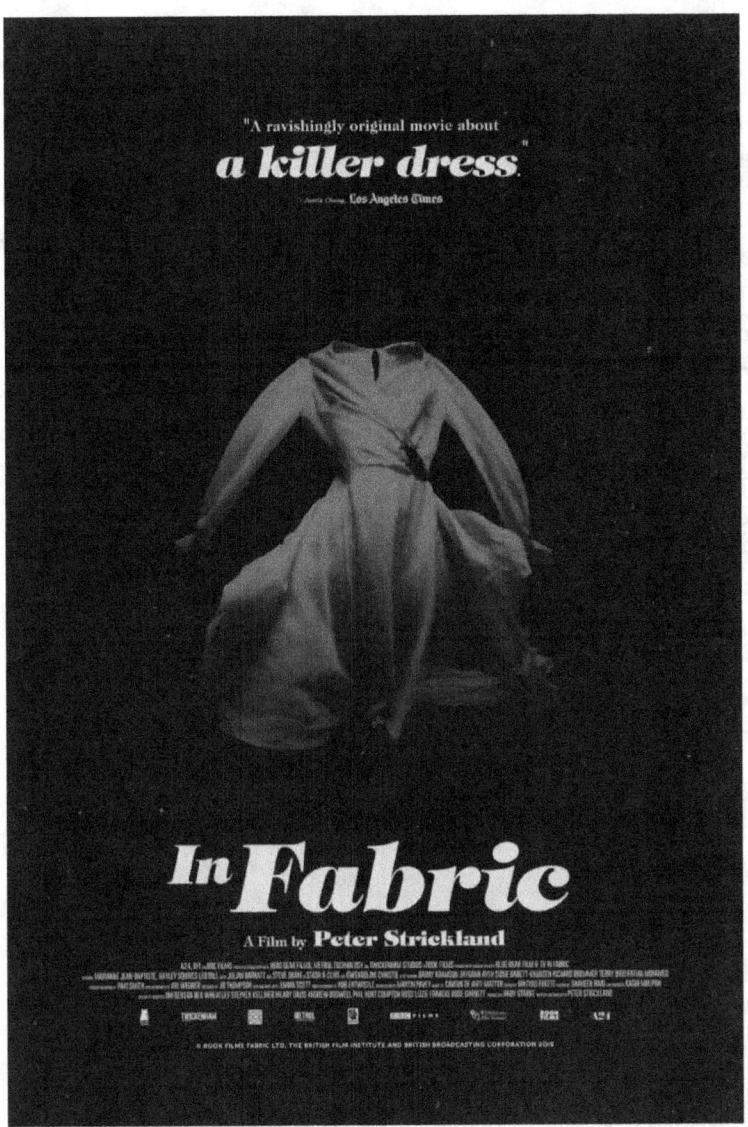

DIRECTED BY: Peter Strickland

FEATURING: Marianne Jean-Baptiste, Leo Bill, Fatma Mohamed, Hayley Squires, Julian Barratt

PLOT: Sheila, a divorcée in the market for a new man, purchases a new red dress for a date; things do not turn out well for her. Reg Speaks is a washing machine repairman about to marry his longtime girlfriend. After wearing the same red dress on his stag night, things turn out poorly for him, as well.

COMMENTS: Among the odd things about *In Fabric* is the fact that this is really two films in one: a pretty good feature-length story about Sheila's experiences with a cursed red dress, and a much weirder, shorter film about Reg's experiences with that same dress. There are plenty of strange things going on in this movie; unfortunately, while the graft is forgivable, it fails as a narrative film, though faring better as a weird one.

Peter Strickland, who wrote and directed, clearly has an obsession with 1970s exploitation movies—his two previous efforts both focus on that decade and that genre—and his penchant for *giallo* shines through brightly. The red of the dress and the red lighting of the strange advertisements for "Dentley and Sopers Trusted Department Store" are the most obvious tributes, with the movie's palette generally mimicking whatever evil form of Technicolor was used by the original giallists. *In Fabric* could be viewed as a love letter to that arty vein of horror, albeit a letter with an incredibly long postscript.

I enjoyed watching this, despite a glaring flaw: it was difficult to commit to the characters. Sheila's tale ultimately left me indifferent, but the story of "Reg Speaks" was more in the transcendent mold, almost literally. Reg's last name is strange, but apt. Though a lowly washing machine mechanic, he has something of a super power: the ability to bring listeners to an orgasmic trance while speechifying on the finer details of the problems vexing broken machines. In the world of *In Fabric* his reputation is such that even the bank managers whom he sees about a loan know about it, and want him to do a "role-playing" exercise so they can enjoy his mesmeric talents. (Julian Barratt plays one of these bank managers, with a performance that expertly rides along the razor's edge of hilarious and mundane. Describing a memo about having a "meaningful handshake", he explains, "It's written in a fun, easy language, with a cartoon at the end that summarizes key points.")

Fatma Mohamed, as the chief store clerk, stands out among the madness. She makes one believe she could be an alien, a demon, or perhaps a mannequin brought to life by some eccentric paranormal force. Her lines ("The hesitation in your voice: soon to be an echo in the spheres of retail" or "dimensions and proportions transcend the prisms of our measurements") sound like ornately translated Italian as delivered by a supernatural facsimile of a sales woman.

Strickland will hopefully sort his visions out enough to make that truly weird, truly worthwhile movie in the future (under the guidance, perhaps, of Ben Wheatley, executive producer here). Measuring *In Fabric*, we find all the pieces are there, but he's crafted something altogether ill-fitting.

In Fabric got a theatrical release in December 2019, too late to qualify for inclusion in last year's Yearbook; it's February 2020 physical and digital release gave us ample excuse to include it in this year's slate.—Giles Edwards

OTHER 2020 RELEASES

The Antenna [Bina] ★★★

DIRECTED BY: Orçun Behram

FEATURING: Ihsan Önal, Gul Arici, Levent Ünsal

PLOT: A building supervisor deals with strange occurrences after a satellite antenna is installed in his apartment building to broadcast government-sponsored news bulletins.

COMMENTS: Set in a Kafkaesque cinder block, but clearly inspired by life in Erdoğan's Turkey, *The Antenna* establishes its propaganda theme right away. Mehmet, an unassuming apartment building supervisor, listens to a government-sponsored radio broadcast as he dresses. Posters of a middle-aged strongman decorate the concrete pillars he passes as he walks to work through deserted streets. The morning report declares that the government will be rolling out an elaborate communications system intended to integrate all media, one which will require the installation of a satellite dish on the roof of Mehmet's building. This achievement will be celebrated with a special midnight broadcast—one which all citizens are strongly encouraged to watch.

Although the contemporary relevance is obvious, *The Antenna* is set in an indeterminately authoritarian time and place. Along with the drab utilitarian architecture, the celebration of satellite antenna television as cutting-edge technology suggest a Communist country in the 1980s. The film's aesthetic is Stalinist: residents' wardrobes are almost all shades of black, white, or gray (Mehmet is praised for the "seriousness" of his utilitarian dress). The cinematography favors shallow-focus shots, with background characters blurred, emphasizing each character's isolation.

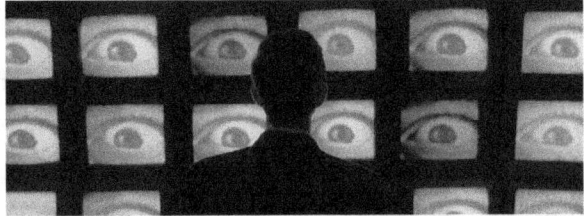

Strong sound design contrasts with the grim visuals. Horror movie music plays from the pipes in the walls, and the noise of the outside world subjectively mutes when characters are in moments of crisis. At one point Mehmet's ears are overwhelmed by a welter of staticky, overlapping propaganda broadcasts.

The Antenna builds an atmosphere of dehumanization and quiet despair, full of subtle threats. It springs some effective horror moments: black goo oozing from the wall and ceiling tiles, a column of anonymous identical silhouettes peering out of compartmentalized windows. Angry synthesizers and VHS quality satellite broadcasts speak to the influence of *Videodrome* and other 1980s dystopias. For all of these virtues, however, the script lacks urgency. It spends too long introducing us to the desperately bland lives of the tenement dwellers; nor does the two-hour journey build to a powerful climax. The ending is a series of weird visual and auditory metaphors, which happen to the characters rather than developing as a consequence of their actions. The grand finale is a confrontation with a lackey, not the source of the evil. Despite these reservations, debuting director Behram shows obvious skill in building fear. It's a talent that might be better harnessed in service of a more propulsive script in the future.

The Antenna went straight to video-on-demand in the United States.—Gregory J. Smalley

Assassin 33 A.D. ★1/2

DIRECTED BY: Jim Carroll

FEATURING: Morgan Roberts, Ilsa Levine, Geraldo Davila, Donny Boaz, Lamar Usher, Jason Castro

PLOT: Muslim extremists use a time machine to go back to 33 A.D. to try to assassinate Jesus; with the encouragement of his Christian girlfriend, an agnostic genius tries to fix the time stream.

COMMENTS: I wouldn't say it's impossible to make a good Christian time travel movie; Andrei Tarkovsky would have nailed it. But I am pretty sure it is impossible to make a good Christian time travel movie that involves terrorist strike teams with assault weapons going back to 1st century Judea to assassinate Jesus. *Assassin 33 AD* is *Donnie Darko* meets *The Passion of the Christ* done on the kind of budget usually reserved for an episode of "The 700 Club."

Assassin 33 A.D. faces a big problem: it wants to be a faith-based movie and a thrilling action sci-fi spectacular at the same time. But those two genres have incompatible messages. Inspirational films require introspective characters who struggle with moral dilemmas to come to a spiritual awakening. Action films require blood squibs and a high body count. Now, when your film is about Jesus Christ, who—little known fact—rejected the use of violence to resolve interpersonal conflicts, there may be a problem satisfying both arcs. Which storyline will win the race for narrative relevance: the hero's gradual acceptance of God's difficult commandment of forgiveness, or his burning desire to make the swarthy guy with a foreign accent pay for his abominable sins? I think you can guess which one this screenplay favors.

Assassin 33 A.D. grows dumber the more you think about it (what is the point in traveling back in time to *kill* someone whose fame comes entirely from his *martyrdom*?) It *is* unintentionally funny, except for one offensive feature: its brazen Islamophobia. All of the Muslim characters are villainous caricatures. The movie progressively assembles a multicultural team of good guy scientists: a handsome agnostic WASP with a Jewish surname, a black dude, a Mexican, even a chick. Americans of every stripe are invited to team up against the Muslims. Jesus commanded believers to "Love your enemies," but that's why he wouldn't last a day as a Hollywood screenwriter. You've got to have somebody the heroes can pump bullets into without anyone feeling guilty about it. Here, the Muslim characters are legitimate targets, outside of God's grace, not eligible for forgiveness. They are not, in this movie's view, people. They are the Other. And although I suspect the writer/director cast them that way more out of thoughtless prejudice than evil propagandistic intent, that dehumanization is an immoral element of this feature that I can't forgive. Maybe Jesus will.

Assassin 33 AD cleaned up at faith-friendly film festivals, where it won numerous "Best Screenplay" awards. In the secular world, it failed hard (although a few critics recommended it as camp). At the time of publication it was available to screen for free on Amazon or for purchase on DVD.—Gregory J. Smalley

Bacurau ★★★1/2

DIRECTED BY: Juliano Dornelles, Kleber Mendonça Filho

FEATURING: Bárbara Colen, Udo Kier, Sonia Braga, Thomas Aquino

PLOT: A group of killers isolate a small Brazilian village intending to massacre the residents for recreation, but find the peasants are more resourceful than they anticipated.

COMMENTS: Seeing mainstream critics use the word "weird" used to describe *Bacurau* reminds us how jaded we are. The only unusual features of this Brazilian export are its blend of art-house drama and ballsy genre filmmaking, along with some mild psychotropic visions and one flying-saucer-shaped drone. It might be a weird brew for general American audiences—ones who would seldom see a foreign or indie film anyway—but this sociological-study-*cum*-shoot-'em-up isn't exactly *Let the Corpses Tan*.

With magnificent landscapes evoking the mythic West of Sergio Leone, *Bacurau* could have been titled *Once Upon a Time in Brazil*. The opening scene reinforces the Spaghetti Western connection with a litter of coffins spilled onto the road. By the end, when the resourceful tribe defends their deserted town from better-equipped invaders, *Bacurau* resembles *The Seven Samurai*.

The first forty-five minutes paint a portrait of the hamlet of perhaps one hundred souls, planted in the middle of nowhere. A matriarch, the ancestor of a large percentage of the population, has just died. The town has a teacher, a doctor, a whore, a DJ who also serves as the town crier and local news anchor, and so forth; it also has a museum devoted to the town's history. Things get strange when Bacurau suddenly disappears from Google Maps and bullet holes are found in the tanker truck that supplies the town with fresh water. The reason soon becomes apparent; a tour group of American thrill-killers have paid a small fortune to hunt these forgotten people for sport. The killing starts in the final act, but although squibs are not spared, it's not the action-packed bloodbath you might predict. The murders are spread out, as the invaders are picked off one by one. You might guess that Udo Kier, the oldest, evilest, and most famous of the bad guys is the last one to go. We'll never tell.

With the sympathetic portrayal of the villagers' "degeneracy," and the presence of con-man mayor Tony Jr. representing provincial corruption, the film takes its shots at right-wing Brazilian president Jair Bolsonaro. Capitalism itself also comes in for quite a thrashing. But Bolsonaro might be pleased with the film's xenophobia aimed at the stereotyped Western interlopers (Kier is *not* a Nazi, he insists, shooting a companion to prove his point), and of the derision heaped on the invaders' traitorous globalist collaborators. The line between anti-colonialism and populist nationalism is thin indeed.

Pulled from American theaters early due to the Covid-19 crisis, distributor Kino thoughtfully set up a system whereby the independent theaters that were supposed to screen the film can share the streaming revenue. It was one of the first movies to test this model, which proved moderately successful and at least lessened the blow for a number of art-house theaters. Since Kino probably could have kept all the streaming receipts for themselves, as Disney did with the digital release of *Onward*, they deserve massive respect for this move.—Gregory J. Smalley

"Boogiepop and Others: The Complete Series" (2019) ★★★

DIRECTED BY: Yōsuke Hatta, Park Myung Hwan, Norikazu Ishigōoka, Mami Kawano, Hiromichi Matano, Masato Nakazono, Shingo Natsume, Kazuo Nogami, Keiichirō Saitō, Katsuya Shigehara

FEATURING: Aoi Yûki, Saori Oonishi (original Japanese); Michelle Roja, Morgan Garret (English dub)

PLOT: The spirit known as Boogiepop fights a succession of "enemies of this world."

COMMENTS: If you enjoyed the enigmas of the anime classic "Boogiepop Phantom" (see p. ___) and want to dip deeper into the lore, "Boogiepop and Others" will scratch that itch. You'll learn more about the Towa Organization, the Manticore, Nagi Kirima, and Boogiepop herself. If you're looking for an introduction to Boogiepop, however, I'd recommend starting with "Phantom"; the more mysterious presentation of the 2000 series plunges deeper into the franchise's dark psyche.

Compared to "Phantom," "Others" is more conventionally structured, although it still hops about in time in a way calculated to disorient newcomers. This eighteen-episode series is split into four separate arcs, with Boogiepop facing off against the Manticore, the Imaginator, rogue psychiatrist Dr. Kisugi, and the King of Distortion. (Not to mention sub-boss "Spooky E," who has his DJ name already picked out for when he retires from his job manipulating mankind's evolution for the Towa Organization.) This structure gives the series a "villain of the week" quality. The stories mostly center around one particular antagonist's effects on regular high school students; we also get a sort-of origin story for the series' namesake in the "Boogiepop at Dawn" arc. "Others" spends time explicitly spelling out mysteries that were left to the viewer to decipher in "Phantom." This Boogiepop is more superhero than enigmatic interloper from some netherworld. Each arc resolves with a *deus ex machina*; Boogie hangs around in the background, then swoops in at the climax to banish another "enemy of this world."

The simplified narrative is, perhaps, an understandable concession, but more disappointing is the fact that the visuals here are completely ordinary. Gone are "Phantom"'s dark, muted palettes, replaced by sunny skies and colorful toons with big eyes. Boogiepop, once a brooding presence, now has a bright, almost Hanna-Barbera quality to go with her increased verbosity. The immersively strange sound design of "Phantom" is also nowhere to be found.

While it's difficult to describe a television show as complicated as "Boogiepop" as "dumbed-down," there can be no doubt that Madhouse's follow-up series is less ambitious and artistically inferior to their first take on the character, aimed at an audience more interested in the series' plot mechanics than its otherworldly mood. Nevertheless, fans of "Phantom" may want to investigate this alternate take for the way it expands your understanding of the universe and the overarching storyline. There's still plenty of strangeness to chew on.

Funimation released the entire "Others" series to Blu-ray in 2020. Currently, the entire run of "Boogiepop and Others" is available for online viewing for free at Crunchyroll.—Gregory J. Smalley

Butt Boy ★★1/2

DIRECTED BY: Tyler Cornack

FEATURING: Tyler Cornack, Tyler Rice

PLOT: I.T. specialist Chip becomes obsessed with sticking items into his rectum; years later, he becomes an Alcoholics Anonymous sponsor for a police detective who grows to suspect Chip is involved in a child's disappearance.

COMMENTS: *Butt Boy* is the inverse of the bigger-budgeted horror/drama *Swallow* (2020), a serious and psychological-minded take on a woman with a compulsion to swallow inedible objects. Superficially, *Butt Boy* is (almost) equally serious in tone, but its focus on the opposite end of the digestive tract (and its title) makes it impossible to take seriously.

Despite lacking the high poetry implied by the term, "magical realism" would be a technically correct designation for *Butt Boy*. What makes the experiment work, to the extent it does, is its dedication to remain absolutely deadpan. It is, most definitely, weird in conception; but not, for the most part, in execution. In fact, the idea of a detective who suspects his A.A. sponsor of having committed a terrible crime is so rife with inherent drama and suspense that, in a fit of spontaneous normality, I almost thought it was wasted in a movie where the chief suspect is—literally, not figuratively—an asshole.

Director Tyler Cornack tackles on the central role with a dull and detached take that suits the dry tone. Tyler Rice, who has sort of a Joe Pesci-in-a-goatee thing going on, brings a needed burst of energy as Detective Fox. The defensive mannerisms of a recovering alcoholic mesh perfectly with the suspicious nature of the archetypal career cop. Passable cat-and-mouse action takes up the second act, although there are no real surprises or standout suspense scenes to be had (at least, not until the blankly funny moment where Chip drops trou during a violent confrontation). It passes time well enough until the movie goes all the way to the end of its alimentary canal of a premise.

Fox falls off the wagon just as things start to get really weird. Naturally, his by-the-book supervisor refuses to entertain his anal explanation for the disappearance, so he's forced to go looking for the missing boy himself. We then get into the bowels of the story, so to speak; and although thankfully things don't get *too* gross, the sights are not for the meek. Then again, the meek probably won't be streaming something titled *Butt Boy* in the first place.

While your attention will naturally be drawn to the *Butt*, but pay attention to the *Boy* as well. While *Butt Boy* may play like a simple parody, if there's any serious subtext under the surface, it's an attitude towards fatherhood that isn't necessarily obvious.

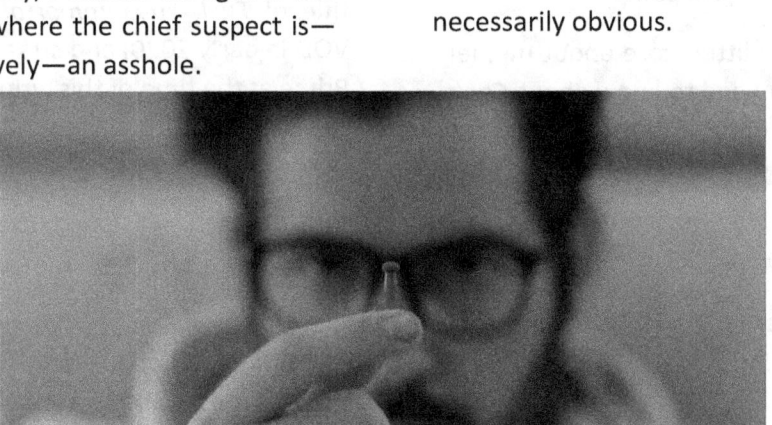

Butt Boy dropped on VOD and physical media in April. At press time it was playing on Amazon Prime for free.—Gregory J. Smalley

Can't Kill This [AKA *Fuck You, Immortality*] ★★1/2

DIRECTED BY: Federico Scargiali

FEATURING: Bill Hutchens, Josephine Scandi, Brutius Selby

PLOT: An old drug buddy from the 1970s appears to be immortal, so Tony and Kacy try to track him down, and then try to kill him.

COMMENTS: A minor character in *Can't Kill This* reminded me of a high school video project that has plagued my memory since its completion. When stumbling around the English countryside looking for Joe, hippies Tony and Kacy accidentally knock on the caravan door of a luchador. Outside his domicile is a junkyard overrun with chickens, which he refers to as "pollo loco"; this happens to have been the original name for my final film project. We had filmed the ancillary shots for what was intended to be a *Blair Witch Project* spoof (those of you who remember that movie's popularity probably cannot blame a flippant seventeen-year-old for feeling inspired). However! (And this is the exciting bit.) About two-thirds through shooting, there was a massive snow storm and we lost all possibility of continuity. And so, on the fly, we threw together an alternative just days before the deadline: "Mister Psychopants".

Now that you know a little more about me, let me tell you what you need to know about *Can't Kill This*: it was likely done with the earnestness of a teenage filmmaker, and, indeed, adopts the same genre (mockumentary). However, Scargiali's movie was not done last-minute by high schoolers. But slogging through the eighty minutes of run-time, I found myself laughing only thrice (and bear in mind that this is supposed to be a stoner comedy). The first time involved a secret "door-knock" bit, touching upon the correct pronunciation of "Fhtang". The second involved Tony in a bathtub having a narrative adventure with two rubber duckies. I do not remember the specifics of the third instance.

Despite my chirpy, mindless optimism about filmmakers and their directorial debuts, I'm not sure I can honestly say that I look forward to what Scargiali gets up to in the future. I did watch all of *Can't Kill This*, and I liked the premise—but I would have much preferred the movie that had formed in my mind when I saw the ominous poster and read whatever bare-bones description came my way before volunteering to watch and review it. To wrap this up with a six-word review, "Totally watchable, but I wouldn't bother."

Can't Kill This (renamed from its original festival title of *Fuck You, Immortality*) showed up on VOD in early 2020, and streams free on Amazon Prime at the time of this writing.—Giles Edwards

Capone ★★★★

DIRECTED BY: Josh Trank

FEATURING: Tom Hardy, Linda Cardellini, Kyle MacLachlan, Matt Dillon

PLOT: Released to his Florida home on humanitarian grounds, Al Capone spends the last year of his life rapidly deteriorating in body and mind, while trying to remember where he hid ten million dollars.

COMMENTS: *Capone* plays like an anti-biopic: there's no glamorization, and virtually no sympathy elicited for its protagonist. As a star vehicle for Tom Hardy, it also veers off the beaten path. Hardy's performance is a strange hybrid of tin-pan-alley grandiosity and bloodshot malevolence. *Capone*'s reception by the common viewer has been unsurprisingly frigid, but for those who want a haunting and uncomfortable dissection of the mental deterioration of history's most notorious gangster, *Capone* is as priceless as the treasure that eludes the titular character.

Al Capone's sentence for tax evasion is cut short to allow him to spend his final days in his sprawling mansion surrounded by a sprawling swamp. His homestead's grounds are infested with crocodiles of the literal variety; its hallways are infested with metaphorical ones. Al Capone sounds like a dying horse, croaking out random threats and random pleas. He is prone to incontinence—so much so that his doctor (Kyle MacLachlan, both slippery and terrified) supplies Capone's long-suffering wife (Linda Cardellini, emanating frustration) with diapers for her husband. When not staring at his lake, puffing endless cigars and listening to his radio, Capone endures encounters with friends both past and present. On a fishing trip with an old criminal associate, he casually lets slip that he has hidden ten million bucks, but he can't remember where.

Capone's mental fragility contrasts with the precise formality of the rest of the movie. Each scene is impeccably orchestrated around Hardy's characterization, the surrounding cast providing the struts on which Capone's quiet madness is displayed. The dream sequences often manage to be unpredictable—the final blow-out only showing its hand at the scene's watery collapse—while at other times there's obvious pathos. The recurring symbol of gold—a young boy's balloon, the metal trim of a shotgun Capone uses to shoot a crocodile that stole his fish, or the gaudy submachine gun used on his rampage—acts as a clue to the viewer, but also as a metaphor for what Capone has lost. His youth and power are gone forever; what's left is a tragic cartoon ever veering between rage and collapse.

Capone was a victim of the pandemic; originally scheduled as a major theatrical release, it ended up debuting on the Internet (and after glum rentals of about $2,500,000 against its $20,000,000+ budget, it was soon written off to Amazon Prime, where subscribers streamed it for free).—Giles Edwards

Cats ★★

DIRECTED BY: Tom Hooper

FEATURING: Francesca Hayward, Idris Elba, Taylor Swift, Judi Dench, Ian McKellan... (Indeed, the cast list is so talent-heavy you couldn't swing a cat without hitting someone with an entertainment award.)

PLOT: Meow.

COMMENTS: Not only did "they" pull the trigger on this one, they emptied all six of the chambers. From the opening nonsense of cat-people-cats spouting the word "jellicle" like it was going out of style, up through to the finale where they send off one of their own to her death, the cataclysm just wouldn't stop, and the transformation I underwent during the movie was comparable to that which bunches of A-list actors and celebrities went through to become *Cats*.

I could discuss the finer points of the plot, but if you know anything about Andrew Lloyd Webber's iconic work, you'll know there isn't really a story. Moreso, you knew whether or not you were the kind of person who'd want to see *Cats* by the time the first hints of its production sprang up.

And why was this movie made? In a way, I think that it had to be. Some critics complain ad nauseum that everything these days is a remake, sequel, or adaptation, but this has been the norm since the earliest days of cinema. As to how the producers got all these big names on board, I do not know; but then, perhaps you have to agree to performing in *Cats* if you are asked. I didn't leave the cinema thinking any less of any of the parties involved, and was actually quite pleased with Idris Elba's performance as the only two+ dimensional character of the bunch.

About fifty-five minutes into the movie, I glanced at my watch for the first time and nearly recoiled in terror. After all the song and dance I had watched these "jellicles" go through, I was only half-way through. Around that time I noticed two things: first, there was an intermittent but persistent clicking coming from one of the speakers; second, the latter half went by far more quickly than the first. I don't know if it's a testament to the powers of Eliot + Webber + Hooper, or testament to brain damage I suffered five-and-a-half years ago, but I actually started to care about these things. The end of times, to be sure.

Released Dec. 20, 2019 as a sort of white/elephant dirty Santa gift to the moviegoing public, *Cats* was almost immediately seen as a historic flop (arguably, it was a historic flop when its first disastrously-received trailer dropped in July 2019). Some reviews acknowledged its camp potential, and Alamo Drafthouses even sponsored "rowdy" screenings where audiences were encouraged to talk back to the screen, *Rocky Horror Picture Show* style.— Giles Edwards

Color out of Space ★★★1/2

DIRECTED BY: Richard Stanley

FEATURING: Madeleine Arthur, Elliot Knight, Nicolas Cage, Joely Richardson, Brendan Meyer, Julian Hilliar

PLOT: A meteorite lands at a remote New England farm and spreads alien madness to a family.

COMMENTS: The color out of space is actually lavender, or maybe it's more of a fuchsia. At any rate, it's in the pink/purple spectrum. Director Richard Stanley is committed to this color palette, which is prefigured in the streak of purple dye in Lavinia Gardner's otherwise golden hair. In Lovecraft's original story, a color never before seen by man was a metaphor for the ineffable quality of the alien visitor. In the movie, that color necessarily must be represented literally, and Stanley takes the literalism so excessively—slathering the film with liquid lilacs and violets—that the effect becomes almost as strange as an indescribable extraterrestrial hue. In fact, you only know when the alien presence has departed because the scene becomes drained of all color.

Bookended by quotations from Lovecraft*'s* text, *Color* follows a standard horror movie arc: character setup, arrival of an evil presence, steadily escalating eerie incidents that come to a climax. There are a lot of unusual sights along the way, however, starting with the purple mutant grasshopper/dragonfly hybrid with tie-dye spider-eye vision and progressing to a Cronenbergian mother/child re-assimilation. The inscrutability of the aliens' nature and purpose is true to Lovecraft. Questions of whether the color arrives on the pink glowing meteor by accident or purposefully, and why it suddenly departs—or perhaps just goes dormant—are left unanswered. "What touched this place cannot be understood or quantified by human science," is the best those hoping for an explanation will get.

Despite being featured in the film's promotion, Cage, as the family patriarch, doesn't dominate the story. He doesn't even start Cage-ing until halfway through, after the kids forget to feed the alpaca, he starts gesticulating wildly and switching accents mid-monologue. Young stars Madeleine Arthur (as Lavinia) and Elliot Knight (as the surveyor) are the main protagonists. I came into the experience looking forward to Cage bringing the crazy, but ended up happy that his peculiar lunacy merely seasoned the film a bit, rather than dominating it.

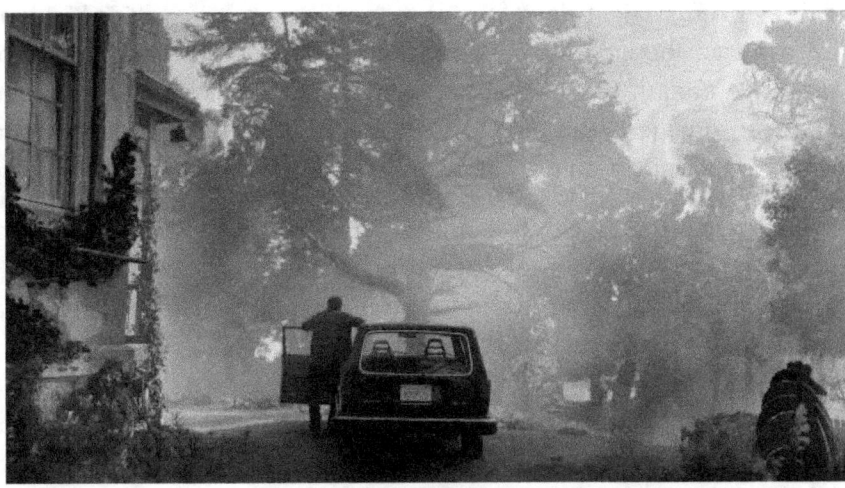

Due to its provenance— a weird fiction classic that's been adapted many times, but never properly; a cult director come out of retirement to helm the project; Nic Freaking Cage— *Color Out of Space* was the hot ticket among cult film fans in early 2020. The movie doesn't actually do anything truly unexpected, but nor does it disappoint. With Cage, a retro-80s horror pace and feel, and pretty swirling colors, it hit the sweet spot for a lot of viewers.—Gregory J. Smalley

Coma [*Koma*] ★★★★

DIRECTED BY: Nikita Argunov

FEATURING: Rinal Mukhametov, Lyubov Aksyonova, Konstantin Lavronenko

PLOT: Viktor awakens in his apartment to find the walls a strange cavalcade of architectural wonders dotting the skyline at improbable angles; then, he finds himself on the run from giant monsters.

COMMENTS: The title gives away the gimmick—but it doesn't matter. From the start, *Coma* smacks us with a beautiful show of some top-notch CGI buildings making up a future city whose center is graced with a modern reimagining of the Monument to the Third International. St. Basil's architectural motifs round out the metropolis. What is *Coma*? It's a vodka-drenched *Dark City/Inception* knock-off. And it's all the more entertaining for it.

Viktor, we eventually learn, was in a car crash. In Coma-land, Viktor immediately has to flee tall, thin-limbed beasts, made of an ever-flowing inky substance, which catch sight of him as he exits his apartment. Just in the nick of time, a grizzled gang of survivors spots him and hoofs him out of trouble to a survivor's camp—reached via a multiplanar, but very stationary, bus wreck—to meet Yal, their leader. Why did Yal send out his crack squad to save this ungainly beardo? We learn through exposition, montage, and a Moment of Trial.

This dismissiveness is meant as no more than gentle ribbing. *Coma* does a number of things well, not the least of which was keep my attention throughout. Argunov provides a ceaselessly interesting vista of interconnected, odd-angled planes: different memories, we are told, of different inhabitants. They're connected by wisps of ground; or not, as Viktor learns when he has to run straight down a pier to jump up into a piazza looming above. Firefights in this realm give "death from above" new meaning. And when our hero—an architect—learns how to use his special gift, things get even cooler.

I shan't reveal the reveal, but suffice it to say, (movie) science has an explanation for all the goings-on, and it seems we may be bearing witness to one man's pursuit of immortality. This being a Russian film, I cannot help veering into some sociopolitical observation. Viktor, in his waking life, is an idiot savant, an architect ahead of his time who was led to believe he could go on to create great, new things. As Yal makes very clear: in modern day Russia, change is only possible in your dreams.

Coma is a rare Russian movie distributors bothered to dub into English (we still recommend watching it with subtitles). It didn't make it into North American theaters but showed up on DVD, Blu-ray and VOD soon after its international release in 2020.—Giles Edwards

Come to Daddy ★★★ 1/2

DIRECTED BY: Ant Timpson

FEATURING: Elijah Wood, Stephen McHattie, Michael Smiley, Martin Donovan

PLOT: Norval receives a letter from his long-estranged father, begging him to come to his remote home to reconnect--but daddy is not who he seems.

COMMENTS: Appropriately for a plot that hinges on a theft, there is a whole lot of stealing in the movie: stealing of scenes (not to mention chewing of scenery). That's to be expected from a film featuring some of the best characters actors in the business, each one-upping the other as the craziness volcano erupts. The heavy lifting (and grand larceny) is done most by Elijah Wood, who surprises equally with his capacity to normalize the narrative while drawing attention to himself with perhaps the most nerdy/hipster/pratt/mama's boy character I have ever seen. (While rocking one of the worst haircuts ever to grace the big screen.)

Wide-eyed, apprehensive Norval (Wood) steps off a bus close to the middle of nowhere, California, and walks on foot while rolling a massive suitcase along with him. When he arrives at "a UFO that crashed in the '60s"-style cabin, he meets his father (Stephen McHattie), whom he has not seen for three decades. They bond, or try to, but mostly Norval endures of varying degrees of abuse. Norval is a recovering alcoholic who describes himself as a combination DJ, pianist, beat-layer, and event organizer; what his father describes him as I cannot type, but the description is apt. At one point mid-rant, his father's dander rises so high that he has a fatal heart attack while threatening his boy with a butcher knife. Then what's actually going on starts coming to light.

Watching it with a packed film festival house on a Friday night, I noticed two related things: the audience was far too eager to laugh at things that probably warranted silence, and *Come to Daddy*'s sheer oddness (and intensity) was insidious. Rabid fans of Stephen McHattie burst out laughing at the drop of a pin; I sat quietly wondering what, if anything, was going to make a payoff that warranted my attention. The arrival of Michael Smiley's character (a kind of a twisted, drunken, deadbeat heir to *A Field in England*'s effete and sinister O'Neal) turned out to be the harbinger of the film's madness, and once this madness set in, it did not relent.

After a successful film festival run, *Come to Daddy* came in just under the wire for a pre-pandemic limited release in February 2020, then went to home video soon after.—Giles Edwards

Dead Dicks ★★

DIRECTED BY: Chris Bavota, Lee Paula Springer

FEATURING: Jillian Harris, Heston Horwin, Matt Keyes

PLOT: Mentally ill and suicidal, Richard tries to off himself, but is repeatedly reborn though an orifice that's growing on his wall, leaving his apartment cluttered with corpses of his previous selves.

COMMENTS: Richie and Becca debate about the orifice that has suddenly appeared on his bedroom wall. He calls it a vagina; she replies "it looks more like an asshole to me." He sees at as a possibility of rebirth, while she sees it as the same shit over and over? (For the record, it's obviously shaped like a vulva: trust me, I've seen one before.)

Whatever the hole is, it's driving the plot. Well, not really. The real conflict in *Dead Dicks* is not the struggle between death and rebirth, but the friction between Richie, a mentally ill artist who annoys his only neighbor with inappropriately loud music, and Becca, who nurtures her brother instead of pursuing her own dreams. A perpetual enabler, cleaning up her brother's spare corpses comes naturally to her.

The bare sets and uneven sound levels smack you in the face with the fact that *Dead Dicks* is a low-budget affair. But the main place where these limitations become intrusive is in the middle act, where cheap conversation takes the place of expensive action. Most of the available money goes into one big effect, a brief but nightmarish scene that does dazzle.

Of the spotty actors, Matt Keyes coming across the best (although there is little nuance required of his perpetually aggrieved neighbor). Jillian Harris has a hard time of it; her character is written to under-react to the insane events. I'm not sure exactly how an actress should play a character asked, by her brother, to hack up her brother's body, but I expected Becca to freak out in a much higher register than she does. There is some black comedy—sis is more shocked by her brother's full-frontal nudity than by the fact that he's returned from the dead—but the script mainly favors a dramatic tone.

Dead Dicks lags in the middle, but it starts the third act with two twists that come in quick succession, and ends on a strong note. The ultimate resolution is unexpected and morally troubling. Some may complain, but this is horror after all, and I'm glad they avoided a conventional feel-good ending. *Dead Dicks* is an ambitious and partly successful feature, though one that might have been scaled back to be an impressive short.

Plus, the body count is much higher than the total number of characters in the film, which is quite a trick to pull off.

Dead Dicks did not get a theatrical release. Artsploitation's 2020 DVD/Blu-ray contains commentary from the two directors and video diaries of the production. These extras are valuable to anyone considering making their own movie.—Gregory J. Smalley

The Dead Ones ★★★

DIRECTED BY: Jeremy Kasten

FEATURING: Sarah Rose Harper, Brandon Thane Wilson, Katie Foster, Torey Garza

PLOT: Four seniors are locked inside their high school at night as punishment for vandalism; characters dressed as the Four Horsemen of the Apocalypse stalk them.

COMMENTS: I'm not the first one to describe *The Dead Ones* as some variation of "*The Breakfast Club* goes to Hell," and I won't be the last. But *The Dead Ones* is a good bit more than that description suggests, digging into the issue of teen bullying and its sometimes apocalyptic consequences, while satisfying the bloodlust of its horror demographic with gore, shocks, and—yes—weirdness.

To continue the *Breakfast Club* metaphor: it should be no surprise that this one won't end with a Don't-You-Forget-About-Me-fist-pump. (Instead, we get an ironic recitation of the title, which is as close to redemption as *The Dead Ones* comes.) Rather than a collection of brains, athletes, princesses, etc., what we have here are two basket cases and two criminals. Three out of the four are fleshed out with backstories of abuse, humiliation, and mental illness. Emily, for example, is a cutter, and the bizarrely calligraphed scarring patterns on her arms and back are the first hints of weirdness in the film (not counting some high school chatter about the ancient Egyptian god Ammit). What begins as a haunted high school spook show is interrupted by a far more realistic horror: four masked figures (the same ones who have locked the teens inside for the night) go on a daytime shooting rampage. *The Dead Ones* alternates between these two stories, and it's not clear whether scenes are flashbacks, flash-forwards, or alternate realities. Meanwhile, weird scenes continue at Midnight Breakfast Club: warping floor tiles, rag-eating ghouls, a precariously perched column made of classroom furniture.

The acting is sufficient. Sarah Rose Harper holds down the main duties (and delivers one fairly chilling monologue). Effects are done on the cheap. Kasten throws a lot of different styles into the film, from horror movie standards like flickering lights to various CGI and post-production tricks, crude stop-motion monsters, and scenes that play out on security cameras or YouTube videos. The welter of techniques keeps you off balance, but it might have been a stronger film had they stuck to a couple of key stylistic motifs. Still, it's hard to complain about a horror movie that has the courage to go full weird.

Surprisingly divisive, *The Dead Ones* garnered positive reviews from critics while earning a shockingly low 3.2 rating (as of October 2020) on IMDB. Maybe it's just a case of the film not finding its way to the proper audience yet.

The Dead Ones was shot way back in 2009; some have speculated that the sad plague of school shootings in the following years scared off investors and distributors who thought the subject matter was too raw for the moment. Once finally completed in 2019, it played at only one film festival (Brussels International Fantastic Film Festival). Fortunately, Artsploitation Pictures rescued it from obscurity and put it out on the Internet and Blu-ray. The disc comes with two short behind-the-scenes featurettes and two commentaries, which are worth listening to in order to catch all the tiny, almost subliminal details that will probably escape you on a first viewing.—Gregory J. Smalley

The Death of Dick Long ★★★ 1/2

DIRECTED BY: Daniel Scheinert

FEATURING: Michael Abbott, Jr., Andre Hyland, Sarah Baker, Virginia Newcomb

PLOT: Two dimwitted band members try to cover up the suspicious death of the third member of their trio in a small town.

COMMENTS: "Hey… ya'll motherfuckers wanna get weird?" asks the eponymous (and still living) Dick Long in the opening scene. *The Death of Dick Long* does get—sort of—weird, though not in the way you might be expecting from half of the directing duo behind *Swiss Army Man*. Like the crude joke in the movie's title, which makes you think you're headed for a raunchy redneck comedy, the word "weird" is a bit of misdirection. Though the movie is set in Alabama, the "weird" here is of the species you'd expect to see in a headline beginning with the words "Florida Man…"

Initially submitted as a regional black comedy, *Death* deals with the consequences of the trio's "weird" night, which we gather must have involved something more intense than the shotgunned beers, joints, and fireworks we see in the opening montage. At first, Dick's body (which his bandmates surreptitiously dump at the emergency room door in the wee hours) is unidentified, and the precise cause of death unknown. Zeke and Earl aren't good at cover-ups, but fortunately for them the hometown cops—led by a sheriff with a cane and her friendly lesbian deputy—are equally inept at solving unexpected crimes, even when the suspects literally hand them clues. The first half settles into a *Fargo*-esque groove, as sleep-deprived Zeke forgets to cover up bloodstains and neither conspirator shows much skill at improvising cover stories under pressure. Then, around the midway point, *Dick Long* takes its outrageous premise and, unexpectedly, wrings serious drama out of it. This tonal shift is a huge gamble, but it pays off.

The acting is universally strong—close to great. Michael Abbott, Jr. handles the lead with tragicomic aplomb. He doesn't want the secret to get out, but he's even more afraid of hurting those he loves, which makes it easier to root for him despite his duplicity. His buddy Earl (Andre Hyland) is a comic foil, a vapin' fool whose philosophy of life distills down to a beer and a shrug. Sarah Baker makes you think she might grow up to be Alabama's answer to Marge Gunderson. Virginia Newcomb has a supporting role as Zeke's wife, but gets a major moment when hubby awkwardly and reluctantly confesses after inconsistencies in his story give him no other choice. The smaller roles are handled with equal facility. Scheinert deserves credit for assembling and guiding this fine ensemble.

The Death of Dick Long put in a token appearance in theaters before showing up on an extras-free DVD and Blu-ray in December. This solo outing for Scheinert does not mean that he's broken up with directing partner Daniel Kwan. The Daniels are currently at work on a new project, *Everything Everywhere All at Once*, described as an "interdimensional action film."—Gregory J. Smalley

Disappearance at Clifton Hill ★★★

DIRECTED BY: Albert Shin

FEATURING: Tuppence Middleton, Hannah Gross, Eric Johnson, David Cronenberg

PLOT: Returning home to Niagara Falls after her mother's death, a woman remembers a childhood incident that haunted her—witnessing a one-eyed boy being abducted in the woods—and decides to investigate.

COMMENTS: Clifton Hill is a tourist trap street in Niagara Falls, Canada. Although a memorable scene in *Disappearance at Clifton Hill* occurs at Clifton Hill, the titular disappearance doesn't occur there. Make of that bit of misdirection what you will.

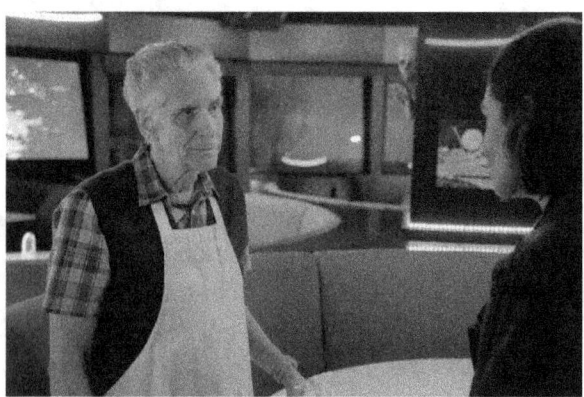

The disappearance we're concerned with occurs upriver, and about twenty-five years before Abby returns to Niagara Falls after her mother's death. Abby wants to preserve Rainbow Inn, the old family business which has fallen into disrepair, from being bought up by the Charles Lake Corporation; her sister wants to sell and move on with life. Browsing through mom's old photographs turns up a picture that sparks Abby's memory of the day she saw the boy abducted, and she begins investigating. Her follow-ups bring her into contact with a podcaster and local historian who operates out of a UFO-shaped cafe and who knows where the bodies aren't buried, a husband and wife magic act modeled on Siegfried and Roy, and the dashing Charles Lake III. Evidence of what might have happened to the boy builds slowly, while a series of glitchy, tiger-infected dreams that look like Ken Russell montages edited on third-generation VHS tapes liven things up (and provide the film's sole weird moments).

The ultimate mystery has as much to do with Abby's slowly-revealed past as it does with the disappearance she's investigating. Her backstory isn't a twist, exactly; it's more of a change of focus that turns *Disappearance* from a thriller into a character study. The movie's eventual revelations about Abby do, however, illuminate a couple of incidents that might not have made complete sense otherwise (for example, why Abby's parents never contacted the police after the incident in the woods). The switch of emphasis works; the script slowly (and purposefully) undermines its own narrative.

Full of psychological unease rather than jump scares, *Clifton Hill* plays well within its budget. Superior writing elevates it from merely a "modest thriller" to a "modest-but-clever thriller." An ace performance from lead Tuppence Middleton carries the film.

Much was made in some quarters of David Cronenberg's small role as the podcaster. While Old Croney holds his own, there's nothing revelatory in his performance. The significance of his presence has more to do with his endorsement of the film, which is a major marketing point for a not-flashy indie that relies on a slow-burn to pull you in.

IFC Midnight gave *Disappearance* a modest theatrical release in February 2020.—Gregory J. Smalley

Dreamland [AKA Bruce McDonald's Dreamland] ★★★★

DIRECTED BY: Bruce McDonald

FEATURING: Stephen McHattie, Henry Rollins, Juliette Lewis

PLOT: A burnt-out trumpeting virtuoso is to play at the wedding at the castle of a disgraced countess, while a burnt-out hitman has a crisis of conscience when he discovers his boss is trafficking young girls.

COMMENTS: The ending credits for Bruce McDonald's latest movie indicate that it was "filmed on location in Dreamland." The non-specific geography encapsulates the overall atmosphere of *Dreamland*: strange goings-on in a shabby metropolis at the foot of an imposing, high-walled fortress. The neon grit of the atmosphere feels like it was scraped off the cracking leather shoes of the protagonist after having just stomped through mean streets on mean business.

Having just looked at some Tinder-style photos of underage girls, a very bad man gets half a sentence out before being shot in the head by his limo driver—none other than our nameless hero (Stephen McHattie). Defiant, with his scraggly haircut and gumshoe get-up straight from the '70s, he's rewarded with a fat wad of cash from his boss Hercules. The nameless gunman's next assignment: collecting and delivering the "right pinkie finger" of a disgraced trumpet player (Stephen McHattie) for an alleged slight against Hercules.

In both roles, McHattie conjures a Dashell Hammet archetype of the world-weary man, each character having its own twist. While the trumpet player's mind has been ground down (in his case, by heroin), it's the hitman's soul that has been hit hard. Combined, they'd make a perfectly broken Sam Spade, and watching them talk with each other is simultaneously eerie and hilarious. This ties in with the stylized interludes: the killer is struck by haunting visions, and the musician is "able to be in two places at once." Their paths keep crossing, and the hitman's fight for what is right contrasts with his counterpart's shame at not being able to take any action.

Some fairly heavy stuff goes on in *Dreamland*, yet the film spins along in a vibrant fashion. Garish nightclubs merge with dispiriting city streets and homicidal pawnbroker's wives aid against gun-toting boy gangs; but the image of McHattie's face—either as the haunted gunman or the wryly smiling maestro—dominates. And once again I find myself making this sound heavy. I suppose that heavy it may be; but it is also, one might say, dreamy.

Dreamland debuted on video-on-demand and later showed up on DVD in 2020. You might see it listed as *Bruce McDonald's Dreamland* to avoid confusion with the Margot Robbie thriller *Dreamland*, also from 2019. —Giles Edwards

Gretel & Hansel ★★★

DIRECTED BY: Osgood Perkins

FEATURING: Sophia Lillis, Alice Krige, Samuel Leakey

PLOT: Cast out by their poor mother, Gretel takes her brother Hansel into the woods, where they come upon a house inhabited by a witch.

COMMENTS: There's no gingerbread house in *Gretel & Hansel*, but there is an unnatural abundance of food that appears on the old woman's table day after day. Near starvation, Gretel and her younger brother Hansel aren't picky about where this abundance is coming from—at first.

Oz Perkins' spin on the ancient fairy tale focuses on the relationship between Gretel and the witch, who is both an antagonist and a perverse mentor. To expand the slim folklore to feature length, the screenplay provides the witch a rich backstory. Wickedly played by a creaky Alice Krieg, she's not just a boogey-woman, but a full-fledged herbalist and pagan practitioner. After a prologue describing her origins—a fairy tale inside the fairy tale—the story begins in earnest with Gretel discovering her prospects are limited in a famine-plagued village. With mom providing no help, she takes Hansel as a ward and sets off in search of a better life. An out-of-place episode involving what appears to be a mutant zombie, and a bout with hallucinogenic toadstools, provide a couple of bumps in the road before they arrive at the mysterious cottage. Once there, the eldritch atmosphere takes over as Gretel settles into a routine: days sparring with the witch, nights filled with nightmares. All the while, Hansel is getting fatter...

This gently spooky middle part of the film is the strongest. *Gretel* ends on a too-short climax that, while true to both the folklore and the revisionist narrative the script builds, disappoints in its obviousness. There's no budget for elaborate effects, but the dark cinematography is dreamy and intoxicating. Shots are filled with occult symbolism: pentagrams scratched on trees, Gretel's eye caught in a triangle like an Eye of Providence, and the pointy roof of the witch's house framed beside an eternally crescent moon.

Thematically, *Gretel* is muddled. It's a coming-of-age story with a blink-and-you'll-miss-it reference to menstruation. Gretel herself changes during the course of the story, growing from an unsure virginal girl to a confident virginal young woman; Sophia Lillis captures the transformation capably. More interesting is the focus on fairy tales as warnings, and particularly a bit of play on the ideas of poison and gifts. The witch explains to Gretel that, although poison tastes bitter, imbibing a bit is salutary because it builds immunity. By contrast, the pastries on the witch's table taste sweet, but hide a bitter reality.

Gretel & Hansel's slow-paced art-house aspirations were designed to please critics more than PG-horror audiences. It's no wonder that it was dumped in theaters in the cinematically lean month of February with little promotion; the bigger mystery is how this mid-budget horror got a relatively large scale pre-Covid release in the first place. --Gregory J. Smalley

Horse Girl ★★1/2

DIRECTED BY: Jeff Baena

FEATURING: Alison Brie, Molly Shannon, Matthew Gray Gubler

PLOT: A young woman with a family history of mental illness becomes paranoid that aliens are affecting her behavior.

COMMENTS: *Horse Girl* conjures up a specific archetype: a girly-girl so relentlessly feminine that she alienates others and relates better to equines than humans. Sarah works at an arts and crafts shop selling beads and yarn, and hangs out at the stable decorating her old horse's mane with homemade lanyards, even though the owners hint that she's not welcome anymore. Other than a kindly older lady at the shop, she has no real friends, and spends most of her time watching the supernatural TV soap "Purgatory." Sarah's social awkwardness takes a turn for the worse after she starts having dreams about a glowing ramp hanging over the ocean and a white-on-white room where she sees comatose people whom she dimly recognizes...

What are we to think of a character who asks her doctor, "Is there a test to see if I'm a clone?" Sarah has proto-schizophrenic fantasies about alien abductions and time travel, but the script never seriously suggests that her theories are more than the ravings of a madwoman. Rather than hoping that there might be an alternate, high-stakes sci-fi explanation for our protagonist's inner turmoil, we're left watching her sad decline into madness. Sarah's psychotic break happens abruptly; the last act is essentially a long hallucination broken up by a few conversations with her caseworker. The scenes are weird, but we never get the psychological depth in her backstory that would make her delusions meaningful. We aren't even explicitly told why she's so attached to her horse—it's left to us to put two and two together. Without much emotional connection to Sarah, or narrative investment in her crazy theories, we're left to pity rather than empathize with the poor horse girl. We watch Brie move through glowing white rooms and wrap herself in a homemade anti-alien suit. But it's a depiction of madness rather than a submersion

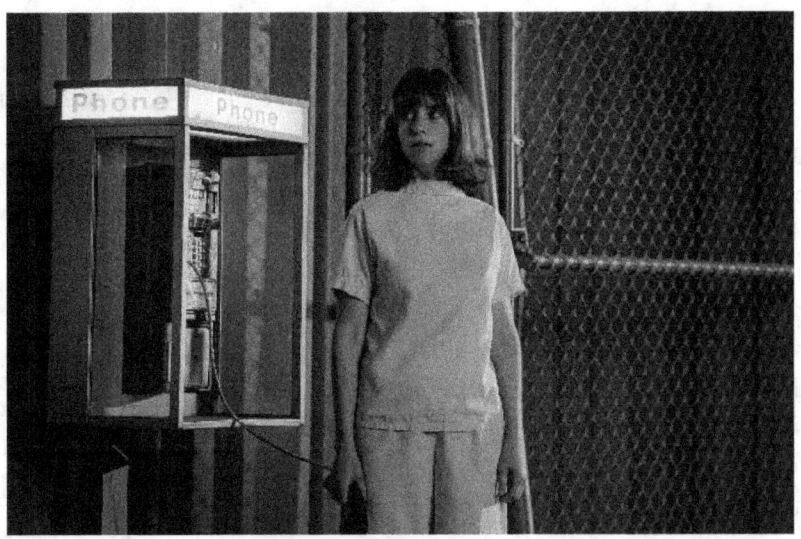

in madness. *Horse Girl* keeps us on the outside of Sarah's head, looking in.

Brie excels in the role, socially stunted during the first half and dazed and terrified when her psychic dam breaks. *Horse Girl* is clearly a passion project for her: Brie co-wrote the script, partly basing Sarah on her own paranoid schizophrenic grandmother. This makes it more tragic that, despite her fervent portrayal, the story isn't as gripping as it might have been.

Horse Girl was made as and currently remains a Netflix exclusive movie.—Gregory J. Smalley

I Lost My Body [J'ai perdu mon corps] ★★★1/2

DIRECTED BY: Jérémy Clapin

FEATURING THE VOICES OF: Hakim Faris, Victoire Du Bois

PLOT: A right hand, severed from its host body, goes on a harrowing journey in hopes of a reunion.

COMMENTS: If the logline, "It's like *The Incredible Journey*, but it's a hand" doesn't raise an eyebrow, then you are impervious to surprise. But the earnestly told, irony-free tale of a hand that is violently amputated and

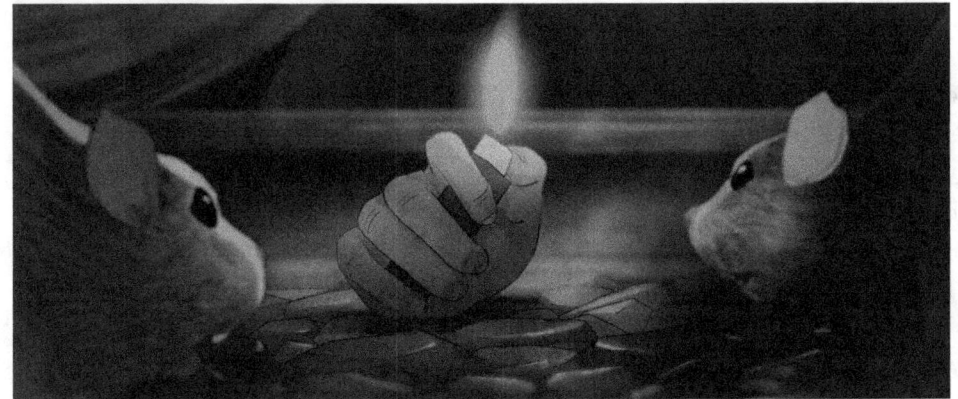

struggles mightily to be reunited with its body is an idea so crazy, and an undertaking so destined to end disastrously, that it just has to work.

Director Clapin raises the difficulty level by balancing multiple narratives and time periods. He juggles present-day Naoufel, an orphaned immigrant who happens to be missing a hand; his backstory as a boy in Algeria; his recent history as an aimless young man hoping to win the affection of a pretty young woman through techniques straight out of a wacky Hollywood rom-com; and, of course, the adventures of a hand loose in the city.

The hand is a riveting character, navigating the streets like a wily insect, triumphing in battles with the city's wildlife, and generally overcoming very long odds. It's worth noting that the title clearly identifies the hand as the star of the show. While we see flashbacks to Naoufel's youth, the loving close-ups of his soon-to-be-separated extremity remind us that this is as much the hand's story.

It is sometimes said that it is harder for animated movies to seem weird because they are already a step removed from reality. But some of Clapin's techniques could be called anti-animation, like the long, static, dialogue-focused meet-cute that takes place in an apartment building lobby as Naoufel chats with the future object of his affection entirely over an intercom. This is animated! And yet, the details are so lovingly captured – his hangdog embarrassment, his resigned eating of a piece of mushed-up pizza – that the format becomes completely irrelevant.

I Lost My Body is a subtle turn of the prism that casts a familiar tale in an entirely new light. Instead of asking "What happened to that boy who lost his hand?" it has the courage to ask, "What happened to that hand?" The answer turns out to be even more affecting.

After an acclaimed festival run, *I Lost My Body* debuted as a Netflix exclusive in December 2019, too late for inclusion in last year's Yearbook.— Shane Wilson

Impossible Monsters ★★

DIRECTED BY: Nathan Catucci

FEATURING: Santino Fontana, Devika Bhise, Chris Henry Coffey

PLOT: With the prospect of a juicy grant on the line, a professor needs to keep his project together; the murder of one of his participants complicates things.

COMMENTS: A social worker, a painter, and a dominatrix walk into a sleep study… but that suggests that *Impossible Monsters* is more interesting than it actually is. It isn't for want of trying. Fulfilling its obligation as a "psychological thriller," there is a twist; in keeping with the "sleep study" premise, there are a lot of dream sequences; and in homage to the title-inspiring quote, there is plenty of mention of Francisco de Goya. But all the pieces add up to a dense sludge of events that awkwardly drips over the edges of its narrative container, making a mess on the floor.

Rich Freeman is a university professor in New York City, focusing on sleep and dreams. To further aid mankind, he proposes a study involving three volunteers who will discuss their dreams, keep a dream journal, and in the process have various socio-emotional-sexual interactions with each other. Meanwhile, Freeman's friend/adversary is busy cheating on his wife with one of Freeman's students, Jo, a "sexual pain exploration specialist." Jo has a crush on Freeman, and is unhappy that Freeman is dating the second participant, a young social worker who dreams of starting a non-profit in

Albany, N.Y. Freeman's mentor, who works with veterans suffering from PTSD, wants Freeman to join him and "make a difference" in... Albany. The university dean, however, wants the prestige that would accompany the Really Big Grant, which somehow hinges solely on Freeman's work. The third participant is Otis, a soft-spoken painter raised in foster care and who may or may not have been raped in his early teens and may or may not have, later, burnt down his foster family's home.

That's a lot of plot write-up, but a sense of the goings-on is necessary to emphasize the importance of telling a story. Not six or seven stories. Everything interrelates, of course (speaking of relations, the lapse of professional ethics on display here is astounding), but if you've only got so much time, cuts needs must. Though not without its charm, *Impossible Monsters* has too much narrative flab supported by too little narrative bone and sinew. As such, it never really gets moving.

Impossible Monsters got a very limited theatrical release in February 2020 before quickly moving to home video and video-on-demand.—Giles Edwards

Knives and Skin ★★1/2

DIRECTED BY: Jennifer Reeder

FEATURING: Grace Smith, Ireon Roach, Kayla Carter, Marika Engelhardt, Ty Olwin, Raven Whitley

PLOT: A teen girl's disappearance affects the residents of a small suburban community.

COMMENTS: Jennifer Reeder's feature debut is a "Twin Peaks"-inspired study of a high school girl's disappearance, decorated with lots of soapy subplots and feminist subtext. It's got a capella versions of 80s New Wave hits like "My Lips Are Sealed" and "Girls Just Wanna Have Fun" that sound like they were arranged for Gregorian chant. It's got high school students roaming the halls in dreadlocks stiffened into tentacle peaks and garish tribal makeup. A girl sells her mom's used underwear to the principal as a side hustle. A pregnant woman hooks up with a mime behind her husband's back. It's got a grieving but horny MILF, vaginal note passing, and a talking tiger t-shirt.

With all that cool stuff going on, it's almost hard to explain why the movie, as a whole, fails. Maybe it's the fact that, other than Marika Engelhardt as the victim's deteriorating mother, every character acts like they've been sneaking too much Xanax from mom's medicine cabinet. A little of the subdued, melancholy mood that Reeder creates goes a long way; the film needed more comedy and more mania for a change of pace. The feminist message is also too on-the-nose, as if Reeder didn't trust her audience to figure out the cruelty of the slut-tease dilemma high school girls find themselves in without spelling it out in cringey explicitness.

More than anything, the problem is with the screenplay. There's no central character, the mystery of Carolyn's disappearance is never resolved, and, like the teens longing to escape their bland suburban existences, the entire enterprise goes nowhere. Since individual scenes are much better than the whole, *Knives and Skin* might have worked better as a TV series, where the leisurely approach would allow character development over longer arcs. As it is, every story the movie embarks on feels shortchanged. And despite being too long for comfort at 111 minutes, the plot feels compressed.

The cinematography is vivid and colorful, the costuming the right shade of bizarre, the music sets the exact mood the movie seeks, and, as mentioned, Reeder has plenty of quirky ideas to surprise you; there's so much that's good here that it's a shame that *Knives and Skin* ultimately rates a near-miss. Younger females with offbeat (or queer) proclivities may really groove to it, however, so it could serve as a good entry point into weirder cinema for your kid sister.

Knives and Skin received a brief pre-pandemic theatrical run starting in December 2019. It's available on Blu-ray, video-on-demand, and, at the time of this writing, on Hulu.—Gregory J. Smalley

Lake Michigan Monster ★★★★1/2

DIRECTED BY: Ryland Brickson Cole Tews

FEATURING: Ryland Brickson Cole Tews, Beulah Peters, Erick West, Daniel Long

PLOT: Having lost his father to the claws of the terrible "Lake Michigan Monster," Captain Seafield assembles a crew of specialists to exact his revenge.

COMMENTS: In the spirit of the movie, this is a DIY review. Feel free to cut and paste the sections below however suits your mood.

Good: There is a jokesy doppelgänger of Guy Maddin at work in *Lake Michigan Monster*. Ryland Tews captures the Canadian auteur's aesthetic—grainy black and white, mythic proportions, and the idolization of a city—and puts it to work for an episodic comedy that would seem ramshackle if it weren't so charming and somehow pinned to what just about passes as a story arc.

Plot: Assembling a mercenary crew comprising a weapons expert, a N.A.V.Y. drop-out, and a "sonar individual," Captain Seafield hopes to hunt and destroy the titular monster that he blames for his father's murder. With half-baked schemes (à la "Nauty Lady" and other pun-driven titles), he fails again and again until he is abandoned by his hirelings and is forced to summon a ghost army (found, incidentally, in an Episcopal cathedral).

Weird: *Lake Michigan Monster* is merely 78 minutes long, but a whole world and mythology is haphazardly crammed into every nook. Seafield begins each outing with a magical, animated map of the action, on which designations for each crew member zip around according to his mad whim. The fourth wall is battered to dust as Seafield, in character, begins to dismantle the narrative shell that keeps the audience separate from his machinations; we become very much the accomplice in his silly work as the movie goes on.

Opening or Closing: So what is it like to watch this movie? Unless you have some very creative film buddies, it'd be hard to get closer to the core of the crafting experience. Mind you, this isn't just some dumb evolution of a movie into a movie about movies. This is just some dumb ~~sea~~-lake-faring yarn that feels like it's being told to you live over a glass of bourbon. But there is a gloriousness to its apparent idiocy. No real actors, no fabricated sets, but one heckuva wild and whimsical outing awaits you.

Release: Made for relative pennies, *Lake Michigan Monster* won the Audience Award for Best International Feature at the 2019. That wasn't enough to earn it an actual theatrical release, but it did receive a spectacular Blu-ray edition from Arrow Video, and certainly earned back its budget multiple times over. But whatever idiot thought the original scratchy, glitchy, warped print was good enough for a so-called "special edition" Blu-ray should have a talking-to. All the blurry black-and-white imagery, silly angles, and 19th-century cinematic effects look just as home-made and... Hang on. [*Checking Notes...*] Ah, it's supposed to be that way. Of course! And what better treatment for the film than to treat it in a manner it wants to be treated. The Arrow edition is all-around great, featuring a handful of interviews, some special effects breakdowns, the classic Seafield sea-shanty, two cast and crew commentaries (one sober, one drunk), and even Ryland Brickson Cole Tews' silly web series about an intergalactic process server. "Criterion"-level treatment for an Ed Wood-level motion picture. Bang-on.—Giles Edwards

Love Express: The Disappearance of Walerian Borowczyk ★★1/2

DIRECTED BY: Kuba Mikurda

FEATURING: Walerian Borowczyk, Noël Véry, Terry Gilliam, Neil Jordan, Peter Bradshaw, Slavoj Zizek, Lisbeth Hummel

PLOT: A talking heads documentary about the rise and fall of expatriate Polish director Walerian Borowczyk, who started out as an enfant terrible of French Surrealism, but ended up stereotyped and dismissed as a Eurotrash pornographer.

COMMENTS: Walerian Borowczyk began his career as an acclaimed Surrealist animator, working in both stop-motion and traditional forms. Over two decades, he produced almost two-dozen award-winning films featuring milk-drinking wigs (*The House*, 1958) and blue-bleeding angels (*Angel's Games*, 1964). His live action debut, 1969's dystopian parable *Goto: The Island of Love*, was a highly-anticipated critical success. His career takes a sharp turn, though, with the arty, titillating erotic portmanteau *Immoral Tales* (1973). *Tales* is a succès de scandale, but Borowczyk loses critical support; that erosion accelerates greatly with his follow-up, the outrageous bestiality tale *The Beast* [*La Bête*] (1975). With *The Beast* banned across the world, Borowczyk's career begins to decline. He is pigeonholed; producers only fund him if he agrees to film overtly erotic movies. He's paired with softcore siren Sylvia Kristel for the flop *The Streetwalker* (1976), and his fortunes fall further. Borowczyk manages to make a few more interesting and ambitious films in the late 70s and 80s, but, in the public and the industry's eyes, he's just a pornographer. By 1987 he has fallen so low that he's called on to helm *Emmanuelle 5*. But he's disinterested in the project, and walks off set after he's disrespected by top-billed scream queen Monique Gabrielle (according to the assistant director who actually completed the movie, she slapped him). He releases one more film, the arty *Love Rites*, but that's it; Borowczyk disappears as a feature filmmaker.

The paragraph above contains all the essential information you'll learn from *Love Express: The Disappearance of Walerian Borowczyk*. There are a few juicy tidbits here and there, but the documentary is essentially an excuse for a parade of high profile cinephile fans---critic Peter Bradshaw, cinematographer Noël Véry, the always delightful Slavoj Zizek, and others---to say nice things about Borowczyk. Indeed, large parts of the movie seem made in the YouTube-inspired "reaction video" genre, as directors Terry Gilliam and Neil Jordan watch clips from Borowoczyk films in real time (admittedly, Gilliam's amused shock at the rape scene in *The Beast* is priceless). Lisbeth Hummel's conflicted reminiscences about filming *The Beast* are interesting; unexpectedly, she was more traumatized by the rose scene than the rape. But overall, *Love Express* is merely an appreciation and celebration of Borowoczyk, as it has to be---because who's going to dial up a Borowoczyk documentary besides a Borowoczyk fan? Someday it will make a fine Blu-ray extra.

Love Express played sporadically on the festival circuit since 2018, emerging on DVD, Blu-ray and VOD in late 2020.—Gregory J. Smalley

Monos ★★★★

DIRECTED BY: Alejandro Landes

FEATURING: Sofia Buenaventura, Julianne Nicholson, Moisés Arias, Wilson Salazar

PLOT: A paramilitary squadron of teenagers guard a hostage at a remote jungle location; bad decisions by the inexperienced soldiers lead to tragedy.

COMMENTS: *Monos* is a movie that reminds everyone of other movies, of *Lord of the Flies* and *Apocalypse Now* and *Aguirre the Wrath of God*. That's not a knock on director Alejandro Landes; there's no need to reinvent the wheel when existing styles are the best means to tell the story you want to tell.

A co-ed group of teenagers are given rifles and tasked with guarding an American hostage (and a cow) on a lonely mountaintop. To pass the time, they play blindfolded soccer and shoot automatic rounds into the air; as the story begins, their life is more like summer camp than boot camp. They have code names like "Rambo" and "Bigfoot" and work for "the Organization," with their single point of contact with the outside world a ripped dwarf dubbed "the Messenger." We do not know why they are fighting or whom they are fighting for or against. Besides providing an ambiguous ambiance, there's an important reason for the lack of specific context to the military campaign—it puts you in the same position as the conscripted kids, who have no ideology and show no understanding of the prospects or merits of their side of the conflict.

Monos is a worthy movie, but it's mostly a work of psychological realism exploring the dynamics of a group of child soldiers. The kids struggle against their hormones, form internal alliances, don't understand why their hostage isn't friendlier to them, and make immature decisions that lead to their numbers being whittled down over the course of the movie. Its slim claims to weirdness stem from a number of impressionistic, ritualistic montages—in particular, one where three of the team discover psychedelic mushrooms on the eve of a government ambush—which gives it that surreal fog-of-war haze found in war films like *Come and See*. Mica Levi (*Under the Skin*) contributes a misty, atonal score that heightens the ethereal unease.

Wilson Salazar ("the Messenger") was himself drafted into the Revolutionary Armed Forces of Colombia (FARC) at the age of thirteen. He was initially brought in to train the kids to act like soldiers, but the filmmakers liked his look and persona so much that they cast him in a prominent role.

Monos played film festivals and got an extremely limited U.S. theatrical release in 2019, but wasn't available to most viewers until it appeared on home video and VOD in December, too late to make it into our 2019 Yearbook.—Gregory J. Smalley

Murder Death Koreatown ★★1/2

DIRECTED BY: None listed

FEATURING: None listed

PLOT: An unemployed man becomes obsessed with a murder that happened in a nearby apartment complex, but his investigation turns paranoid as he imagines a wide-ranging conspiracy.

COMMENTS: Though taking its starting cue from a real-life murder, *Murder Death Koreatown* is, it's safe to say, fictional, as you will doubtlessly decide for yourself by the time its deranged protagonist starts spouting theories about the Pastors, ghosts, and voices speaking to from the sewers. It's like a re-edited version of one of those paranoid YouTube videos that leave you wondering whether the uploader is genuinely crazy or is just pranking you, or like *Under the Silver Lake* remade on a $100 budget in the style of *The Blair Witch Project*.

Our unemployed, over-stressed narrator begins by following blood splatters on his sidewalk, discovering that one of his neighbors murdered her husband in a neighboring apartment complex in L.A.'s Koreatown. He finds some minor inconsistencies, and interviews (real-looking) locals to see if they noticed anything unusual. As his investigation continues, he starts uncovering connections which aren't really connections—and which sometimes don't even rise to the level of coincidences—but which are completely obvious and convincing to the protagonist. But unless you're Dale Cooper, it's never a good idea to admit evidence from your dreams into a murder investigation. It's not really a spoiler to suggest that the movie is a study of one man's descent into delusional paranoia.

Your enjoyment will be linked to your tolerance for watching feature-length shot-on-cellphone vlogs. The movie is, by necessity, talky—there are no significant effects or action sequences. Unfortunately, the narrator's voice isn't compelling: he delivers most of his lines in a drab "woe is me" tone, and at one point his bleats of terror make him sound like a Muppet startled by a spider. On the plus side, the actor they found to play the shifty-eyed homeless vet in the alley is so convincing that you might believe he's a real hobo, and that the plot was actually built around his schizophrenic ramblings. The effective horror soundtrack is another element that supersedes the budget; in fact, it's so well-made that it at times undermines the film's found footage credibility. Ironically, it's too professional a touch for a movie that's trying to make its amateurism into a selling point.

If you're willing to overlook the budgetary issues, however, *Murder Death Koreatown* is a solid watch that holds your interest for just over 70 minutes—and if you plot it on a dollars spent to entertainment value curve, it's off the chart.

Murder Death Koreatown did a reasonable job of viral marketing, keeping its director and actors secret to preserve the illusion that it was an actual found-footage artifact. You can read some of the movie's promotional gimmickry at https://imgur.com/gallery/UPnp5U0. It debuted on Amazon Prime (for free) and you can also buy it on DVD or Blu-ray; they don't have to sell many copies to recoup the budget.—Gregory J. Smalley

The Platform [*El hoyo*] ★★★★

DIRECTED BY: Galder Gaztelu-Urrutia

FEATURING: Ivan Massagué, Alexandra Masangkay, Zorion Eguileor

PLOT: To qualify for an "accredited diploma," Goreng volunteers to spend six months on "the platform": a vertical prison with one feeding tray that allows the inmates, from floor one down to the bottom, a mere two minutes to eat their daily sustenance before it moves on, emptier and emptier as it descends.

COMMENTS: As a social experiment, watching *The Platform* with like-minded 366ers in a group setting was a real treat. But the social experiment explored by film itself is nothing but harrowing. Though he takes some visual (and, doubtless, budgetary) inspiration from other near-future tracts about human nature, Galder

Gaztelu-Urrutia is making his own movie, telling a story whose scale and brutality can make you lose your appetite.

Like the titular conveyance, *The Platform* begins piled high—but with intrigue, instead of food. The (literal) platform's food, we learn, diminishes during each section of its downward journey. Concurrently, our insight into the film's premise increases. Goreng is the lens through which we watch the system, administered, of course, by "The Administration." He is an academic, established not only by his demeanor, but also by his sole possession: a copy of Cervantes' *Don Quixote*. His only companion is an older gentleman. He's affable enough, to be sure, but also armed with a "SamuraiPlus": a knife with the almost magical ability to self-sharpen with use (or so claims the advertisement). Goreng learns the hard way that an accredited diploma might not be worth this ordeal-by-privation.

Rarely have I ever seen "drab industrial" captured so well–and so simply. *The Platform* hinges wholly on the script and its characters, since we spend almost the entire film on a simple, concrete cell. Massagué and the rest are all top notch, imbuing a believability into what are effectively expositional conversations interspersed with some not-so-light-handed social commentary. Capitalism is skewered, then roasted to perfection by some of the top cooks in the business. Having such an obvious agenda often does a disservice to a film, but Gaztelu-Urrutia tempers the preachifying with humor, pathos, and some incredibly well maneuvered dei-ex-machina sleights-of-hand. *The Platform* is an impressive movie, though perhaps not best enjoyed with a good meal.

Netflix snapped up *The Platform* and debuted it as an exclusive offering.—Giles Edwards

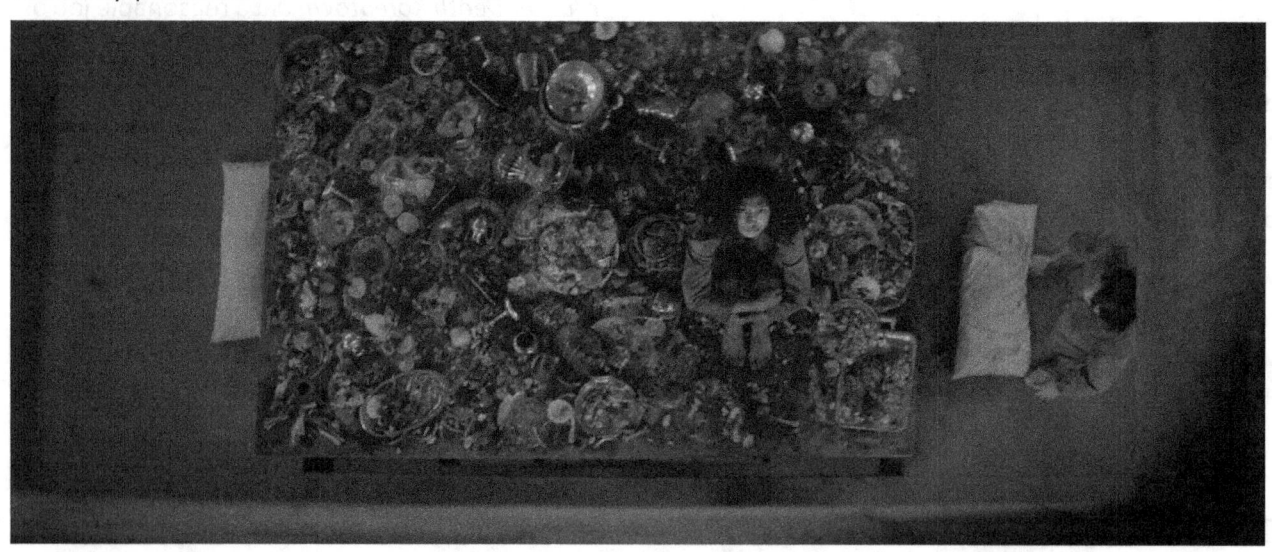

Possessor [AKA Possessor Uncut] ★★★★

DIRECTED BY: Brandon Cronenberg

FEATURING: Andrea Riseborough, Christopher Abbott, Jennifer Jason Leigh, Tuppence Middleton, Sean Bean

PLOT: In the near future, elite assassins carry out their work by possessing the bodies of innocent parties through a neural implant; Taysa, a top Possessor, has trouble on her latest assignment when the subject proves capable of sporadically suppressing her control.

COMMENTS: "This film has not been modified from its original version" is an odd notice to see on a first-run movie. Releasing *Possessor* as *Possessor Uncut* plays on the fact that Brandon Cronenberg declined to make cuts necessary for an "R" rating. Thirty years ago that would have been a big deal, but nowadays, unrated movies—especially provocative art-house pictures and sordid genre films (*Possessor* fits both categories)—get theatrical releases all the time with little hoo-ha. Still, after watching a possessed hostess plunge and twist a knife repeatedly into her target in *Possessor*'s opening sequence, you will understand why marketers made a big deal out of the "uncut" nature of this project. *Possessor*'s violence is graphic, well-done, and sociopathic.

A few details of the technology that allows *Possessor*'s assassins to ply their gruesome trade are plot-important: possessors are tested to make sure their individual memories remain intact after each job, and warned that it's safe to inhabit the host bodies for only about 72 hours. Storywise, there is not too much to follow: top hitwoman Taysa Vos (Risenborough, looking like she's inhabiting the body of a young Tilda Swinton) is feeling the stress of her lifestyle, spontaneously recalling grisly work scenes as she's trying to re-establish her bond with her estranged husband and son. Her boss offers a lucrative job that involves possessing a man so as to murder his CEO father-in-law-to-be as part of an extremely hostile takeover scheme. Things go badly, as Taysa finds her neural connection with her target isn't as steadfast as usual. The subject retains some measure of free will, complicating the job.

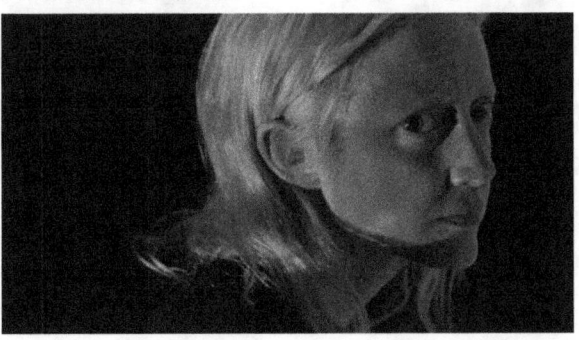

Like his father, Cronenberg *fils* knows when to ratchet up the unease with subtle touches and when to unleash the hounds. Our protagonist is, by necessity, off screen for most of the action. Her motivations are equally absent; we don't get any overt explanation as to why she's willing to risk her family—and her sanity—for her distasteful job. This blankness makes her all the more a monster, a perfect parasite. The trippy sequences where she and her target battle for control feature images of mannequin heads melting and reassembling, and Risenborough trapped in an ill-fitting mask, suggesting not so much a *Persona*-styled existential crisis as a character battling for her own humanity. While not as aggressively weird as Cronenberg's 2012 debut *Antiviral*, *Possessor* will satisfy your desire for soul-freezing chills.

A highly buzzed-about horror release, *Possessor* debuted (as *Possessor Uncut*) in pandemic-dampened theaters in October 2020, on VOD in November, and is scheduled to drop on Blu-ray in early December, soon after this Yearbook is released. It's the perfect stocking stuffer for the psychopath on your Christmas list.—Gregory J. Smalley

Psychomagic, A Healing Art ★★1/2

DIRECTED BY: Alejandro Jodorowsky

FEATURING: Alejandro Jodorowsky

PLOT: Surrealist director-cum-therapist Alejandro Jodorowsky describes his own variant of psychotherapy, which involves patients undergoing rituals such as smashing pumpkins with family member's faces on them or recreating their own births.

COMMENTS: *Psychomagic, A Healing Art* raises three questions: 1. Is "psychomagic" a revolutionary form of psychotherapy? 2. Does *Psychomagic* tell us something about Alejandro Jodorowsky? And, 3. Is it worth watching?

Most people will answer the first question "probably not." Jodorowsky walks us through a dozen handpicked case studies, all apparent successes, but with no long term follow-ups. A man who seems to be cured of his stuttering looks like an impressive triumph, but for all we know he's stumbling over words again as you read this. Jodorowsky's theories aren't peer reviewed, but he does characterize psychomagic is a healing *art*, not a healing *science*. It may be closer to faith healing than to either. Among people already motivated to fix their emotional problems, a ritual recommended by a trusted guru can surely invoke the placebo effect. But only dedicated Jodoworskians will buy that psychomagic is the therapeutic breakthrough the director wants us to believe in.

You'll more likely answer the question of whether *Psychomagic* reveals something significant about Jodorowsky "yes." In this final stage of his career, Jodorowsky's work has turned from the explicitly mystical to the explicitly autobiographical. In *Psychomagic*, he illustrates each case with a clip or two from his own movies, e.g., a man fastens a photograph of his father to a helium balloon and sends it to the heavens, similar to a balloon scene from *Endless Poetry*. You may begin to wonder: have the ritualistic scenes in Jodorowsky's movies been self-therapy all along? Is his whole corpus self-psychomagic?

And even though there may not be too much to psychomagic, is the film worth watching? For deep Jodorowsky fans, of course. For casual followers, it's iffier. I'd prioritize the narrative films first, then tackle this if you're fascinated by the man behind those extravagantly esoteric movies. *Psychomagic* resembles a Jodorowsky movie enacted by amateurs on a low budget. For example, our stutterer dresses up like Donald Duck and rides the teacups at Euro Disney, then lets Alejandro grab his testicles to transfer manly energy, then is painted gold and sent out into the streets to recite poetry. Some of the patients' confessions are so painfully raw that it feels unpleasantly voyeuristic to listen to them, and there's also some menstrual self-portraiture to be wary of. But it wouldn't be much of a Jodorowsky movie if there weren't moments that made you want to look away, would it?

Psychomagic was originally available only as a virtual theatrical release via Alamo Drafthouse, then as bonus disc in the Jodorowsky 4K restoration box set (reviewed later in this volume). It was a good excuse to buy that set and upgrade your Jodo collection. Late in 2020, however, *Psychomagic* came out separately on VOD and physical disc.—Gregory J. Smalley

Queen of Paradis ★★1/2

DIRECTED BY: Carl Lindstrom

FEATURING: Reine Paradis

PLOT: After a sold-out exhibit of her "Jungle" photography series, Reine Paradis goes around the United States to find the perfect locations for her follow-up, "Midnight."

COMMENTS: When I experience art, I try to do so with a degree of ignorance—I typically neither know, nor care to know, anything about the artist. I eschew "director's commentaries" for films because I want to see the work, and experience the story, on its own. I found *Queen of Paradis*, a documentary about an artist making art, somewhat awkward going—and knew half an hour in where it was going, and how it was going to get there.

We follow Reine Paradis, a Surrealist photographic artist, and her husband (who handily fills the roles of driver, prop repairman, photographer, and all around supportive swell guy) across the country as she puts lime plexi-plastic on display, making unreal, still life vignettes from a real, photographed setup. The tone is typical talking heads-style documentary interspersed with intimate scenes (socially and emotionally intimate, that is)—including more breaking-and-entering segments than I was expecting, as Reine and hubby sneak into a salt mine for a white "mountaintop" shoot, or onto a fenced-off billboard for a neon-lime-green spaghetti dinner "restaurant" shoot. It is a credit (I presume to director Lindstrom) that the tone never quite veers into satirical—any other movie with the line, "Okay! I have the fish!" shouted by a French woman standing beside a train track would doubtless smack of parody.

But an interesting topic does not an interesting movie make. While *Queen of Paradis* is competent, adequately assembled, and informative about its subject matter, that only hits a documentary's minimum requirements. (Upon reflection, it seems unfair to be so dismissive of a documentary that does those three things; oh well.) Still, all in all, I found Reine's imagery fascinating and playful and that, ultimately, is the point. *Queen of Paradis* could be dismissed as an advertisement for the artist, but I don't begrudge her that. It worked on me.

Queen of Paradis showed up on Amazon Prime (for free), and has not appeared in other formats.—Giles Edwards

Redoubt ★★1/2

DIRECTED BY: Matthew Barney

FEATURING: Anette Wachter, Matthew Barney, Eleanor Bauer, Laura Stokes, K.J. Holmes

PLOT: In remote Idaho, Diana and her two assistants hunt, observed by an Engraver.

COMMENTS: A dialogue-free exploration of the myth of Diana the Huntress set in Idaho's ridiculously beautiful Sawtooth Mountains, *Redoubt* is a level beyond art-house; it's art installation. Diana (played by U.S. National Rifle Team member Anette Wachter) is a mysterious sharpshooter camping in a tent in the wilderness. She's accompanied by two female assistants, contortionists who sleep together in a hammock high in the pines and who express themselves solely through interpretive dance. Meanwhile, an Engraver (played by director Barney himself: the character seems to be both a forest ranger and an artist) ventures into the mountains and etches landscapes. At night, he returns to his trailer, where a woman (presumably his wife) electroplates the day's metal engravings; she's also working on an abstract sculpture based on a constellation. We observe every step in the creative process. At one point the Engraver watches a Native American woman perform a hoop dance at an American Legion building in an otherwise deserted town. The "action" is divided into a series of "hunts," although there is little story development. Eventually, Diana catches the Engraver spying on her, shoots one of his engravings, and finally sets a pack of wolves loose in his trailer. Unlike the mythological Acateon, who was transformed into a stag and killed by his own hunting dogs after catching a glimpse of the goddess bathing nude, the Engraver merits divine wrath simply by the act of creating his art, as if the act of reimagining nature is itself a transgression.

There is fantastic imagery here, capped by the National Geographic-style mountain cinematography (at one point, Barney captures an avalanche) and the finale which shows the artist's lair chewed over by lupine chaos. If you enjoy the kinesthetics of the human body in motion, the limber dancing (by professionals who are often clad in long johns) will have an additional appeal. The austerity of the glacially-paced, low-narrative presentation, accompanied only by minimalistic music and the sounds of footsteps in snow and occasional bird calls, is as cold as an Idaho morning, however, and will limit *Redoubt*'s appeal. Nonetheless, this is Matthew Barney's version of an accessible art-house film.

At this point, you might be wondering, "where have I heard the name Matthew Barney?" Barney is the sculptor/filmmaker responsible for the celebrated/infamous films that comprise the "Cremaster" cycle (which featured hermetic symbolism, bizarre costuming, and such provocative imagery as a bee flying out of a man's penis). He followed that performance up with the 330-minute scatological film opera *River of Fundament*. His films incorporate his sculptures and other multimedia (a book accompanies each), and are typically screened only at museums. In fact, Barney almost never allows his work to appear outside of a museum setting: a few extremely limited-edition Cremaster DVDs command outrageous prices on the secondary market. *Redoubt* represents, to my knowledge, the first time he has worked with an actual film distributor (Grasshopper). In a welcome expansion of venue, it was released in late 2019/early 2020 to select art-house cinemas as well as the usual museums. The scarcity of Barney's work contributes greatly to its legendary status, but let's hope that the increased distribution of *Redoubt* represents a loosening of the artist's strictures. Maybe as he ages and mellows he'll break his vow to never release the *Cremasters* commercially. Or at least let us poor schlubs see *River of Fundament* on Blu-ray. Probably not, but hope springs eternal.—Gregory J. Smalley

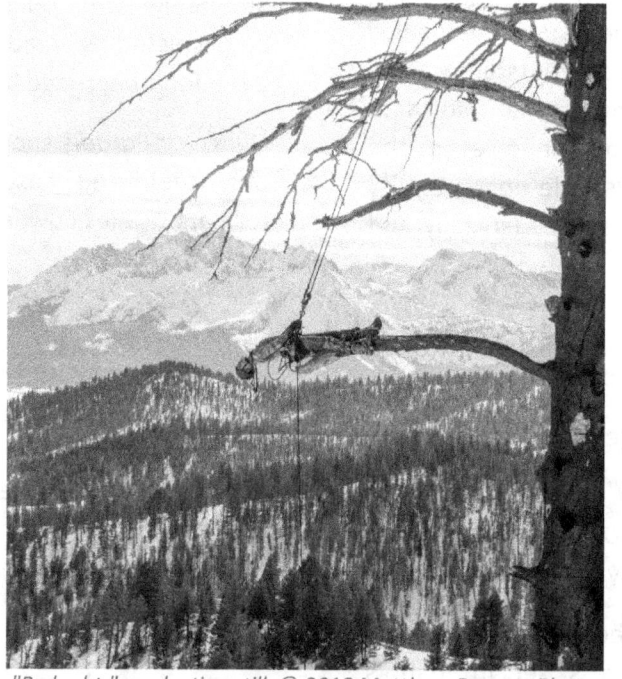

"Redoubt," production still, © 2018 Matthew Barney, Photo: Hugo Glendinning

Seven Stages to Achieve Eternal Bliss [AKA *Seven Stages to Achieve Eternal Bliss by Passing Through the Gateway Chosen by the Holy Storsh*] ★★1/2

DIRECTED BY: Vivieno Caldinelli

FEATURING: Kate Micucci, Sam Huntington

PLOT: Claire and Phil move to a spacious L.A. apartment with suspiciously low rent and discover it's not a lucky find.

COMMENTS: *Liberate yourself from the shackles of your thought.*

Or so goes the opening tract from the Book of Storsh. An absurdist comedy that explores the space where "self-help" and "suicide cult" intersect, this movie's relentless energy is to its credit. By the end, though, *Seven Stages* descends into a nihilistic abyss that papers over human despair with a folksy, up-tempo delivery.

For reasons explained during a bathtub vision, Paul and Claire find themselves in an impressively large apartment in downtown Los Angeles. Claire is doing her damnedest to get ahead in the advertising business; Paul is doing his damnedest to loaf around their new home and avoid reality. On their first night in their new home, a fanatic sporting a red spiral mark on his forehead breaks in and engages Paul in a bizarre quotation challenge (somehow involving esoteric civil infraction statutes from Iowa), then tap-dances to the bathroom and slices his own throat with a cake knife. When the police are summoned, Detective Cartwright explains that it's just another case of a Storsh disciple knocking himself off ("Didn't you read the lease?").

Seven Stages has the feel of an "Upright Citizen's Brigade" sketch stretched out a bit too long and never quite hitting top gear. There were a number of laughs (often involving the detective, who is hell-bent on pitching his screenplay to Wesley Snipes). When Paul and Claire decide to follow only the "good" parts of Storsh's religion, it's a clear indictment of the whole self-improvement media complex. But when the final sections—*Let the Tub Runneth Over* and *Change Your Story*—begin to unravel, the often-silly tone plummets into something far more sinister.

I may be overreacting here, perhaps having mentally shifted into a wholly unintended direction, but the feeling I was left with afterwards was not one of comedic satisfaction, but of emptiness. I have more of a fatalistic joie-de-vivre than many, but the lesson hammered home here—delivered glibly in the opening scene by Storsh himself, "That's what death is: eating that ice-cream on your own terms"—suggest that this movie's screwball antics merely mask a dark mind.

Seven Stages debuted at the Tribeca Film Festival under its complete title (*Seven Stages to Achieve Eternal Bliss by Passing Through the Gateway Chosen by the Holy Storsh*) in 2018 and received a limited, pre-pandemic theatrical release in early 2020.—Giles Edwards

Shadowplay ★★★

DIRECTED BY: Tony Pietra Arjuna

FEATURING: Tony Eusoff, Megat Sharizal, Juria Hartmans

PLOT: Anton Shaw is an unlicensed detective hired to track down a missing college student, but his own traumatic past keeps derailing his investigation.

COMMENTS: Under a glaring neon sign, at the cross-section between pulp-detective and pulp-romance, you will find *Shadowplay*—a movie with ambition. Among the themes explored are:

- The effects of childhood trauma
- The influence of dreams on reality
- The slipperiness of identity
- The cross-section between the written word and real life
- The unreliability of memory

The question then becomes, does Arjuna's reach exceed his grasp?

Shadowplay's story, as best as one might decipher, involves a would-be private investigator named Anton Shaw, as he minds the shop for a friend and mentor. To kill the time, Anton reads a "choose your own adventure" novel, one with no author credited and no publishing house mentioned. The phone rings. Does he choose to answer? Turning to page 18, he does so, and thus begins the investigation of a young woman's disappearance—an investigation that neatly mirrors his own past. His choices in the book are shown in real life, or perhaps vice-versa. For Anton, nothing is made clear until the end—and even then, he may have gotten no further than the chair in his friend's office.

This movie does have problems. The acting quality is very inconsistent, particularly with the female characters. This being a "hard-boiled detective" story, there needs must be a femme fatale–several, in the case of *Shadowplay*. This numerousness is fine, but hearing a sultry dame huskily inquire, "Are you of indigenous descent?" strained even my generous incredulity. Perhaps it's the script: the story is truly novel (so to speak), but many of the players are stuck with platitudinous lines that even the best actors would have difficulty giving weight to. Also, the scattered nature of the narrative leaves a lot of unhelpful ambiguity.

But, *Shadowplay* succeeds in two key ways. It's beautifully shot, with a clever lighting and color scheme that creates a genuinely otherworldly aura. The aerial shots—of a very '80s-looking Kuala Lumpur—ably define the environment, a nighttime hybrid of neon reality and neon dreams. The soundtrack, also very 1980s, enhances this effect, and by the film's end I was in one of those pleasantly altered states of contemplation; the movie had transported me from my viewing room to its twilight vision of shadowy luminescence.

Shadowplay was released in its native Malaysia in 2019, and showed up on multiple streaming services on these shores in 2020. —Giles Edwards

The Shasta Triangle ★★★

DIRECTED BY: Barry W. Levy

FEATURING: Dani Lennon, Ayanna Berkshire, Helenna Santos, Deborah Lee Smith, Madeline Merritt

PLOT: Paula returns to her hometown of Shasta, CA where unexplained phenomena regularly occur, to look further into one such instance—the disappearance of her father.

COMMENTS: *The Shasta Triangle* is an above-average low-budget genre film of the type that you'd expect to see on the SyFy Channel on a Saturday night, and if you temper your expectations to that level, you'll enjoy the film. There's nothing that's particularly new here in terms of playing with the tropes, but it is refreshing to have the "group going into the woods" be all-female in this variation. You might recognize some of the cast from other genre work, particularly Lennon, Berkshire, and Santos (also a producer and the co-story writer). These three also give the film's better performances.

The premise is solid for what's essentially a friends-go-into-the-scary-woods movie. It all plays out fairly well, although the ending is somewhat muffed and may leave some dissatisfied; there's a resolution, but it also feels like the filmmakers left themselves room to continue the story. Some may not feel a compelling need for them to do so.

This microbudget indie was released on VOD in December 2019, too late to make it into last year's Yearbook.—El Rob Hubbard

A Ship of Human Skin ★★1/2

DIRECTED BY: Richard Bailey

FEATURING: Hilly Holsonback, Hannah Weir, Ike Duncan, Cameron McElyea

PLOT: Jeanie, an aimless young woman, is arrested after she murders a man with an axe; a cult of personality forms around her after a prison guard claims to see her levitating.

COMMENTS: Richard Bailey's *A Ship of Human Skin* is first and foremost a minimalist character study. It's a film clearly aware of its limited budget, which opts to incorporate these limitations into its surreal nature. The cast is small, and sets are limited, and lengthy, loving shots of the Texas landscape make up a good portion of the film. At one point, a segment implied to take place over several months is shot entirely in a single room. The emphasis is on examining Jeannie, prostitute turned messiah figure, as a character. Throughout the film, we're slowly familiarized with a sharp-minded young woman who, due to her underprivileged upbringing and lack of formal education, is forced to channel her considerable intelligence into seeking meaning in abstract concepts and alternative belief systems, leading her down a path of paranoia that ultimately drives her to violence.

Elements of *A Ship of Human Skin* come off as underdeveloped, however. In particular, the film is premised on the notion that Jeannie has amassed a global following; but due to limited resources, this can only be conveyed through sporadic scenes with a handful of extras.

In terms of acting, the film is also a mixed bag. Hannah Weir does a solid job as Jeannie's meek but loyal sidekick Saribeth. Jeannie, played by Hilly Holsonback, however, just does not exude the charisma and conviction that the film would have us believe the character possesses. This is problematic, since that's the core of the film.

A Ship of Human Skin is, for the most part, a sensitively made film that did not have the resources to fully convey the vision behind it. Nonetheless, Bailey's feature-length directorial debut shows a resourcefulness and a talent for evoking a strong atmosphere that will surely serve him well in any future forays into weird cinema.

A Ship of Human Skin was released on DVD, Blu-ray, and video-on-demand in the summer of 2020. At the time of this writing it was free for Amazon Prime subscribers.—Simon Hyslop

Sleepless Beauty [Ya ne splyu] ★★

DIRECTED BY: Pavel Khvaleev

FEATURING: Polina Davydova

PLOT: Two orderly researchers trap unsuspecting Russian, enacting potent operational reprogramming, neurologically.

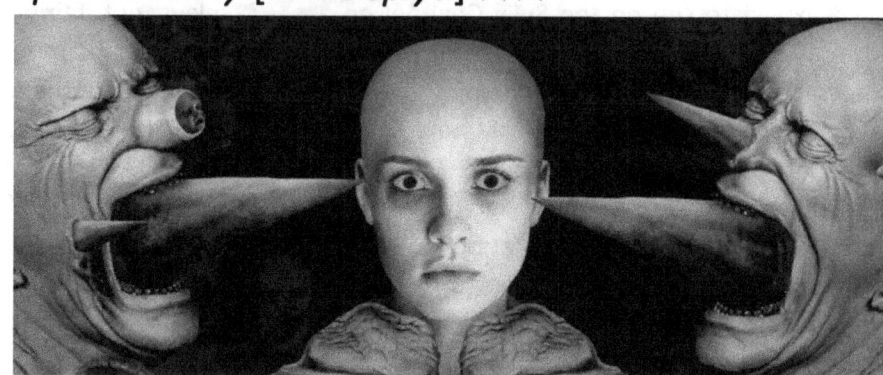

COMMENTS: In case my subliminal message didn't sink in, here's an illustrative rhyme to clarify:

"T" is for "trying", the squeamish beware;
"O" is for "overt", showing all it dares.
"R" is for "retching", a result that's sought;
"T" is for "tension", one's throat in a knot.
"U" is for "ugly", most violent of crimes,
"R" is for "razor", it's used oftentimes.
"E" is for "endless", may blood never cease,
"P" is for "prodding", in places liked least.
"O" is for "offal", of the human kind,
"R" is for "rotting", of body and mind.
"N" is for "nasty", how it has to be—
It spells "Torture Porn", unsettling with glee.

Like most porn, "torture porn" is an "I know it when I see it" kind of thing. In Pavel Khvaleev's latest film, *Sleepless Beauty*, I saw plenty of it. Khvaleev takes cues from the *Saw* franchise, the *Dark Web* franchise, and the Hieronymous Bosch franchise—illustrated by an extended animation sequence that can only be described as "Boschian".

For the most part, *Sleepless Beauty* is spot-on. The introduction gives the viewer enough grounding to follow what's happening to "Mila", even if we don't necessarily know what all this Sturm und Drang is storming and driving at. Joining us in our confusion is a peanut gallery of chatroom personalities who have opted to watch the web broadcast of the ordeal in pursuit of lurid thrills. Two chatroom "Admin" voices have a conversation during the feed that increasingly hints at what is actually going on.

To the extent torture porn can work, *Sleepless Beauty* works well. The chatroom vignettes provide some great black comedy moments. And the seemingly-unrelated framing story about a Russian ambassador nicely wraps everything together. However, whoever cast the English-dub actors should be ashamed. This is a dark Russian movie, and its tone is crippled without bleak, Russian voices. The low-rent Californian-English "coming" from Mila's somber-looking parents effectively ruins the movie every time they appear—and the less said about the C-grade vocalizations for the world-weary Russian detective, the better.

If you find yourself curious at this point, seek out the subtitled version and I can all but guarantee that you will enjoy yourself tremendously as horrible things are enacted on the protagonist-cum-test subject.

Sleepless Beauty's film festival run was cut short by the pandemic, and it dropped on VOD in the U.S. in November 2020.—Giles Edwards

Spindrift's Haunted West ★★★1/2

DIRECTED BY: Burke Roberts

FEATURING: The members of "Spindrift"

PLOT: Four musicians record sights and sounds from their "Ghost Town Tour" in a pastiche of performances, wandering about acid-infused scenery.

COMMENTS: What better way to write a movie review than while listening to that movie's music in the background? Normally I don't have the film playing while I write my reviews, but having reached the half-way mark in *Spindrift's Haunted West*, I have figured out what's going on and can be certain of two things.

The first thing: this isn't really a movie. *Haunted West* begins in wide (wide wide) screen, its opening credits over what could be the establishing shot of a top-tier spaghetti western. Blue sky, jagged hillside, and a day-time moon lurking above. But Spindrift quickly show their hands in the opening scene: the band wanders around a derelict town while their music plays non-diegetically. Things move forward, in their meandering way, with shots from performances in historical saloons, shots from performances around campfires, and the occasional music-video-esque backdrop of gibbets, "Olde West" thoroughfares, and some neat-o pointy rock sites.

The second thing: *Haunted West* is the perfect thing to play on a grainy projector with dodgy speakers during your next Western-themed party. Delaware-born band leader Kirkpatrick Thomas must have spent a youth saturated in Western movies, Western television shows, and acid rock. His band's sound veers from Prog-Western to Ballad-Western to Acid-Wibblies, with even some visits from what I can only describe as "Mariachi Luau." The one constant is an Ennio Morricone vibe, as might be expected; Morricone was God's gift to Spaghetti Westerns.

I often mention the length of short movies—whether it be a comment on efficient story-telling or a bafflement at how something so short could seem so long. *Spindrift's Haunted West* moseys onto the screen, showcases some considerable musical talent, and then moseys away. This travelogue music video is a much better investment for your seventy-seven minutes than some movies I could mention, so pull out the Bulleit, slap on a Stetson, and rock on, rock in, and rock out with Spindrift.

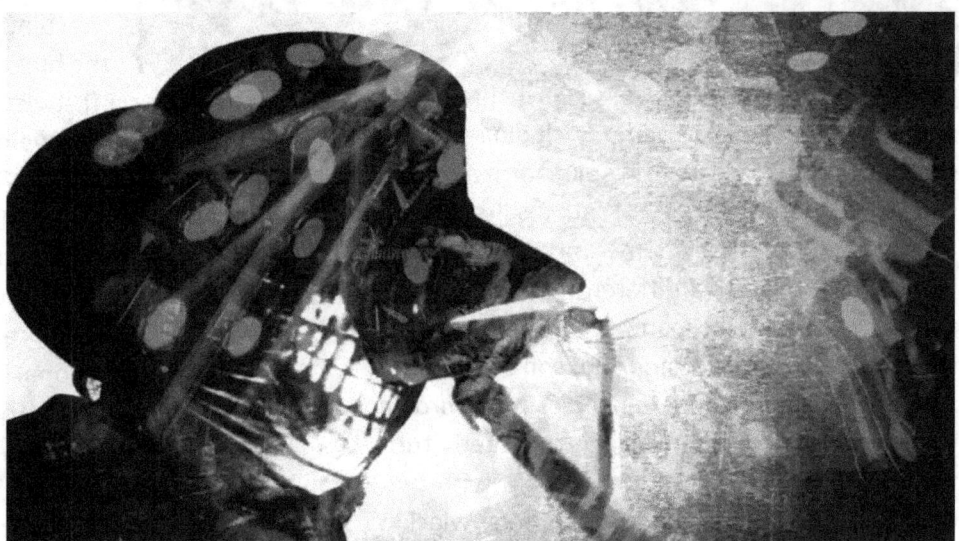

WHAT THE TOMBSTONE SAYS:

"Here lies George Johnson / Hanged by mistake / 1882 / He was right, we was wrong / But we strung him up & now he's gone."

This visual album was released on DVD and VOD in 2020. Somewhat surprisingly, the soundtrack was not available for purchase separately, at least not yet.—Giles Edwards

Synchronic ★★1/2

DIRECTED BY: Aaron Moorhead, Justin Benson

FEATURING: Anthony Mackie, Jamie Dornan, Ally Ioannides

PLOT: New Orleans paramedics discover that a series of bizarre deaths are linked to a new designer drug called "synchronic."

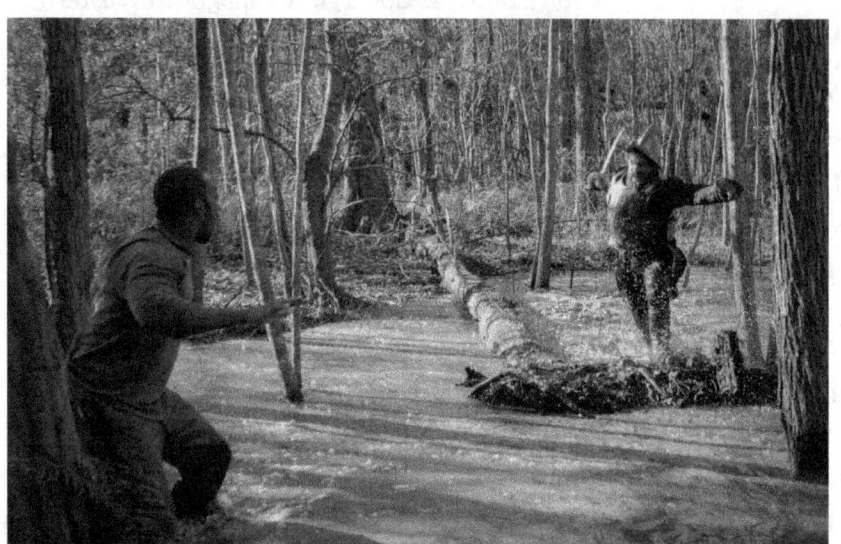

COMMENTS: The designer drug "Synchronic" is not "red marijuana," as some (including us) had speculated, but comes in pill form and is passingly described as "bath salts." The "chronic" in the drug's name doesn't reference weed at all, but has a different derivation, and the movie doesn't have any relation to the story shared in Moorhead and Benson's previous features *Resolution* and *The Endless*. *Synchronic* is, instead, a slightly bigger-budgeted turn towards the mainstream for the pair, with two moderate movie star leads in Anthony Mackie (Marvel universe's "Falcon") and Jamie Dornan (*50 Shades of Gray*).

Synchronic's dramatic setup is more entertaining than its sci-fi twist. Steve (Mackie) drinks a lot and pops codeine pills. Is he turning into a "junkie paramedic cliché," as his partner fears, or is there a deeper reason? While Steve is an aging bachelor still playing the field, Dennis (Dornan) long ago settled down with a wife and kid. Each partner envies the other's lifestyle just a little bit. Dennis' daughter, Tara, is a good kid but, like a lot of 18-year-olds, unsure what she wants to do with her life; right now, her passion is for staying out all night partying. Meanwhile, the two paramedics are called into scenes where they find zonked-out druggies with strange, sometimes inexplicable injuries—like the skull-faced voodoo practitioner who won't stop laughing despite his compound fracture—all linked to a new designer drug that's plaguing the city.

So the characters are likable, their situations dramatic and relatable, and they're all set up for a speculative blast that will blow the hinges off. The problem is that when the sci-fi twist arrives, it's basic and contrived, and not weird enough to compensate for its unbelievability. The drug's mechanism is revealed in explicit detail less than halfway through the movie, taking away a potential source of mystery. If you accept the silly premise, what follows is logical—too logical. Even the characters' emotional arcs are predictable. The trippy promise of the opener, with reality dissolving and reassembling as the synchronic kicks in on an elevator ride, never materializes. All in all, it's like a run-of-the-mill episode of the "X-Files"; watchable, but nothing special. *Synchronic* would have been a promising debut film from a new director, but it's a bit of a letdown from a duo who looked like they were pushing boundaries and getting weirder and weirder.—Gregory J. Smalley

Time Warp: The Greatest Cult Films of All Time ★★★
Vol. 1: Midnight Madness; Vol. 2: Horror and Sci-Fi; Vol. 3: Comedy and Camp

DIRECTED BY: Danny Wolf

FEATURING: Joe Dante, John Waters, Ileana Douglas, Kevin Pollak

PLOT: A three part documentary on cult movies.

COMMENTS: The charm of Danny Wolf's three-part talking-heads-plus-clips documentary *Time Warp: The Greatest Cult Films of All Time* is that, at bottom, it's just a bunch of knowledgeable film fans sitting around yakking about some of their favorite films, which just also happen to be some of the wildest and weirdest visions ever committed to celluloid.

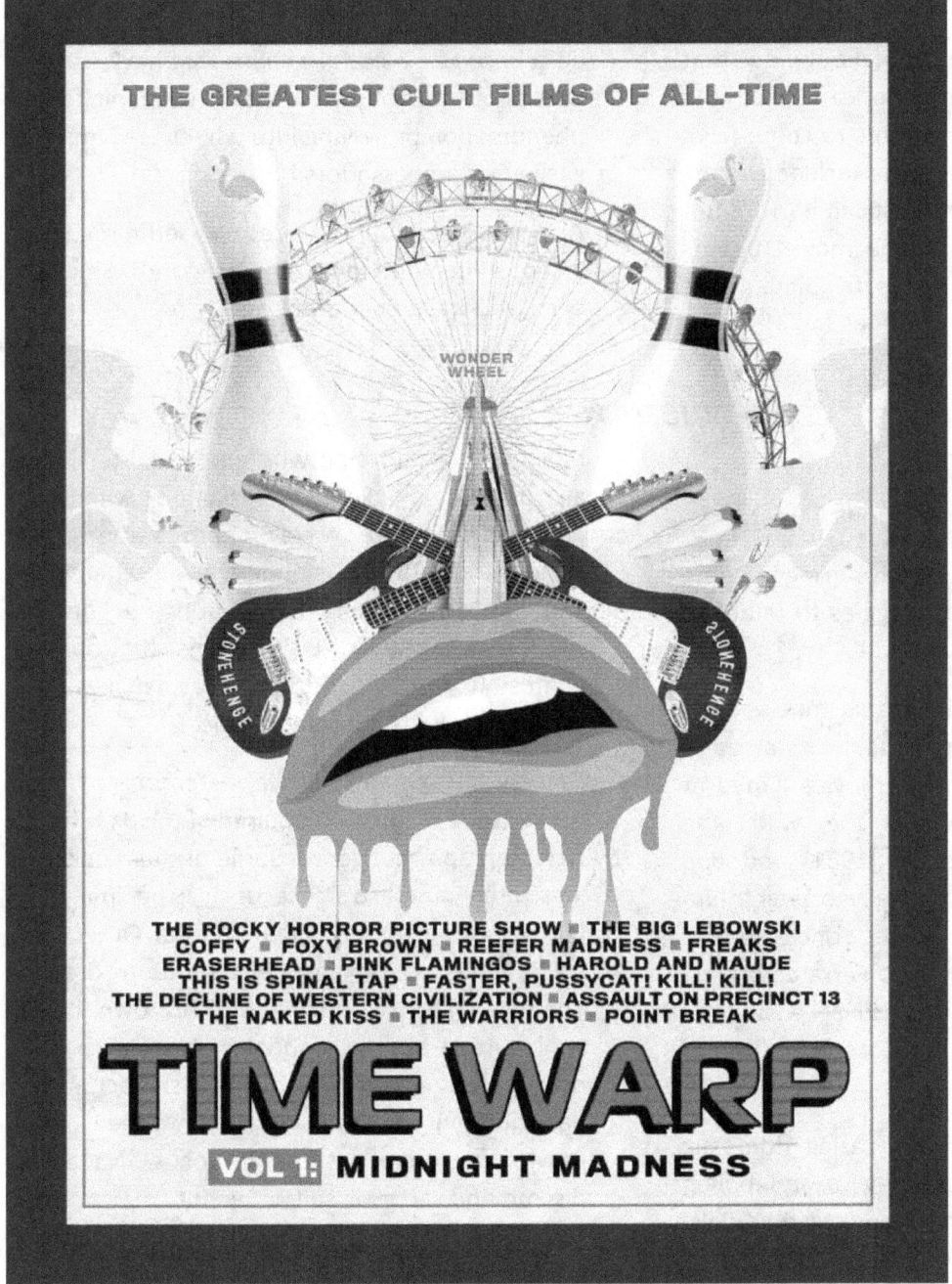

Volume 1, "Midnight Movies," covered obvious territory like *Rocky Horror Picture Show* (but notably omitted any mention of Alejandro Jodorowsky). Gregory J. Smalley observed "most true 'midnight movies' dive deeper into the cult catalog than *Time Warp* cares to go... But we'll give them a break, because *Time Warp* isn't a graduate cinema course; it's a freshman 'Introduction to Cult Movies 101' offering."

Of Volume 2 (Horror and Sci-Fi), Terri "Goregirl" McSorley said "There is something to entertain everyone in this documentary, from the seasoned horror and sci-fi fan to the newcomer" and was "particularly thrilled they included *Liquid Sky*. The absolute definition of a cult classic; a genuinely weird and one-of-a-kind flick." She quibbled over two inclusions: "*Texas Chainsaw Massacre* is without a doubt one of the greatest horror films ever made. It does buck all the rules of cultdom, though. It was successful on its release, was well-reviewed, and is probably one of the best known and most loved horror flicks of all time. Secondly, *Human Centipede* is the only film to make the cut that was not made in North America. Of all the amazing and unique horror films to come from other countries, they decided to include *Human Centipede* as one of the greatest cult horror films of all time! I actually liked the movie, but its inclusion here sincerely boggles my mind."

Shane Wilson assessed the "Comedy and Camp" installment: "*Time Warp* just wants to have fun and share some rabidly adored films. And there's nothing necessarily wrong with that. But... the whole enterprise carries about as much weight as 'VH-1's 100 Greatest One Hit Wonders.'" He speaks for the whole team with his final summary: "To spend a decent amount of time with 47 films in less than six hours is really a solid achievement. But it still feels like the format makes it impossible to do much more than pay lip service to a handful of films that have earned passionate devotion, without examining the phenomenon or delving into why these films are such good ambassadors."

All three installments were released directly to video-on-demand in 2020.—Gregory J. Smalley, Terri McSorley, Shane Wilson

Tommaso ★★1/2

DIRECTED BY: Abel Ferrara

FEATURING: Willem Dafoe, Cristina Chiriac

PLOT: An aging American director living in Rome goes to AA meetings and struggles to relate to his much younger Moldavian wife.

COMMENTS: It may be inevitable that as Abel Ferrara has aged and sobered up, he's started to make self-consciously serious movies aimed at art-houses, as opposed to the wild and exploitative hits like *Ms. 45* (1981) and *Bad Lieutenant* (1992) that originally brought him cult fame. While his movies once graced grindhouses, prior to *Tommaso* Ferrara was last seen at the Venice Film Festival pushing a prestige biopic about fellow bad-boy director Pier Paolo Pasolini.

Now, he's back with a navel-gazing domestic drama that's heavy on scenes of squabbling spouses and Alcoholics Anonymous testimonials. There is no doubt that Tommaso is Ferrara: an ex-alcoholic movie director living in Rome with a much younger foreign wife and daughter (who are played by Ferrara's real-life wife and daughter). Ferrara wisely chooses the great Willem Dafoe as his stand-in: even when he's cheating, or thinking of cheating, or having messianic fantasies, Dafoe finds the human confusion and suffering that makes us sympathize with every indulgence.

Fantasy segments give *Tommaso* the Felliniesque credibility required of the directorial autobiography subgenre. Some of them nakedly illustrate Tommaso's insecurities: he imagines his child in danger, his wife unfaithful. Others are inscrutable: a Kafkaesque detention dream, Tommaso literally pulling out his own heart while sitting around a squatters' campfire. But no matter their tone or subject, the hallucinations do not seriously impede the movie's basic plotlessness, its focus on marital discord and sarcastic self-reflection.

Tommaso's struggle with his own controlling nature---even with yoga and breathing exercises, he's high-strung and quick to jealous anger---form the essence of his internal conflict. Although his wife Nikki can occasionally seem a little immature ("I want to do what I want, when I want..."), Tommaso consistently comes off much worse. At one point, he spends his entire turn at an AA meeting complaining about his spouse; the next speaker empathizes with him, but also offers some wisdom: "this program teaches me to stick to my side of the street... whenever I'm pointing a finger, I've got to look at myself." The message is lost on Tommaso, however, who persists in his arrogance.

This unflattering portrayal is Ferrara's way of working out his own issues and anxieties on film---a public confessional that is as brave as it is uncomfortable for the viewer. After watching *Tommaso*, I feel like I know Ferrara intimately---more intimately than I should know a stranger.

Due to the pandemic, *Tommaso* was released online in June 2020. It probably wouldn't have gotten more than a token release in art houses, anyway. It's more natural home is on video-on-demand or DVD/Blu-ray, which is where you can find it today.--Gregory J. Smalley

Verotika ★

DIRECTED BY: Glenn Danzig

FEATURING: Ashley Wisdom, Rachel Alig, Alice Haig, Scotch Hopkins

PLOT: Three tales of "violent eroti(k)a": a woman's albino spider kills when she sleeps, a stripper cuts off women's faces, and a Countess bathes in blood.

COMMENTS: I've got this theory that heavy metal musicians shouldn't be allowed to make horror movie vanity projects. Rob Zombie directed a couple that weren't totally embarrassing; after that, the field was slim... until *Verotika*. You may have heard this film is bad. It's worse than that.

Each of the three segments—adapted from Danzig's horror comic series of the same name—is introduced by a nondescript goth chick, who's comelier than the Cryptkeeper but has nowhere near the sense of humor (after gouging out a woman's eyeballs in the opening, the best she can come up with is "Welcome, my darklings, this is *Verotika*." Whatever happened to lines like "Welcome to our cornea-copia of horror, my pupils!"?)

The first story, "The Albino Spider of Dajette," is the "best." A French girl with eyeballs on her nipples has an albino spider who turns anthropomorphic whenever she falls asleep, and goes out and snaps hooker's necks. The spider-man makeup is not bad, but the best part is Wisdom's Pepe le Pew accent. (Lines like "keeler... keeler... you... are a murder*air*!" are a lot funnier when delivered in an emotionless French accent.)

"Change of Face" is about a stripper who steals the faces of pretty girls. No reason is given. (Beat cop, standing over the corpse of a face-stripped victim: "We've got nothing. Zero evidence, which means no leads or motive." Detective: "There's your motive. They wanted her face.") When a detective chases her, she just moves to another gentlemen's club and changes her stage name from "Mystery Girl" to "Mysteria." Now, the heat will never catch her, and she will continue to de-face harlots for eternity.

"Drukija: Contessa of Blood" is the final story: the familiar old tale of a decadent Eastern European noblewoman who bathes in the blood of the local village virgins to keep up her youthful appearance. She indulges in jugular showers, enlists the help of a wolf, and pulls the beating heart out of a nude girl. She doesn't, however, follow any kind of plot arc—she starts out bleeding virgins, continues to bleed virgins, and ends up bleeding virgins. None of the locals care, and neither will you. This isn't the metalhead horror movie version of *The Room*, folks. You've been warned. AVOID.

Verotika played three film festivals in 2019, found little enthusiasm, and went straight to Blu-ray/DVD/VOD in March 2020.—Gregory J. Smalley

Vivarium ★★★★

DIRECTED BY: Lorcan Finnegan

FEATURING: Imogen Poots, Jesse Eisenberg, Jonathan Aris

PLOT: A young couple visit a realtor's office and find themselves trapped in an empty, endlessly repeating suburban hellscape.

COMMENTS: Gemma, a kindergarten teacher, and her boyfriend Tom, her school's groundskeeper, have finally started to think about "settling down." While a cookie-cutter house in the suburbs isn't anything like what they want, they decide to have a laugh and follow Martin, the unnerving real estate agent, and visit housing unit number 9 in the new "Yonder" development; a subdivision with the tagline: "Quality homes. Forever." The couple's attempts to leave are thwarted by the development's labyrinthine repetitiveness, and their car runs out of gas—conveniently in front of their designated unit. Soon a parcel with food and supplies arrives. Soon after, a parcel with a live infant is left by their curb.

Vivarium is one of the creepiest and dystopian-est stories I've seen in. By the film's end, I was experiencing what can be best described as "the jibblies". It opens ominously with a murder of one baby chick by another in the nest before nestling into a cutesy boy-and-girl story. The eccentric and over-eager realtor even makes the opening comedic. But hope collapses quickly as the story's narrative groove is dug within the first ten minutes. The boy that shows up isn't human—he reaches a physical age of 5 or 6 by "Day 94", as marked by the couple on a door frame in their purgatorial domicile. He's given to mimicry, much like the real estate agent. And he screams whenever something does not go exactly according to routine. Tom is the first to break, attempting initially to starve the creature, then taking solace in an ever-deepening hole he's digging in an attempt to escape. Gemma unwillingly becomes a mother figure to the creature, and seesaws between frustration at the situation and hope at discovering the reason behind their imprisonment.

Lorcan Finnegan captures us along with the couple, and lets us grope blindly along with them. While there is something of a reveal in the final moments, it raises at least as many questions as it answers, with hints of extraterrestrial and theological oddness. Its near-ceaseless malaise, mitigated only by the occasional flicker of human hope and kindness, makes *Vivarium* like a shot of Novocain to the soul, putting you under into a minty-green coma of unease.

Vivarium was released to VOD and physical media in March 2020.—Giles Edwards

The Wave ★★1/2

DIRECTED BY: Gille Klabin

FEATURING: Justin Long, Sheila Vand, Donald Faison, Tommy Flanagan, Ronnie Gene Blevins

PLOT: A corporate lawyer decides to cut loose one night, but regrets it when a strange drug dealer convinces him to try an exotic hallucinogen whose effects last several days and make him randomly skip forward in time.

COMMENTS: It's hard to pigeonhole *The Wave* in a genre. It isn't reality-based enough to be science fiction, and nor is it divorced enough from reality to be fantasy. It might be a psychological thriller, but it's much lighter than that term usually implies. The pacing and light mugging from the leads suggests that it wants to be taken as a comedy. Indeed, the setup, with straight-laced corporate lawyer Frank sneaking out for a night on the town with his more adventurous buddy, suggest suits-cut-loose shenanigans are coming. But the movie also takes itself seriously, and lacks moments played for big laughs.

"Dramedy" might fit, but in the end I think *The Wave* really belongs to that disreputable subgenre, the "trip movie." It's not an exploitation piece—although it has its drug porn moments. *The Wave*'s money shots are its wavery lysergic visions—especially when one of the hallucinogenic "waves" kicks in at a corporate board meeting, turning executives into Mammon-channeling demons. (The visuals here are simple but effective—it looks like they digitally painted over every frame of film, like rotoscoping done in MS Paint). At its core, the script posits that psychedelics have legitimate spiritual healing qualities—that all a self-centered lawyer needs is a dose high enough to turn himself on, grok karma, and become a self-sacrificing hippie.

The script is naive at heart, but hides it well. After Frank takes the mystery drug, the plot barrels along, lurching forward in time. Frank might suddenly find himself in a deserted house, or in the middle of a car chase, without explanation. Blackouts are a side effect of the drug, but there's something mystical about the process, too. By the end, the plot points snap into place nicely. The leads are all pro. Donald Faison provides good buddy support, playing the bad or good angel as needed; Sheila Vand, the mystic pixie dream girl, is luminous in her dream sequences; Ronnie Gene Blevins overacts appropriately as the hell-bent drug dealer. Justin Long has a pleasant John Krasinski-meets-Fred

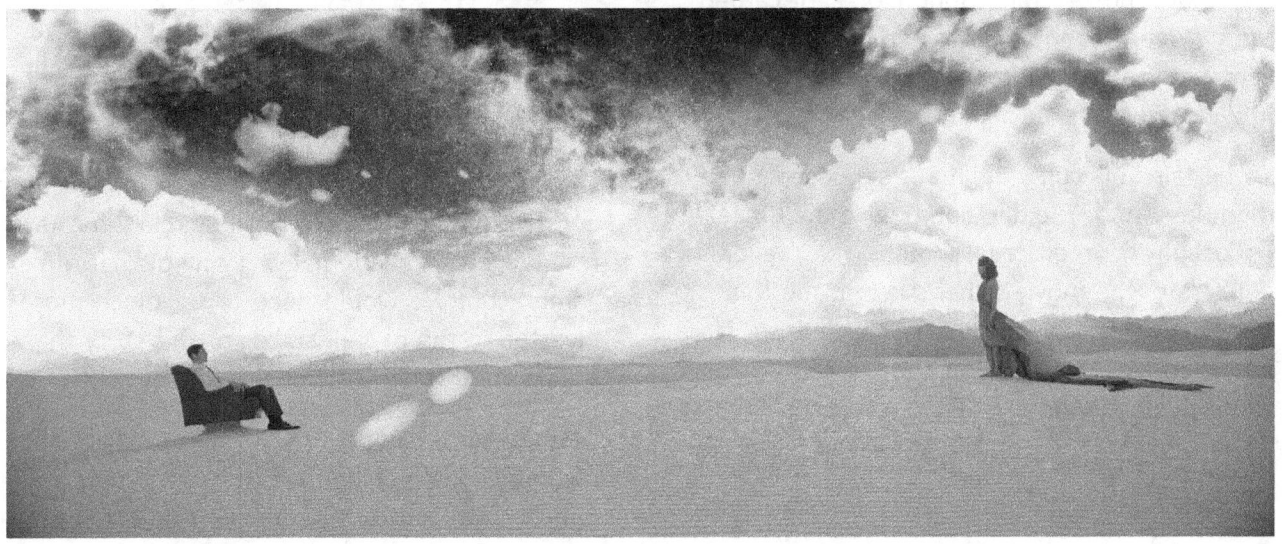

Armisen quality; you can't stay mad at him, even when ambition leads him to screw over the beneficiaries of a dead firefighter. Not everything works as it should: some characters, like the shrewish wife and the ruthless CEO, are cardboard caricatures. But, rough patches aside, the visuals and speedy pace make it a trip you *probably* won't regret taking.

The Wave showed up in selected cinemas, and more widely on video-on-demand, in January 2020.—Gregory J. Smalley

Welcome to the Circle ★1/2

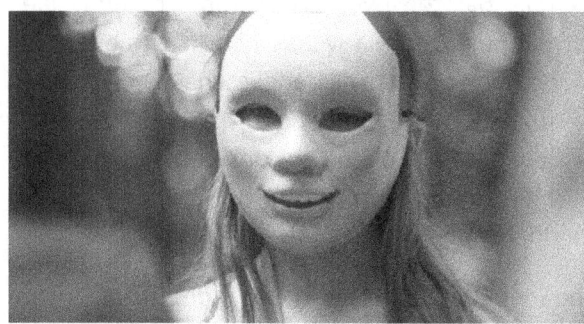

DIRECTED BY: David Fowler

FEATURING: Taylor Dianne Robinson, Ben Cotton, Matthew MacCaull, Hilary Jardine, Cindy Busby, Andrea Brooks, Michael Rogers

PLOT: After a bear attack, a man and his daughter are rescued by a cult in the woods.

COMMENTS: "The meaning is the message." "And the message is the meaning." "So what is the message?" "That is exactly the question." "What is?" "We have to figure out what it is." "What, the message?" "The meaning."

No, that's not a transcription of a discarded sketch where Abbot and Costello meet the Dalai Lama; it's a typical "circular" dialogue exchange in *Welcome to the Circle.*

To be fair, this cult's dogma is supposed to be mumbo-jumbo. The decision to give the Circle's philosophy no intellectual content whatsoever is deliberate; the movie's thesis is that the things we believe can override reality, and so it's important to focus not on the strings, but on who's pulling them.

It's a thoughtful idea rife with potential allegories, but unfortunately the message gets lost under too much obfuscating trickery. It's relatively straightforward ride through the first act, but then the plot loses its way with information overload (founder Percy Stevens' strange and confusing backstory) as it's simultaneously diving into an anything-can-happen abyss. It's a nice touch that cult membership includes an unusually high number of creepy mannequins—most of the prop budget went to this small army—but other ideas don't pay off. Too many sudden cutaways to stock footage montages (marionettes, chess moves), too many portals that pop characters from one location to another, too many ostentatiously delivered Zen warnings. It's tough for a movie founded on such a free-floating structure to work, unless it has the budget to pull off some majorly distracting special effects, or a series of catchy surrealist ideas consistently pitched on the level of a David Lynch.

Needless to say, *Welcome to the Circle* can't match these standards. There's no one we strongly care about to interest us in entering this circular labyrinth. Greg, bear victim and loving father, should be the character we identify with, but he's pushed to the sideline relatively early in favor of a new main character: a stoic cult deprogrammer headed into the Circle intent on rescuing one of the females. It's a bold narrative gambit, but we would need to be much more invested in the overall stakes of this story than we are for this perspective shift to pay off.

Ultimately, *Welcome to the Circle* lacks the budget and, unfortunately, the imagination to fulfill its lofty ambitions. The film's meaning gets lost in its message—or maybe it's the other way around.

David Fowler's previous credits were mostly writing the narration for Disneynature documentaries like *Elephant* and *Penguins*. A low-budget surreal horror film was an unexpected choice for a directorial debut. Artsploitation Films picked it up and debuted it on VOD and physical media in late 2020.—Gregory J. Smalley

Why Don't You Just Die! [*Papa, Sdokhni*] ★★★★★

DIRECTED BY: Kirill Sokolov

FEATURING: Aleksandr Kuznetsov, Vitaliy Khaev, Evgeniya Kregzhde

PLOT: Matvey intends on doing in Olya's father with a hammer, but complications—and Matvey's uncanny indisposition to dying—derail his straightforward plan.

COMMENTS: To paraphrase one of my peers who attended the 2019 screening at Fantasia Festival, this movie has "Chekhov's shotgun, Chekhov's hammer, Chekhov's power drill, Chekhov's handgun…" I added, "Chekhov's chandelier." It also had the most consistent laughs of any Fantasia comedy so far. Perhaps all of us are just terrible people, but I lay the blame squarely on directing neophyte Kirill Sokolov (who also wrote the film) for creating such a side-splitting violence chamber play.

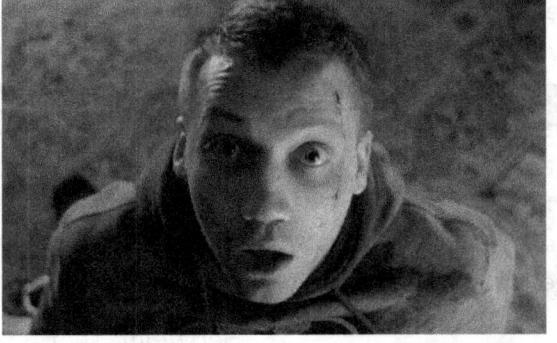

During his brief introduction, Matvey seems like a regular fellow, albeit a regular fellow furtively hiding a hammer behind his back as he rings an apartment doorbell. He intones "One, two, three, evil can't touch me" as he buzzes and is greeted by Andrey, an intimidating, hefty man in his fifties, who reluctantly invites him in. Andrey's wife Tasha offers the boy something to drink. When Matvey and Andrey sit down, so begins a very awkward conversation after Matvey's hammer slips out of his pants, clattering to the ground. "Is that your hammer?" "Yes. A friend wanted to borrow it." And soon a room-busting mêlée ensues.

This violent battle of wills continues throughout, interrupted on only three occasions by vignettes concerning pertinent back stories. All very "Guy Ritchie", but there is a point at which the whole affair careens over an edge and becomes ludicrous. No more hemming-and-hawing for me, but a quick flash of realization that this movie had just entered the world of crazy-go-nuts. Within its tiny setting, nearly everything becomes saturated with someone's blood as TVs bludgeon, shotguns blast, drill bits spin, and kitchen knives cleave.

Near the end, when all the facts are on display and poor Matvey is sitting in a sorry state on the tattered couch (middle finger still flipped up in defiance), Andrey muses aloud to his daughter, "How is this guy still alive?" What, indeed, is this bloodshed for? Part of me suspects it's allegorical: Matvey, the Russian everyman, enduring and outlasting every abuse from a government system that's against him. But this red-spewing fountain of black comedy needn't be approached with any lens, political or otherwise. Just make sure you can stomach ninety straight minutes of top gore.

Why Don't You Just Die? didn't get a stateside theatrical release, but Arrow Video picked it up this year for home video distribution in all territories.—Giles Edwards

"World of Tomorrow, Episode 3: The Absent Destinations of David Prime"

DIRECTED BY: Don Hertzfeldt

FEATURING: Julia Pott

PLOT: A time-traveling clone appears to David Prime to warn him of future danger.

COMMENTS: Few will brave "The Absent Destinations of David Prime" without having seen the Oscar-nominated "World of Tomorrow" first—but this short does stand alone, and knowledge of previous episodes isn't absolutely necessary. The rest of us will find this new World of Tomorrow familiar, yet different. What's most obviously missing is Winona Mae, the child star of the first two episodes. Her imaginative, candid chattering provided both a launching pad for writer/director Hertzfeldt's speculative ideas, and a comic foil for Julia Potts (who voiced Winona's adult clones). The first two episodes' dynamic was the tension between adult realities (represented by Potts' hilariously damaged clones) and the innocent potential of Winona Mae. Now, the child has aged out of the role, and Hertzfeldt has adapted. Potts still voices an Emily clone (Emily 9, to be precise), but the protagonist is now the silent David, Emily's love interest, referenced in the original through a brain-dead clone on display at a museum. The wistful melancholy for childhood is replaced by the wistful melancholy of love—romance complicated by the fact that it occurs between various permutations of clones, each of whom share incomplete and sometimes faulty memories with their originals.

"Episode 3" is less explicitly philosophical than previous installments, driven instead by an intricate time-travel narrative. What remains the same is Hertzfeldt's incisive satire, the absurdly quotable dialogue, and the animation, which, although continuing to advance into ever more elaborate and psychedelic landscapes, remains stick-figure-based. (David's hallucinatory journey to a distant moon could be Hertzfeldt's stickman tribute to *2001*'s Star Gate.) The satire, in particular, hits a high note in this episode: the World of Tomorrow is a cybernetic nightmare of data overload chillingly reminiscent of our own fast-moving times. Humans have neural chips—like iPhones implanted directly inside our brains—that allow them to install and delete functions as needed. Apps like Chinese fluency or basic ambulation can be removed to free up space for new content. Advertising is omnipresent; Emily's memory cache is partly funded by pop-up ads, including one for "holograms that yell at you!"

"The Absent Destinations of David Prime" is the most ambitious "World of Tomorrow" yet, clocking it at over thirty minutes long, double the previous two episodes lengths. Having survived the maturation of Winona Mae, it appears that Hertzfeldt's imagination is capable of spinning out the series indefinitely into the ever expanding World of Tomorrow.

Hertzfeldt sent "The Absent Destinations of David Prime" into the world in fall 2020 without much prior warning. It is currently available exclusively for purchase or rental on Vimeo. Someday all three episodes (and maybe even a future episode) may be available bundled together on physical media, but no time traveler has yet divulged the release date.—Gregory J. Smalley

CHANNEL 366: THE WEIRDEST TV OF 2020

"The Midnight Gospel" [Netflix] ★★★★

CREATED BY: Pendleton Ward, Duncan Trussell

FEATURING: Voices of Duncan Trussell, Phil Hendrie, various guests

PLOT: Clancy lives by a run-down farm in a run-down house and uses a run-down multiverse simulator to find interviewees for his spacecast.

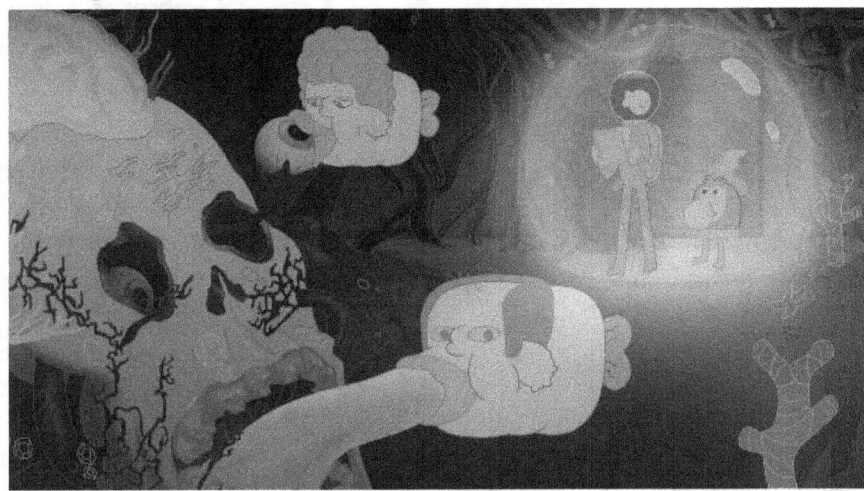

COMMENTS: The first thing you'll notice when beginning Netflix's new series *The Midnight Gospel* is that it is not of this Earth, at least not of a specific time and place. The landscapes, décor, and props evoke everything from '50s sci-fi novels to hippie chic to '90s CD-ROM games, with a color scheme that blasts through it all with as much brightness they can get away with while still being easy on the eyes.

The main focus of each episode is the conversation between Clancy Gilroy (Duncan Trussell) and his special guest for that adventure, but I'd like to talk first about "The Midnight Gospel"'s visual appeal. The drawings have a meditative quality. The line work is all soft; even the corners feel soft. While it never quite spills over into "organic", the movement of characters (and despite this television show's origins, there's plenty going on on-screen) is somewhere between easy-going and fatalistic. I bring up that word, "fatalistic," because more likely than not, Clancy and his guests will suffer through some sort of massacre or dismemberment each episode. Whether being gored by undead hordes, or traveling through a meat processing plant as the meat is being processed, there's a happy squish for the eye to go along with the philosophical/sociological discussion dominating the dialogue.

When you boil it down, *The Midnight Gospel* is a podcast between a somewhat enlightened, somewhat leftist fellow as he speaks with all manner of intellectuals about drugs, life, death, and so on. That isn't to say that there's a strong demarcation between the conversation and the visuals. During a discussion of drugs, "little president" is busy defending the White House against invading zombies. At the meat processing plant, a different guest has his eye removed and consumed by one of that world's clown children, exclaiming, "That kid just took my fucking eye!"

If you aren't interested in informed-but-meandering discussions, you will find this cartoon rather trying. If, however, you are looking for a little consciousness-expanding conversation paired with some casually-extreme outlandish visual back-drops, then you are in for a treat.—Giles Edwards

"The Third Day" [HBO] ★★★1/2

DIRECTED BY: Marc Munden, Felix Barrett, Philippa Lowthorpe

FEATURING: Jude Law, Naomie Harris, Katherine Waterston, Emily Watson, Paddy Considine

PLOT: A bereaved father saves a suicidal girl and returns her to her home on a remote strip of land off the English coast, only to discover an undercurrent of violence and a weird theology permeating the island; months later, a mother brings her children to the same island for a vacation that quickly goes from bad to worse.

COMMENTS: *The Third Day* falls neatly within the popular "outsider goes to strange little northern European village" genre. As such, there's a powerful and ever-present vibe of discomfort seasoned with folk cult horror that intentionally distances the hero and viewer alike. The show revels in being vague and mysterious, resolutely playing hard-to-get, and the overall mood is effectively creepy. But it's hard for our protagonists to do much besides feel lost and confused. *The Third Day* might have a classier presentation and finer pedigree than, say, *Children of the Corn*, but they're cut from the same cloth. The story of *The Third Day* is undeniably strange, but still familiar to anyone who has come this way before.

The six episodes that make up *The Third Day*'s main storyline are relatively anodyne when compared with its centerpiece: a 12-hour immersive theater spectacle in which an unbroken single shot takes us through a grand pagan passion play. It's a massive technical achievement that simultaneously captures the sheer mundanity of the enterprise. Our opening tracking shot down the gravelly causeway is a full half-hour. Jude Law is put through every manner of abuse: dragging a heavy boat through the town square, being dunked in a barrel of blood, digging a muddy grave, and all without a scrap of dialogue. Even his brief nap is captured in its entirety.

You may ask, "But is it any good?" It's certainly expertly crafted with strong performances. It makes you uncomfortable, like any good horror flick. But *The Third Day* seems to think it's about something more than it really is. The 12-hour telecast is a great stunt, but it's still a stunt, as impressive as flagpole sitting or goldfish swallowing. And while it touches on themes like the insidious nature of religious extremism or mob psychology, it's really just a horror show. It plays with your head. You get freaked out. Then you leave the island.

"The Third Day" debuted in the US on HBO and in the UK on Sky Atlantic in September 2020. The 12-hour "Autumn" episode was broadcast live on Oct 3. The entire package is now available for VOD rental.—Shane Wilson

REDISCOVERIES: OLDER MOVIES AND TV SERIES DEBUTING ON HOME VIDEO OR STREAMING IN 2020

Kinetta (2005) ★

DIRECTED BY: Giorgos Lanthimos

FEATURING: Evangelia Randou, Aris Servetalis, Costas Xikominos

PLOT: "At a Greek hotel in the off-season, a chambermaid, a man obsessed with BMWs, and a photo-store clerk attempt to film and photograph various badly reenacted struggles between a man and a woman." [IMDB synopsis]

COMMENTS: If I am reviewing a film I enjoy or respect (or better yet, both), I am often apprehensive when I sit down to write about it. This is because I am always fearful I won't find my "window" into the movie: that first sentence, or first idea, that opens up the rest of my thoughts as I write. If I am reviewing a film that I did not care for, there's usually at least one withering put-down that acts as my window. With *Kinetta*, I was spoiled for choice. A high point came early on when I was relieved to find that I wouldn't, as I was fearing, have to make use of "Closed Caption" subtitles: it turned out the film already had standard subtitles burned in the stream. This resolved, I watched and took notes; to my right, my cat did the sensible thing, and slept soundly through the entire film.

Whoever provided the summary on IMDb which I lifted straight from the site is very well-spoken. That is exactly what *Kinetta* is "about", and no amount of "walk time" padding or shaky-cam "fight" footage can stop my train of thought from slapping quotations around everything in a vain attempt to convey how mind-numbingly pointless this cinematic exercise is. Of the three leads, the least charismatic (the "BMW"-fanboy, who may be a cop [?]) gets by far and away the most dialogue. Cameraman, with beard, has perhaps half a dozen short lines, but comes across as the only reasonable person of the bunch. The scene in which he saves the hotel maid from a drug overdose makes for the only worthwhile stretch of movie—right in the final minutes. But well before that point, a question came unbidden to my mind, "Why don't the MST3K or RiffTrax people make better use of their skills by tearing art-house garbage to pieces?"

While the likes of *The Killing of a Sacred Deer* and *The Lobster* prove Lanthimos knows how to make really good movies, *Kinetta* stands as proof-in-celluloid that he can make a really horrible one if he puts his mind to it.

The experimental *Kinetta* did not gain much notice on its initial release, and Kino only released it 15 years later to capitalize on interest in the director, who has since become kind of famous (and Oscar-nominated).—Giles Edwards

The Mad Fox [*Koiya koi nasuna koi*] (1962) ★★★★

DIRECTED BY: Tomu Uchida

FEATURING: Michiko Saga, Hashizô Ôkawa

PLOT: An apprentice astrologer, betrayed and driven mad, flees to the countryside where he meets both the twin sister of his lost beloved and fox spirits.

COMMENTS: *The Mad Fox* begins on a grandiose note when a "white rainbow" portentously appears in the sky. The Emperor summons the court astrologer, who predicts doom for the kingdom. Before the sage can divulge the remedy suggested by the astrological scroll that holds the answers to the future, he is slain by bandits. Only his chosen successor can read the scroll, but the astrologer died without choosing between his two disciples. Much scheming and intrigue follows, and the first act ends with Yasuna, the good and faithful disciple, fleeing to the countryside after the death of Sakaki, his beloved and the astrologer's adopted daughter.

This section of the film is a Technicolor spectacle played out on lavish courtyard sets with characters kneeling in embroidered silk robes, a *mise-en-scène* that wouldn't be out of place in an Akira Kurosawa period piece. Things shift towards the abstract once Yasuna's insanity hits, however. The exiled apprentice finds himself in a sea of glowing sunflowers while butterflies on visible strings flit by and a singer warbles a warning to "never fall in love." After this Expressionist interlude, act two begins when mad Yasuna stumbles upon Sakaki's twin sister and mistakes her for his lost love. Things are further complicated when Yasuna rescues a wounded fox spirit transformed into human shape. The fox's granddaughter falls in love with him, and when Yasuna is later wounded, she assumes the likeness of Sakaki and appears to him and licks his wounds clean. It's like *Vertigo*, but with the hero desperately falling for *two* separate specters of his lost love. As Yasuna and the fox build an illusory family, the final act leaves realism even farther behind, turning into a kabuki performance played out on an obvious stage set.

Synopses and reviews often stress that the movie is "hard to follow." Although details of Tokugawa-era society might be unfamiliar to Western audiences, this concern is greatly overblown; it's no more difficult than a Shakespeare adaptation. Another common complaint among the movie's few detractors is that Uchida's stylistic transitions are jarring. But the second half of the film, when we follow Yasuna into his delusions, are more engaging and moving than the realist set up—at least, for those of us who value deep imagination over shallow authenticity.

Though respected in his native Japan, Tomu Uchida never broke through to international audiences, for reasons that probably have more to do with bad luck than anything else. *The Mad Fox* was seldom exhibited outside Japan. Arrow Academy rediscovered and restored this minor classic in 2020 and released it on Blu-ray, where it can now be experienced by the adventurous cinephile with moderately deep pockets.— Gregory J. Smalley

My Hindu Friend (2015) ★★1/2

DIRECTED BY: Hector Babenco

FEATURING: Willem Dafoe

PLOT: Diego Fairman is an Argentinian filmmaker of modest fame whose apparently terminal cancer has prompted him to be a jerk to all of those around him.

COMMENTS: Like most of you, I'm a fan of the musician Taco Ockerse. With his smooth crooner's voice, he dragged hits from the mid-20th century into the 1980s' New Wave. Three such songs featured in Hector Babenco's *My Hindu Friend*. That's not to say they used Taco's versions, but "Ma Vie En Rose," "Dancing Cheek to Cheek," and "Singin' in the Rain" form a trifecta of "Why is this song here, now, doing this?" in a movie ripped straight from *The Hallmark Channel Presents: Fellini's Night of Melodrama*.

Babenco presents a film variant of himself, like Fellini did. Babenco revels in whimsical dream interludes, like Fellini did. Babenco's movie just sort of trails off at the end, like Fellini's... Suffice it to say, *My Hindu Friend* is intensely personal: the upshot of which is that those of us not actually in the movie can merely try to enjoy Willem Dafoe moping around various domiciles.

After untold days/weeks/months in hospital, Diego starts hallucinating Death—who, in a refreshing twist, is just a work-a-day guy who's having problems with his wife. There's talk of the afterlife, but no secrets are revealed; apparently such revelations are above Death's pay-grade. There are discussions about cinema. And, of course, there's a game of chess—'cause that's something a film fanatic might hallucinate while weakened to the core and dosed up on morphine.

Morphine. Yes, I would have preferred more morphine shots, as that not only brought forth the affable Death character, but also the only show-stopping scene in *My Hindu Friend*. In the middle of the night, the heavily-drugged Diego awakens singing a song through his breathing apparatus before removing it and, wonderfully, crooning into it as if it were a microphone. The song going through his dope-addled mind? "Dancing Cheek to Cheek."

And that titular Hindu friend? A young boy he meets in the infusion room at the hospital during his cancer treatment. The ailing director tells this narrative crutch anecdotes, ultimately living through fantasy stories as he does his best to comfort the eight-year-old whom the cosmos considered deserving of such a terrible fate. I'm rambling at this point, but I blame the movie

Babenco (*Kiss of the Spider Woman*) completed the autobiographical *My Hindu Friend*, which describes his battle with (and recovery from) lymphatic cancer, in 2015. It did reasonably well on its festival release, with Willem Dafoe gathering a Best Actor award at 2016's Montréal World Film Festival. Ironically, after recovering from cancer, Babenco died in 2016 of a heart attack. *My Hindu Friend* was forgotten until it was given a limited theatrical release in 2020, followed by a stint on home video.—Giles Edwards

She's Allergic to Cats ★★★★

DIRECTED BY: Michael Reich

FEATURING: Mike Pinkney, Sonja Kinski, Flula Borg, Honey Davis

PLOT: Mike Pinkney is an aspiring director living in East Hollywood, where he dreams of making his passion project: a remake of *Carrie* featuring an all-cat cast. No one is interested in his work, so he makes ends meet by working as a dog groomer, where he meets a beautiful woman who improbably agrees to go out on a date with him. Unfortunately, his run-down rental house suffers from a rat infestation that threatens to ruin his big chance with his dream girl.

BACKGROUND:

- Director Michael Reich and star Mike Pinkney had previously worked as co-directors on music videos for Ryan Adams, the Shins, My Chemical Romance, Yuck, and other bands.

- Reich wrote the part explicitly for Pinkney. They took acting classes together to prepare, which is where they met Sonja (daughter of Nastassja, granddaughter of Klaus) Kinski.

- The movie was shot in Reich's own house and neighborhood. Honey Davis, who plays the landlord in the movie, was Reich's landlord at the time.

- Parts of *She's Allergic to Cats* were inspired by director's Michael Reich's work as a dog groomer in Hollywood, where he expressed the anal glands of pooches belonging to George Carlin and Jake Gyllenhal, among other celebrities.
- It took the movie four years from its film festival debut to finally be released on video-on-demand.
- Not debuting on home video until after the list of the 366 Weirdest Movies of All Time had been completed, *She's Allergic to Cats* was the sixth movie inaugurated onto our supplemental "Apocryphally Weird" list.

INDELIBLE IMAGE: Take your pick from two briefly glimpsed images from the climactic montage: a naked woman holding a bowl of rotting bananas while rats crawl over her, or a naked woman whose upper half *is* a banana. We'll accept either answer. (If you're looking for a non-nude pick, Sonja Kinski posing seductively with a DVD of *Congo* is your go-to).

TWO WEIRD THINGS: Sensual dog grooming instructional video; anal gland expression

WHAT MAKES IT WEIRD: In *She's Allergic to Cats*, dog groomer Mike Pinkney bashfully confesses to "making weird video art that nobody wants to watch." He's wrong. Somebody wants to watch this portrait of a pathetic artist struggling to make an all-cat version of *Carrie* while dealing with a rat infestation and an internal video monologue that consists of glitchy nightmares run through a circa 1989 public access AV board. That somebody is you.

COMMENTS: The old writer's cliché is to "write what you know." The danger of this advice, of course, is that, if every aspiring writer faithfully followed it, massive deforestation would result as slush piles overflowed with autobiographical novels about struggling novelists struggling to write their first novel, and autobiographical scripts about struggling filmmakers struggling to make their first film. The self-indulgent navel-gazing opus is a tricky proposition even for established writers; for first-timers without an established navel to gaze at, it looks like a death

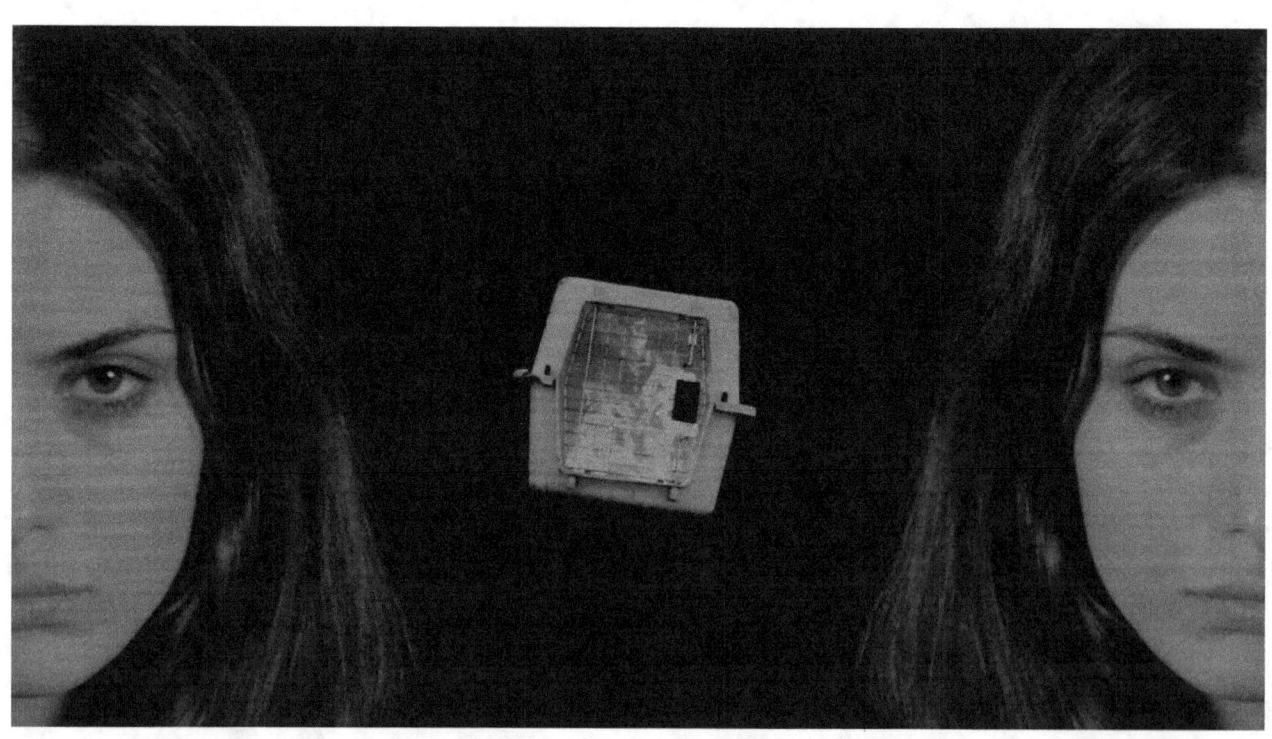

trap. And yet, sometimes, despite these dangers, the ploy can work, and work beautifully. Michael Reich's *She's Allergic to Cats* successfully navigates the minefield of self-reflexive works about the self-doubting artist, not so much avoiding clichés as tramping down hard on them, relishing the beautiful chaos that results.

A couple of elements make *Cats* succeed where other experiments of its type might come off as insufferably self-indulgent. One is the movie's embrace of absurdity, its ability to laugh at itself. There could hardly be a more ridiculous day job for an aspiring artist than dog groomer. The opening montage features Mike Pinkney's boss instructing his protégée, in velvety tones, on the art of grooming—"slowly and sensually, yes," he croons seductively—as blurry slow-motion hands soap up a pooch and oh-so carefully snip the hair around its anus. The scene is simultaneously ominous—because of the low-frequency rumble mixed with canine woofs and whines on the soundtrack—and hilarious, because the groomer takes his vocation with an impossible degree of seriousness. It sets a mixed tone that the movie stays faithful to, mixing nightmarish mundanity with puckish mockery. In the movie, Pinkney is so consumed with self-doubt he can't confront his landlord about the rat infestation without apologizing for bothering him. He's so hapless that he falls face-first into dog shit, which amuses a passing tow-truck driver to no end. The indignities he suffers are amplified by his producer and only friend Sebastian (played with broad Teutonic comedy by Flula Borg), an externalized voice of self-loathing who constantly reprimands the artist ("I say this because I am your friend... you are just a giant, sad, dirty man-baby.") Pinkney's social abasement is so grand and melodramatic that it's a parody of artistic self-pity rather than a wallow in it. It's hard for us to think of a man who dreams of a feline remake of *Carrie* as a great, misunderstood artist. Reich pokes fun at his own archetype; but at the same time, a sense of surreal danger constantly lurks in *Cats*' shadows. It's an absurd, nightmarishly funny evocation of the life of a creative schlub trying to grind out a living in an indifferent L.A, and the comic scenes are like catching a spastic case of the giggles just as a panic attack is coming on.

Besides the humor, the second element that elevates *Cats* is Reich's interjection of his own "weird" video art into the story. Greatly reminiscent of the retro-VHS aesthetics of fellow Los Angeles kitsch artists Everything is Terrible!, these lightning-paced montages are full of static, distortion, purposeful artifacting, superimposed images, and oversaturated and solarized colors spanning the low-tech VGA palette. Parts put me in mind of the then-avant-garde techniques used in 1982's *Liquid Sky*. These moments show us Pinkney's life work, but they also comprise his nightmares, his internal monologues, and, in the 12-minute climax, they serve as the movie's final, in-your-face statement of artistic purpose. A movie about someone who makes "weird video art" should rightfully be full of examples of "weird video art"; and here they aren't just curious exhibits designed to amuse us for a brief moment, but integral components a larger narrative, and illustrations of the movie's theme of cluttered creativity and its celebration of outsider aesthetics.

Cats teems with a rich vein of imagery, revolving around animals, eroticism, and art. Cats are right there in the title. The main character is a dog groomer. Felines and canines are conventionally opposed, and also traditionally represent the feminine and the masculine dichotomy. We also see rats, symbols of disorder and disease; and Cora somehow manages to associate ducklings with death. Then there's a lost dog named Karma, and a man whose DVD collection consists entirely of talking animal films. The movie also makes major use of bananas, an obvious phallic symbol, which here are limp and rotten and nibbled on by rats. Art and sex are linked as the two great creative impulses. Cora may be more symbolic muse than flesh and blood woman. When she first meets Michael, the camera keeps Kinski out of focus or shows her only in silhouette, reinforcing our impression of her as someone unreal, perhaps even imaginary. (Beautiful women don't flirt with their dog groomers every day; and particularly not when he's visibly nervous and making her pet's nails bleed while cutting them.) All of the imagery Reich builds comes together at the climax, in a sprawling "weird video art" montage with torrents of blood, rotting bananas, flaming pet carriers, ghost cats, rats crawling over naked women, mutant woman/banana hybrids... The film tosses you all the pieces you need to build your own allegory about the artistic process, without providing a strict blueprint to follow. The consistency of the imagery gives *Cats* coherence and personality, while the controlled delirium thrills us with an intoxicating sense of freedom.

The end result of all this is a surprising level of authenticity amidst the absurdity. The unglamorous East Hollywood locations, peopled by genuine eccentrics like the brash Sebastian and shifty-eyed hippie landlord Honey Davis—characters who somehow exist in the same milieu as Kiniski's radiant but damaged dream woman—add to this effect. Hollywood is a weird place, especially when you're an outsider dreaming of being an insider, but instead stuck clipping the hair of stars' pets. Reich's surrealist spin on this crazy milieu is much more interesting than a straightforward story about an aspiring indie director could ever be. More importantly, the technique penetrates deeper into the heart of its subject: the insecurities and travails of the unestablished artist.

And, if that's not enough to sell you on this underground gem, it also features graphic depictions of canine anal gland expression, which is something you don't see every day. Unless you're so down on your luck that squeezing anal glands is your day job.

HOME VIDEO INFO: At this time, *She's Allergic to Cats* is only available for video-on-demand purchase or rental.—Gregory J. Smalley

"Small Talk" (2016) ★★★★

IRECTED BY: Terrisha Kearse

FEATURING: Farelle Walker, Jared Benjamin, Scott St. Patrick, Kiya Roberts, Jermaine Jercox, David Chattam, Gayla Johnson, Mia Sun

PLOT: Ahmed attends a dinner party with Corah, his fiancée, to meet his prospective in-laws. Did we mention that they live in Wonderland?

COMMENTS: "Down the rabbit-hole" is as apt a phrase to use with "Small Talk"—literally as well as figuratively—since the film is a very clever bounce off of Carroll's "Alice in Wonderland." The original story has been adapted and interpreted as everything from social commentary to political allegory, but writer/actor Farelle Walker uses it as a pointed and even more surreal look at information overload, behavior defined by social media, and any "ism" (race, sex, class, etc.) that she can come up with—and that's quite a lot.

It's a chaotic package; quite a lot is thrown at the audience, and at "Alice," in this instance represented by Ahmed Mogadam (Jared Benjamin) as the voice of reason. He (and we) are introduced to the Hamner Family, described in the opening statement as an "interesting family of strong opinions and disturbingly small-minded chatter." There's Corah (Farelle Walker), Ahmed's fiancée, an African Goddess (we meet them as they're listening to her podcast on her "Yanniverse"; she refers to Ahmed as a "Moor") and a conspiracy believer (trying to avoid chemtrails as planes fly overhead). Her sister, Senna (Kiya Roberts) is "White" based, having ties to the "White Lives Matter" movement. Her husband, Edwardian "Eddie" Licenter (Scott St. Patrick) is a "White" rabbit ("Creole," he insists). Brother Grant (Jermaine Jercox) is a sinister army officer, describing himself as "the Black Man They can trust." Poppa Hamner (David Chattam) is a pig who acts and talks as a stereotypical black patriarch, and matriarch Athyna Hamner (Gayla Johnson)—The Red Queen —is a pious Christian for White Jesus, who watches all via a portrait on the wall.

Amongst all of this is the Asian housekeeper, Soon Yook (Mia Sun), who gives condescension as good as she gets it; and the constantly streaming "Wonderland News" with the Mad Hatter, Dormouse, and Rabbit as news anchors in the background. It's a dense package that might seem, at first glance, a mad cluster... but it's a film that one needs to pay close attention to, especially the wordplay. It's for smart people. Some of the banter may go over a lot of heads, especially as far as specific cultural aspects are concerned, but for those willing to go on the ride down the hole, they'll have a wild time.

Completed in 2016 but first offered to the public in 2020, you can watch the 45 minute feature for free at www.flyrenegadeproductions.com or on Vimeo.—El Rob Hubbard

Suburban Birds (2019) ★★

DIRECTED BY: Sheng Qiu

FEATURING: Mason Lee, Zihan Gong

PLOT: A team of engineers investigate the sudden appearance of sinkholes which are forcing them to condemn buildings; the story changes to follow a group of suburban elementary schoolers, with parallels developing between the two tales.

COMMENTS: If *Suburban Birds* is any indication, the growing Chinese art-house movement will be founded in the spirit of Bi Gan. Cinematography will be privileged over narrative, hazy mysticism will pervade, and timelines will go out of focus as multiple histories coexist at once.

Suburban Birds begins slowly, develops slowly, and ends with two men falling asleep. We begin by following Han, part of surveying team investigating unstable buildings in a Chinese city. After a while, Han enters an evacuated school and finds a diary. As he reads, we follow the story of a boy—also named Han—and his school chums. They hunt for birds eggs, engage in pre-adolescent flirtation, and eventually trek off on a long journey to find one of their number who didn't show up to school that day. This section of the film takes up an inconclusive hour in the middle of the film, and is almost entirely realistic. The temptation is to assume that young Han and old Han are the same character at different times of their lives, but the story steadfastly refuses to commit to that interpretation, and in fact undermines it. When we return to old Han—seen awakening from a nap—the movie seems less connected to reality than before, although the dissonances are always subtle. Motifs such as haircuts, a riddle, and a stray dog recur in both stories, and it's possible to draw parallels between Han's companions in each hemisphere. It ends with a coda that brings in two new characters out on a birdwatching trip in the forest young Han once roamed.

What it all signifies is anyone's guess; it's impossible to tease out a moral from the odd story, which never develops a consistent tone or obvious theme. It does features good, if restrained, acting; the children, especially, are a believable ensemble, without a weak link. The cinematography is superior, with intelligent zooms and pans highlighting important characters and spatial relationships. Memorable visuals include a shot of tufts of grass that change color, and a dreamlike interlude where the engineers examine "clues" from inside separate plexiglass enclosures, each lit in a different neon lighting scheme. *Suburban Birds* may be enjoyed by fans of slow, obliquely mystical cinema in the mold of Apichatpong Weerasethakul and the aforementioned Bi Gan, but I found it took far too long in developing its enigmas, which didn't seem worth the journey.

Suburban Birds got a very limited U.S. release in 2019; a DVD/Blu-ray showed up in 2020, and it can be found for VOD rental on some of the smaller, art-house oriented streaming services.—Gregory J. Smalley

Vampire Burt's Serenade (2014/2020) ★

DIRECTED BY: Ken Roht

FEATURING: Kevin Richardson, Brandon Heitkamp, Sharon Ferguson, Dylan Kenin, Diva Zappa

PLOT: Burlesque stars and drag queens team up to defeat a vampire, singing forgettable songs along the way.

COMMENTS: A horror-comedy-musical seems like an easy bet for moviemakers on a low budget; the only problem is, great musicals require great music. That isn't easy to come by. If it lost the lame tunes and focused more on pure craziness, *Vampire Burt's Serenade* might have been a better film, although it would distinguish itself less from the crowded camp-horror field.

Who would have guessed that someday Kevin Richardson would be working with even weaker material than when he was in the Backstreet Boys? True, he sings well, but given the generic pop-rock beats and uninspired lyrics he has to work with, it's for naught. The rest of the cast doesn't have Richardson's chops going for them: it's painful to hear Diva Zappa sing "Sex Toy." The lip-syncing is clumsy; it's obvious when the soundtrack switches to the studio, making it difficult to suspend disbelief that the characters are spontaneously singing about their desire to stake a vampire through the heart. Only a couple of numbers are memorable: one where drugged ballerinas stagger around singing a nursery-rhyme track (the ladies all affect little girl voices, so singing ability isn't an issue), and one absurd bit sung by lovers rendezvousing in a toilet stall ("Here in this scuzzy little toilet… in this crazy insanity/with its lack of any sanity…").

The action begins at a burlesque cabaret where Burt is well-known to everyone; he bites three main characters in one night, setting his own undoing in motion. In a movie populated entirely by vampires, zombies, strippers, and a drug-dealing snuff performance artist, all of whom sing and dance, it seems odd to complain about a lack of believably. But this universe doesn't feel like somewhere anyone could live in. Nor does it feel like a delirious dream. It's just a collection of vampire clichés and tropes thrown together.

This *Rocky Horror* wannabe earned a few mild recommendations from the "good try, old chap" school of pat-on-the-back film criticism. If you're looking for pluses, Richardson is believably douchey, having a ball as the titular coke-snorting bloodsucker; the comedy is sometimes effective (e.g. a running joke about bisexual vampires); the idea of a vampire later becoming a zombie is cute; and the finale, with the entire cast coming together in a battle to the death, is bloody and chaotic. I can see someone tolerating it as a fast-paced time-waster. Still, it's nothing to sing about.

Released free on Amazon Prime to sate an entertainment-starved country just as the pandemic struck, it turns out that *Vampire Burt's Serenade* is actually a slightly re-edited version of a 2014 movie called *Bloody Indulgent*. *Indulgent* runs two minutes longer than *Serenade* and can still be found on the Amazon channel "Fear Factory," although the DVDs have been removed from circulation.—Gregory J. Smalley

"What Did Jack Do?" ★★★1/2

DIRECTED BY: David Lynch

FEATURING: David Lynch

PLOT: A detective interrogates a monkey suspected of murder.

COMMENTS: David Lynch made the curious short "What Did Jack Do?" in 2017 for a French museum exhibit, and screened it once more at his own Festival of Disruption in 2018. Other than that, this bit of monkey business was an overlooked footnote in his filmography, until Netflix dropped it onto their streaming service on January 20, 2020 (on Lynch's 74th birthday).

Shot in *Eraserhead*ian black and white, with Lynchian signatures like coffee and a left-field musical number, "Jack" is basically a two-hander (almost a one-hander, since Lynch not only plays the interrogating detective, but also provides the monkey's voice). There is a plot, of sorts, but mostly, it's the detective and his simian suspect trading absurdist quips that occupy a space between the ineffably sinister and the ambiguously clichéd: "Don't worry. I've heard the phrase 'birds of a feather flock together.' A perceived fundamental. There are, of course, exceptions."

"What Did Jack Do?" is Lynch futzing around with the Surrealist potentialities of Syncro-Vox—the technique pioneered in the 1950s in which human lips are superimposed over animals or animated characters. Lynch's experiment is extremely sophisticated, with his usual attention to detail: visually, the lips are blended so well that they almost pass as a real feature of the Capuchin monkey, remaining just "off" enough to supply an uncanny undertone that harmonizes wonderfully with the overt absurdity of a talking monkey in a suit and tie. Jack's face is, of course, blank, and his gaze flits randomly, but depending on dialogue Lynch chooses to put in his mouth he can appear lovesick, resentful, or nervous. That's a wonderful surrealist illusion. The result, while arguably slim, is still arresting and worth your time—and, it goes without saying, a must-see for Lynch completists.

Netflix's business practices give them a lot to answer for, but they deserve credit when they get it right. "What Did Jack Do?" is a super-niche offering that won't be bringing the streamer new subscribers, but they've done a hell of a service to the cinephile community by making it available at all.—Gregory J. Smalley

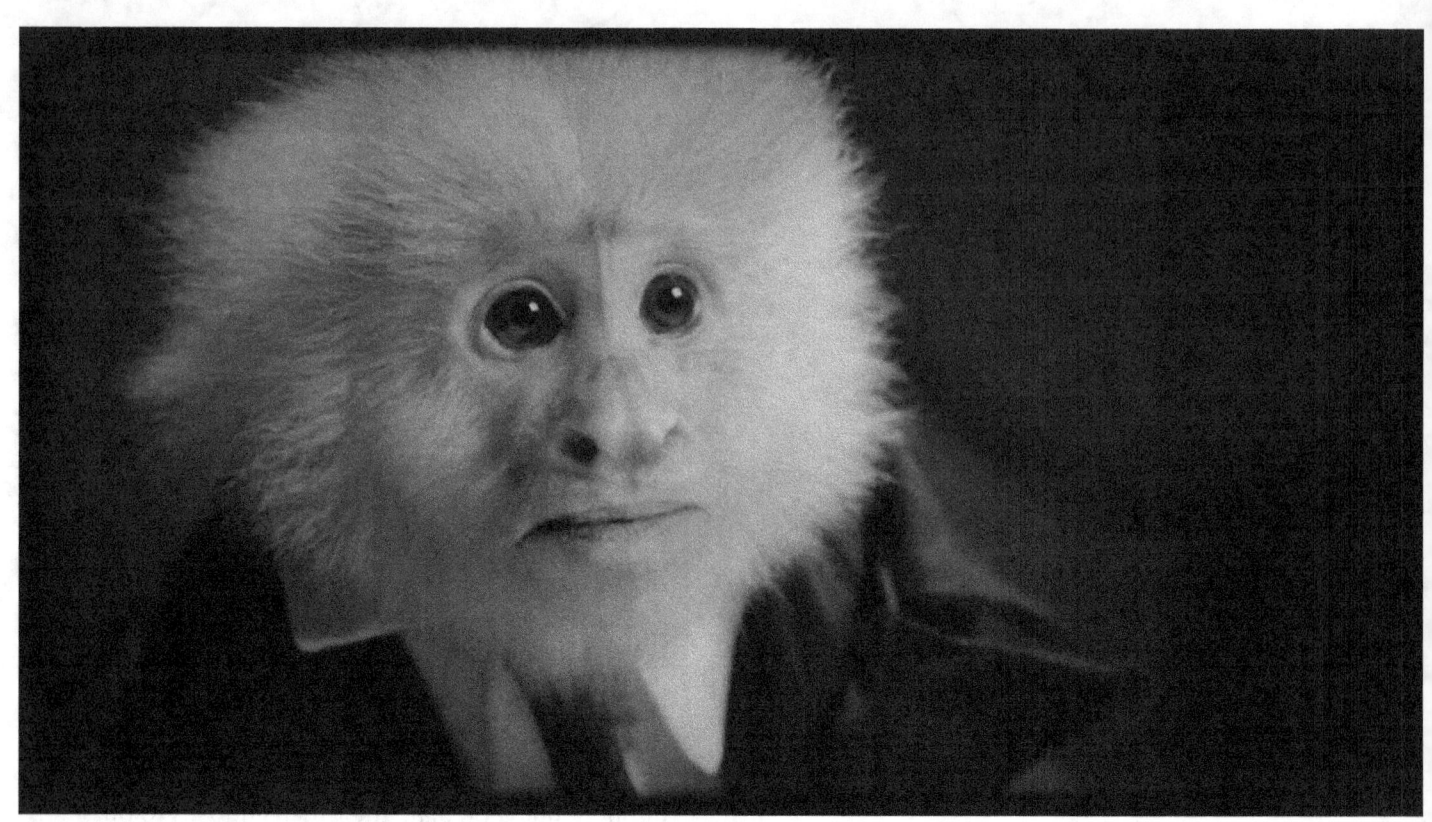

Jack Cruz in "What Did Jack Do?", courtesy Netflix

NOTABLE 2020 HOME VIDEO RE-RELEASES & SPECIAL EDITIONS

"Alejandro Jodorowsky: 4K Restoration Collection" ★★★★★

This 2020 box set, which brings the hippie-era cult films *Fando y Lis* (1968), *El Topo* (1970), and *The Holy Mountain* (1973) together with the director's latest, *Psychomagic, A Healing Art* (reviewed separately above), is not the first Jodorowsky collection from ABCKO. The three early films had been released previously on DVD as "The Films of Alejandro Jodorowsky," and many of the extra features here are recycled from the earlier set. It's understandable that some fans who bought the previous collection may wonder whether double-dipping is worth it. So to begin, here's what's recycled from the older set:

- Jodorowsky's commentary tracks for *Fando y Lis*, *El Topo*, and *The Holy Mountain*

- *La Cravate*, Jodorowsky's 1957 debut film, a 20-minute mime/surrealist short about severed heads, based on a Thomas Mann story

- The soundtrack CDs for *El Topo* and *The Holy Mountain*

- Deleted scenes from *The Holy Mountain*, with select commentary by Jodorowsky

- *The Tarot*, a short providing Jodorowsky's own interpretation of the symbolism of the Tarot deck

- *La Constellation Jodorowsky* (1994), a feature-length documentary which includes an early mention of psychomagic

- "The Father of Midnight Movies," a 2007 interview with Jodorowsky

- Various trailers

- Image galleries of production stills, press materials and posters, screenshots of original reviews (including Pauline Kael's infamous savaging of *El Topo*), script pages from *El Topo* and *The Holy Mountain*, and other odds and ends (a section of images called "set panels" looks like Jodorowsky's Tarot card deck). I can't guarantee that all of this material is recycled; some could be new.

Besides *Psychomagic* (whose disc contains no extras except its own trailer), here's what's new in this set:

- The brilliant 4K restorations, which are doubtlessly the best these films have ever looked. Of special note is the fact that *El Topo* appears in 1.85:1 widescreen for the first time on any disc.

- New "Jodorowsky Remembers" introductions for each film from the 91-year old director, each about 15 minutes long

- Introductions to each film from Columbia film studies professor Richard Peña, each about 10 minutes long, all informative and supplying great context for the movies and their times

- "A Conversation with the Son of El Topo," an interview with Brontis Jodorowsky

- "Pablo Leder: Jodorowsky's Right Hand Man," an interview with Jodorowsky's personal assistant during the period covered in the set

- "The A to Z of The Holy Mountain," a video appreciation by Ben Cobb, which is a work of critical art on its own merits
- The packaging: the set contains six collectible postcards (reverse images from *El Topo* and *The Holy Mountain*), a reversible fold-out poster (an Italian poster for *El Topo* and a French poster for *Holy Mountain*), and a 78-page illustrated booklet with intellectual essays from Virgine Sélavy, Michael Atkinson, Bilge Ebiri, and Mark Pilkington. This booklet is Criterion Collection quality in terms of content, but my copy, at least, had a problem with flimsy binding. Several pages fell out the first time I paged through it. This could be an isolated case, but I advise handling it with extra care if you want to keep your copy pristine.

You could easily get lost for hours in the extra features. Watching all of them should earn you at least a master's degree in Jodorowsky studies. It's impossible to imagine a more complete compilation of video materials for Jodorowsky's first three feature films; this will go down as the ultimate set. It's like finding the lost city of Tar, defeating the Fourth Gunfighter, and scaling the Holy Mountain all at once.—Gregory J. Smalley

"Boogiepop Phantom" (1999) ★★★1/2

DIRECTED BY: Takashi Watanabe

FEATURING: Voices of Yuu Asakawa, Kaori Shimizu, Rakuto Tochihara (original Japanese); Rachael Lillis, Debora Rabbai, Jessica Calvello (English dub)

PLOT: A Japanese high school is the epicenter of odd events involving a pillar of light, a series of serial killings, and whispers of sightings of the mysterious spirit known as Boogiepop.

COMMENTS: Certain features of "Boogiepop Phantom" remind me of "Twin Peaks": the limited setting (a Japanese school rather than a Northwestern U.S. town); the dark, melodramatic subplots from a large cast of interconnected characters; possession by supernatural entities that are allegorical renderings of psychological traumas. The world of "Boogiepop" is more logical and tightly connected to its fantastical central conceits, however, lacking the free-floating surrealism and absurdity of its American cousin. There's still plenty of weirdness to soak in, though.

"Boogiepop" deals with a plague of strange "evolutions" in Japanese teenagers, including a boy who sees (and eats) bugs in people's hearts, and another who dresses like a Pied Piper and causes people to disappear by convincing them to revert to childhood. Is "Boogiepop," an apparition who appears in a dark billowing cape and tall Cossack hat, responsible? Each episode focuses on a different character, and each installment jumps about in time. The same event may appear in different character's storylines, and the second occurrence may shed light on the first.

"Boogiepop"'s visual palette is muted, although frequently filled with bright glowing objects like cellphone screens or magical butterflies. The action is enclosed in a circular iris that dims into darkness around the edges. This effect makes each episode feel like a faltering memory. The sound design is even more notable than the visuals: distorted background static, electronic glitches, mysterious chimes, and Gregorian chant appear, with the main theme from "Meistersinger von Nürnberg," Boogiepop's signature tune, floating through the entire series. At the end of each episode, a cacophony of overlapping dialogue from the next installment whets your appetite (and furthers your bewilderment).

One time through the series may not be enough to understand what's going on. It's particularly challenging to keep track of the large cast of characters, and to figure out how each fits into the whole. If you're also confused, you may want to supplement your viewing with a quick peek at Wikipedia or online guides. Or, you could just watch the series a second time, taking notes. This kind of elaborate worldbuilding tends to create a devoted fanbase of decoders, and such is the case with the "Boogiepop" franchise. With its theme of alienated teenagers neglected and betrayed by their parents' generation, "Boogiepop" is aimed at bright youngsters, but the artistry of the presentation will draw in adventurous older viewers, as well.

"Boogiepop Phantom" was adapted from a series of light novels by Kouhei Kadono (the series has fourteen entries; "Phantom" is an original story, but relies on established characters and events from the novels). It was written by Sadayuki Murai (who also wrote the screenplay for *Perfect Blue*) and produced by Madhouse, who animated all four of Satoshi Kon's movies, along with many other classic anime series and films. Nozomi's English-language Blu-ray release, which arrived in December 2019, features the series' entire 12-episode run. It includes numerous small extras, like the "clean" openings and closings beloved of anime fans, and, more substantially, an English-language commentary track from a couple of Americans who worked on the dubbed version. (Recommendation: as always, turn off the English dub and listen to the Japanese with subtitles. The English voice acting is uneven.)— Gregory J. Smalley

Death Laid an Egg (1968) [*La morte ha fatto l'uovo*, AKA *Plucked*]
★★★★1/2 (Director's Cut Special Edition)

DIRECTED BY: Giulio Questi

FEATURING: Jean-Louis Trintignant, Gina Lollabrigida, Ewa Aulin, Jean Sobieski

PLOT: We open watching a prostitute killed in a hotel room. The action then moves to an experimental poultry farm, largely automated but overseen by Marco, his wife Anna, and their beautiful live-in secretary Gabri. The plot slowly reveals a love triangle, with multiple betrayals, with Marco's growing disgust at the poultry business brought to a boil when he finds a scientist has bred a species of headless mutant chickens for sale to the public.

SPECIAL EDITION COMMENTS: *Death Laid an Egg* was not a hit on release. By 1970, however, the success of Dario Argento's *Bird with the Crystal Plumage* created an international market for the Italian giallo. At 104 minutes, the already challenging (some would say incoherent) *Egg* featured far too much arty oddness and socialist satire to please the punters, but it did boast an exploitable amount of blood, sex, and a pair of gorgeous female leads in Gina Lollabrigida and Ewa Aulin. About fifteen minutes were trimmed, and it was dubbed into English and released as *Plucked*, in the version that most of the world has seen since.

Most of the newly restored fifteen minutes seen for the first time here involve a character named Luigi, an old amnesiac colleague of the protagonist whose significance (like so much in the film) is never made clear. Other restored bits involve gritty scenes of real poultry processing, Lollabrigida making elliptically morbid comments while looking at chicken embryo slides, and another encounter with the dispossessed farm workers. In a film where so many details are merely playful wild goose chases, the newly restored footage is, in some sense, inconsequential. But fifteen or twenty additional minutes of *Death Laid an Egg* is a blessing to be relished.

This edition gives you the option to watch the 90-minute dubbed version or the 104-minute director's cut. The dubbed dialogue is superior: it's a relief to have lines like "I think that's a peculiar way to put it, men and chickens mixed up like that" and "Your bra and panties are almost as important as what's under them" restored, instead of the more prosaic and literal subtitle renditions. Some of the original cast (the four principals included two Frechmen and a Swede) were dubbed into Italian anyway, so there's no question of linguistic authenticity: go with the superior English dub.

Giallo scholar Troy Howarth and "Mondo Digital"'s Nathaniel Thompson provide an informative commentary track, wisely eschewing interpretation and limiting themselves to supplying context and background on Questi, the cast and crew, and the Italian film industry. Other special features include trailers, a video review, Questi's last recorded interview (he doesn't discuss *Death Laid an Egg*), and one of the director's final short films, 2002's "Doctor Schizo and Mister Phrenic." In the interview Questi seems quite proud of the short, but it is somewhat sad to see a man who once shot big-budget films with movie stars on location reduced to starring in his own camcorder-shot YouTube uploads, set entirely in his own apartment.

Early editions of this set come with a slipcase and a package of collectible postcards. This is the *Egg* we've been dying for.—Gregory J. Smalley

The Fabulous Baron Munchausen [*Baron Prásil*] (1962) ★★★★★

DIRECTED BY: Karel Zeman

FEATURING: Miloš Kopecký, Jana Brejchová, Rudolf Jelínek

PLOT: An astronaut, Tonik, discovers that he is not the first man on the Moon, having been beaten there by literary figures Cyrano de Bergerac, Jules Verne's protagonists of "From the Earth to the Moon," and Baron Munchausen. Mistaking the astronaut as a native moonman, Munchausen volunteers to take him back to Earth to show him the ways of Earthmen. The pair there encounter a sultan and are swallowed by a fish, among other fantastic adventures.

BACKGROUND:

- The character of Baron Munchausen comes from Rudolf Erich Raspe's 1785 novel "Baron Munchausen's narrative of his marvelous travels and campaigns in Russia." Raspe based Munchausen on a real-life German officer who was notorious for embellishing tales of his own military exploits. Czechs traditionally called the same character "Baron Prásil."

- Munchausen's stories have been adapted to film many times, beginning with a Georges Méliès short in 1911.

- Karel Zeman's previous film, the black and white *Invention for Destruction* [*Vynález zkázy*], won the Grand Prix at the International Film Festival at Expo 58, and was considered the most successful Czech film of all time. *Baron Prásil* was even more ambitious, adding a luscious color palette and expanding on the techniques Zeman had pioneered in his previous work.

- *Home Cinema Choice* named *The Fabulous Baron Munchausen*'s 2017 remaster the best restoration of the year.
- Though not making the List of the 366 Weirdest Movies of All Time, *The Fabulous Baron Munchhausen* became the tenth film added to our supplemental "apocryphally Weird" list.

INDELIBLE IMAGE: Red smoke billowing in a yellow sky as the Baron and companions escape the Sultan's army on horseback.

TWO WEIRD THINGS: Cyrano and pals on the Moon; Pegasus-drawn spaceship

WHAT MAKES IT WEIRD: *Baron Prasil* is a stunning visual feast combining live-action and animation, the effect far surpassing the modest means (by then-current standards) with which it was made.

COMMENTS: "If he's endowed with such imagination, let's see some grand display of it!" – Baron Munchausen (Miloš Kopecký)

That line could just as easily be spoken by the audience, throwing down the gauntlet to the storyteller to entertain them. That it is spoken by one of the grand storytellers (liars?) in literature, near the end of the film after having witnessed such a grand display, is cheek of the highest order. The success is even more ironic considering that such an imaginative work was made under the auspices of the Communist Government, not an institution noted for embracing imagination.

Baron Munchausen has been a popular figure for adaptations over the years. A 1943 German production and Terry Gilliam's 1988 version bookend Zeman's 1962 vision. (Gilliam freely admits he borrowed considerably from Zeman.) The major difference among the three films is the production. The 1943 and 1988 versions were each, for their time and place, big-budget live action spectacles. Zeman worked on a smaller scale using a combination of animation and live action, giving his film a very stylized look; in this case, evoking the artwork of Gustave Doré, who illustrated the Munchausen stories in the 19th century.

Zeman showed an affinity for such romantic fantasy. 1958's *Invention for Destruction* was based on a Jules Verne tale, as were two of his subsequent works, *The Stolen Airship* and *On the Comet*. Two of Verne's characters from "From the Earth to the Moon" make cameo appearances in *Baron Prásil*. The adventures themselves, which range from the Moon to the Ottoman Empire to under the sea, are the stuff of romantic fantasy; visions which might be in danger of being crowded out by the approaching world of science. Sighting a witch riding a broomstick as they make their way back to Earth, the Baron points out to Tonik that not even the witches take chances anymore: her broom is held aloft by two balloons tied at each end.

In Gilliam's take on the legend, Munchausen's adventures are exaggerations of rationality (that turn out to be true—possibly), centered on fantasy vs. reality, and the interdependence between the two. Zeman's film tackles that theme in a different form. The Baron considers himself to be the "realist" and "moonman" Tonik (who is a scientist) to be the "lunatic fabulist." Observing Tonik's attempt to build a steamship (after the company has escaped the belly of a fish that has carried them across the seas), the Baron notes: "such nonsense requires a hefty dose of imagination. No one enjoys a wild ride more than me, but I generally prefer to remain on terra firma." Upon uttering this declaration, the Baron is suddenly carried off by a huge bird.

The competition between fantasy and science is like the rivalry between the Baron and Tonik for the affections of the Princess. But it proves to be a friendly rivalry; as their adventures progress, the Baron comes to have some respect for this lunatic moonman who, in the end, manages a feat worthy of Munchausen himself. And even though Tonik claims that "the stars will cease to be a mystery to us – there will be no mysteries anymore, except the mystery of love," the last word is had by Cyrano. He doffs his hat, which spirals into the stars, welcoming "all you brave souls hurtling at breakneck speed into the arms of the Cosmos." A very romantic thing indeed.

HOME VIDEO INFO: *The Fabulous Baron Munchausen* is part of the Criterion Collection's recent Blu-ray box set, "Three Fantastic Journeys by Karel Zeman" (fully reviewed later in this volume). It's an excellent introduction to his work. *Munchausen* can also be streamed on the Criterion Channel (subscription required).—El Rob Hubbard

"Scorsese Shorts" ★★★★

To most cinephiles these days, Martin Scorsese might seem like an untouchable symbol of classic Hollywood, one of the last quintessential "great" filmmakers, whose new films are treated with solemn reverence and his old films spoken of in hushed tones as some of the greatest of all time. With their 2020 release of "Scorsese Shorts," the Criterion Collection has compiled three of the master's pre-fame short films (including the rare *What's a Nice Girl Like You Doing in a Place Like This?* and *It's Not Just You, Murray*), along with two documentaries: *Italianamerican* (a lovingly direct portrait of Scorsese's parents) and *American Boy* (a monologue portrait of the larger-than-life Stephen Prince). But the most famous film in this collection is a brief five-minute short called *The Big Shave*. A gory allegory about the Vietnam War, *The Big Shave* is unlike anything in Scorsese's filmography--and it's now available to revisit in gloriously bloody HD.

Shave starts by establishing its setting: a sparkling white bathroom filled with sparkling silver fixtures. There, a wholesome-looking young man wets his face, applies shaving cream, and starts giving himself a nice, clean shave. So what's wrong with this picture? At first, nothing. But as soon as the second coat is applied, the blood begins to flow. Just a few cuts at first, drawing a bit of blood to be washed into the sink. But the man doesn't stop, and neither does the blood. He's alarmingly calm throughout it all, as if this is business as usual.

Then, in the film's big knockout moment, he grips the razor tightly and pulls it firmly across his throat, sending blood streaming down his chest. Scorsese didn't use any elaborate make-up effects in this film. For all the bloodshed, we never actually see any chunks of skin or tissue. The gobs of bright red paint hitting the pure white porcelain tell the story in Technicolor clarity, and the man's decisive suicidal action drives home the finality of his self-mutilation.

The Big Shave offers something rarely seen in Scorsese's later work--a pure visual metaphor that operates without the aid of narrative or dialogue, leaving the viewer to interpret its meaning. After listening to Stephen Prince's stories about heroin addiction in *American Boy*, it's possible to interpret *The Big Shave* as an allegory about substance abuse rather than an anti-war statement. But regardless of how you interpret it, *The Big Shave* remains a gloriously bizarre five-minute oddity stranded amongst the many masterworks of one of the greatest American filmmakers of all time.—Jake Fredel

"Solid Metal Nightmares: The Films of Shinya Tsukamoto" ★★★★★

Shinya Tsukamoto is more than the sum of his parts--his cold, greased parts. During my progression through Arrow's 2020 release of *Solid Metal Nightmares*, I became familiar with the director/actor/screenwriter/producer/creative designer. From his roots as a glibly nihilistic visionary, he grew into a sanguinely nihilistic storyteller. Arrow's box set puts much of his history on display for enjoyment and dissection.

The dissection comes in the form of the many extras, some of which are bulleted below:

- Audio commentaries on all ten features (or near-features) from Tom Mes, a Japanese cinema expert
- Half-a-dozen-or-so interviews with the director from over the years, including one exclusive to the set
- Archival featurettes, documentaries, music clips, and trailers
- A beautiful, hard-bound book with essays about each of the films included, typically in thematic pairings
- Reversible title sleeves for the individual Blu-ray discs
- The requisite double-sided poster
- And a box

I knew "Solid Metal Nightmares" would soon become a collector's item, even beyond its designated collector status. I ordered this set back when it was new and paid some sixty bucks for it (it now fetches close to two hundred on the secondary market). The box I received showed up a bit damaged. I felt the damage was appropriate to the collection, however: every hero and heroine Tsukamoto puts to screen is irrevocably damaged in some way. I'm thinking of sending the package back to the director for him to spruce up with some bolts and metal filings.

As is always the case, the movie is the thing to judge--how it's transferred visually, how the audio feels on the eardrums, and whether the framing integrity is maintained. Rest assured, dear reader, that all the films—*Tetsuo: the Iron Man*, *Tetsuo II: Body Hammer*, *The Adventure of Denchu-Kozo*, *Tokyo Fist*, *Bullet Ballet*, *Haze*, *A Snake of June*, *Vital*, *Kotoko*, and *Killing*--look and feel as close to Tsukamoto's celluloid (and later, digital) dreams as possible. Nothing is too crisp (I'm looking at you, *Tetsuo*), nothing is washed-out, and every clink, slam, kachunk, sigh, scream, whisper, and driving soundtrack blasts---or not---as appropriate.

Just about every film included is at least recommendable, but I cannot help raise an eyebrow at one exclusion and one inclusion. The exclusion first: for reasons beyond my understanding, Tsukamoto's early (and color!) short film, *Futsû saizu no kaijin*, is nowhere to be seen---which is a pity, as it laid the ground work for the more expansive *Tetsuo: the Iron Man* that followed a few years later. Ah well.

The odd inclusion---which I was more than happy enough to watch, mind you---is his latest film, *Killing*. This movie does have some "metal" in it, albeit only in the opening scene where we witness a katana being forged. However, it is a contemplative period drama set in the late Edo period, a very calm (albeit depressing) vision of Imperial decline. It is a good movie, to be certain, and watching Tsukamoto as an aging ronin is a treat. But as the finale in a collection dubbed "Solid Metal Nightmares," it's a bit incongruous.

Fans of Shinya Tsukamoto who don't already own this are probably few and far between. To those who didn't have the good luck of snapping this up on pre-order, I would still argue that the current $200 price tag is well worth the outlay. With a little luck, the folks at Arrow will re-release this, and then put together a set of the director's other features. (May I suggest "Solid Metal Daydreams"?)—Giles Edwards

"Three Fantastic Journeys by Karel Zeman" ★★★★★

Czech animator Karel Zeman created some of the most lavishly stylized Jules Verne-inspired fantasy films ever made, combining live actors and eye-popping sets that defy imagination with cutout animation. In Zeman's playful spirit, the Criterion Collection's Blu-ray set comes in fold-out packaging with pop-up art (a dinosaur, a balloon, and Baron Munchausen riding a cannonball). The DVD set costs a few bucks less and is more modestly packaged; otherwise, the features are the same. Either set includes a foldout Michael Atkinson essay that's presented like a vintage newspaper or playbill.

1955's *Journey to the Beginning of Time* is an easy introduction to Zeman. It tells the story of four boys who take off downriver, traveling backwards through time as they row along, first encountering woolly mammoths, then dinosaurs. At times, it plays more like a trip to the natural history museum than a rousing adventure yarn; but the kid actors are surprisingly good, and the stop-motion animation compares favorably to Ray Harryhausen's. It's unmistakably a kid's movie, more simplistic than Zeman's future features, but you can already tell a sure hand is on the rudder.

Invention for Destruction (1958) is a massive leap forward, the full blossoming of Zeman's distinctive style. In black and white, with every prop and cutout pinstriped to create the illusion of cross-hatching, it looks like a Gustave Doré woodcutting come to life. *Invention* freely switches between animation, live-action, and combinations of the two, and conjures numerous "how did they do that?" head-scratching moments. The plot is a simple anti-nuclear parable, serving mainly as a structure to support outrageous set pieces like an undersea manhunt and a daring balloon escape from a pirate's hideout inside a dormant volcano.

1962's *The Fabulous Baron Munchausen* builds on *Invention for Destruction* with luscious color (and a colorful character). The scenario begins with a modern astronaut discovering Munchausen living—with Cyrano de Bergerac and others—on the moon. The pair fly back to earth on a sailing ship drawn by flying horses to rescue a woman abducted by a sultan, and have other adventures (including more deep sea environments). The absurd exploits of the legendary blowhard allow Zeman to add comedy to the spectacle.

Each disc includes the Czech trailer and a selection of short "museum documentaries." *Film Adventurer Karel Zeman* incorporates most of this footage into a full-length documentary, supplemented by a running challenge to a group of Czech film students to figure out how Zeman accomplished some of his illusions and to recreate them. The *Journey to the Beginning of Time* disc hosts the complete dubbed, Americanized version of the film from 1960, a curiosity that you could show to children too young to read subtitles. *Invention for Destruction* provides the Hugh Downs-narrated opening to the U.S. version of the film (titled *The Fabulous World of Jules Verne* and hawking the film's animation technique as "mysti-mation!") Criterion also throws in two short docs created especially for this edition: "Directed by Karel Zeman," a 12-minute appreciation by director John Stevenson (*King Fu Panda*), and "Making Magic," an informative 20-minute conversation between special effects veterans Jim Aupperle and Phil Tippet. The most important supplements in the set are four short films Zeman made in the late 1940s. "A Christmas Dream" is a charming diversion about a little girl dreaming that her rag doll comes to life on Christmas Eve. "A Horseshoe for Luck" is a little comedy featuring Mr. Prokouk, Zeman's signature character, who went on to star in a popular series of shorts. In the luminous "Inspiration," glass figurines come to life and go ice-skating. "King Larva" is a wordless 30-minute fable about a barber and a king cursed with donkey ears, done in a style resembling Rankin-Bass. With the possible exception of "Inspiration," these shorts don't approach the majesty of the features, but each is entertaining on its own.—Gregory J. Smalley

Until the End of the World (1991) ★★★1/2

DIRECTED BY: Wim Wenders

FEATURING: Solveig Dommartin, William Hurt, Sam Neill, Rüdiger Vogler, Max von Sydow

PLOT: A disillusioned young woman follows a mysterious stranger across the globe, only to become transfixed by a device which allows the user to record and replay their own dreams.

COMMENTS: Usually the term "Director's Cut" suggests that a film was extended by 5 or 10 minutes by restoring a few deleted scenes for home video release. But in the case of *Until the End of the World*, it meant doubling the film's original running time from two and a half hours to almost five. With this film, German auteur Wim Wenders intended to make "the ultimate road movie," building on a career of road movies such as *Kings of the Road* and *Paris, Texas*. Now, thanks to the Criterion Collection, his vision can finally be seen as originally intended.

The original cut was a breakneck sci-fi chase movie, with the directionless Claire (Solveig Dommartin) following the elusive Sam Farber (William Hurt) around the globe in a confusing leap-frog from one country to another. There was little actual travel involved, with the characters seeming to beam from one destination to another. There's more character development in this version, but it still doesn't feel like the road movie it was intended to be. However, the characters' journeys do lead them all to a common destination--Central Australia, where Sam is reunited with his estranged father, the mercurial scientist Henry Farber (Max von Sydow).

In the film's final section, Henry invents a camera that can record and playback dreams on handheld devices that drive their users into isolation and addiction. Today, this plays like a commentary on the smartphone era, but at the time it was made, Wim Wenders was actually looking towards the near future (the film is setting in 1999). For a time when the words "digital" and "the Internet" were obscure technological jargon, Wenders made a lot of astounding predictions in *Until the End of the World*. Maybe that's why, watching it now, it feels less like a science-fiction film and more like an alternate vision of our world today.

Until the End of the World's gargantuan length makes it difficult to watch in a single viewing, but it's easy to drop in and out at any point, taking in the beautiful cinematography and hypnotic atmosphere. With so many great visuals, cool original songs, and the potential to expand even more on the characters' adventures (the original rough cut was 12 hours long), this could have made a good Netflix original series. It's too bad Wim Wenders wasn't able to see that far ahead.

Of course, since 2020 release is on the Criterion Collection, there is much more than just the five-hour director's cut to be seen in this Blu-ray edition. There are a number of interviews with Wim Wenders regarding his influences and the arduous shooting process, a Japanese documentary about the groundbreaking HD digital dream sequences created at the NFK offices in Tokyo, and a number of extras focusing on the film's soundtrack (which includes contributions from U2, Nick Cave and Julee Cruise)—which ended up being the most popular aspect of the film.—Jake Fredel

FANTASIA INTERNATIONAL FILM FESTIVAL 2020: PANDEMIC EDITION

The March cancellation of the South by Southwest festival led the vanguard. The Tribeca Film Festival quickly followed, and soon enough, all spring and early summer film festivals of note, including Cannes, fell like dominoes, cancelled due to the global Covid-19 pandemic.

It was a huge blow to small independent films, which depend on the boost that a successful festival run can create to find a distributor for their movies. Initially, suggestions to hold festivals online were met with a big "blah" from the cinephile and critical communities. Links watched on a computer, it was argued, are no substitute for seeing a film on a big screen with an audience reacting in real time. South by Southwest tried hosting a virtual festival on Amazon, but few selections agreed to participate—no auteur dreams of debuting their beloved project to an anonymous online audience full of potential pirates for free—and the stunt did not appear to be a success. Twenty-one canceled or suspended festivals—including Annecy, Cannes, Karlovy Vary, Sundance, Toronto, Tribeca, and Venice–banded together for the "We Are One" online festival streamed live on YouTube. Again, a number of the more promising releases declined the opportunity—although Ugandan "Wakaliwood" auteur Nabwana IGG (*Bad Black*) eagerly seized this chance to debut *Crazy World*, about a gang of child-kidnappers in Kampala's slums who accidentally capture a pint-sized team of kung fu masters.

On April 29, Montreal's Fantasia became the latest festival to announce that they would be holding their event entirely online. The cancellation was bad enough, but worse yet, the online screenings were geolocked to Canada. 366 Weird Movies has attended Fantasia since 2016, using their slate to locate the some of the weirdest upcoming movies—so, while disappointed by the loss of a physical venue, we gladly accepted their offer of remote virtual screenings. Giles Edwards and I divided up the most promising candidates between us, with voracious Fantasia fanatic Giles plunging far deeper into the online catalog after I gave up.

Keep in mind that, for directors and producers, film festivals are primarily auditions for distributors. The most marketable movies may be picked up and be available for viewing by the general public as soon as 2021. (On the other hand, *She's Allergic to Cats*, reviewed herein for the first time, went four years between its Fantasia debut and its 2020 video-on-demand release; some others may never appear). So, for the reader, this is just a heads-up on weird movies that *may* be coming down the line, at an indeterminate time. With that disclaimer in mind, what follows is a brief survey of 366 correspondents' couchbound festival experience.

I saw two forgettable films (well, one forgettable and one debatable, as you'll see) and two I'd advise you to look out for in the coming year(s). In the forgettable category, Minoru Kawasaki's *Monster Seafood Wars* is a straightforward, low-budget kaiju spoof: a giant octopus, crab, and squid terrorize Japan. The foam-rubber seafood suits are expectedly cheesy, and there's barely enough budget to stomp the Lego scale model cities. Kawasaki (*Executive Koala*) is capable of better, and weirder. *Fried Barry*, about a South African heroin addict possessed by an alien, falls into the "debatable" camp. It's a shaggy-dog story that reminded me of better movies about mute outsiders holding up a mirror to society, in particular, *Brother from Another Planet* (1984) and *Bad Boy Bubby* (1993). Giles was more favorably disposed to this one, however, enjoying the psychedelic sequences and general aura of detached oddness, so you may give it a shot if the idea of an exploitative, low-budget, drug-porn alien abduction flick shot in the seedy parts of Cape Town appeals to you.

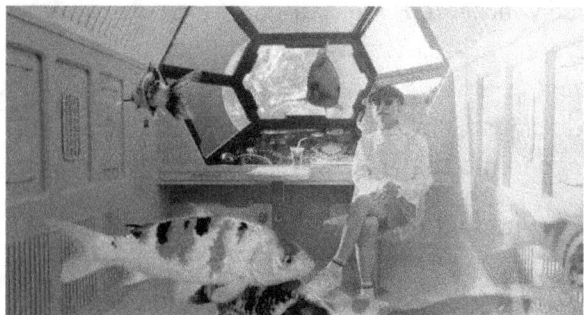

Labyrinth of Cinema

The two memorable offerings come from two very different artists—each distinguished in his own way—at the end of their careers. From Nobuhiko Obayashi, the mind that brought us the deranged pop-art haunted *Hausu* (1977), comes *Labyrinth of Cinema*, a three-hour epic tour through Japanese cinema in which four teenagers are sucked into the movies they watch at an all-night marathon. It's an exuberant, monumental, and poetic ode to the power of cinema to bend reality; it arguably could have used some editing, but much of the movie's ramshackle extravagance would have been lost. And, lest you doubt its weird credentials, it's introduced by "Fanta G," a time-traveler who arrives in modern-day Japan in a spaceship with goldfish floating inside it. Equally epic, but on the other end of the taste spectrum, is Lloyd Kaufman's *Shakespeare's Shitstorm*, an extremely loose, politically-incorrect retelling of "The Tempest." The aptly named *Shitstorm* is one long hedonistic orgy of grossout comedy and Bardic references, with musical interludes in praise of crack, William Shakespeare telling a donkey show joke to a panel of Ph.Ds, and a climax that is accurately characterized as "like a Hieronymus Bosch painting" (if Bosch had been just a bit fonder of green slime, prosthetic boobs, and punk rock anthems). Unlike *Labyrinth*, it's not a posthumous film, but Kaufman is now 74 years old and may not see a budget like this

again; the feeling that *Shakespeare's Shitstorm* is intended as his final trashterpiece is inescapable. It's a shame that Covid-19 robbed this hilarious atrocity of the rowdy premiere to a packed house of eager deviants that it deserved.

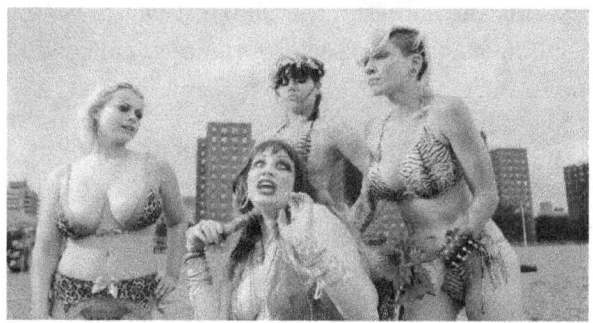

Shakespeare's Shitstorm

And with that, I turn the floor over to Giles to discuss the remainder of Fantasia's 2020 online slate.—Gregory J. Smalley

Greg's gotten the bad news out of the way. The good news: there were still plenty of movies to cover, and what follows is merely the tip of the iceberg. I began my screenings with an Estonian animation, *The Old Man Movie.* Oskar Lehemaa's and Mikk Mägi's ridiculous paean to rural life is filled with Claymation silliness, some social commentary, and plenty of milk--as well as featuring filmdom's only "cowju" monster. Madness continued in another way with Yûji Shimomura's *Crazy Samurai Musashi*, the brainchild of weird violence auteur Sion Sono. In one seventy-seven-minute cut, we see almost six-hundred chumps being iced by one man. Not much story, but plenty of style, action, and even a few dashes of humor.

Melodrama--which has lurked in most corners of every Fantasia Festival we've covered--took the center stage with Mickey Reece's *Climate of the Hunter* and Macoto Tezuka's *Barbara*. In the former, we make the acquaintance of a definitely writer, possibly vampire, as he reconnects with a couple of old flames in a '70s-style drama piece set in a remote hideaway.

Bonus points for narrating all the meal selections. Young Tezuka's take on papa Osamu's iconic work has plenty of brooding, but vanishingly little momentum; it appears that the original manga still awaits a worthwhile translation to the big screen.

The Oak Room (dir. Cody Calahan) and *Kriya* (dir. Sidharth Srinivasan) explore the nature of storytelling and father-son relationships-- one through a series of tall tales set and told in rinky-dink Canadian bars, and the other set on a remote estate in the sweltering Indian countryside. While *The Oak Room* is clearly a thriller and *Kriya* is clearly a horror movie, they stand out in the same manner that they stand together: both meditate on the death of a patriarch, and both explore the vagaries of human memory and tradition.

For some silly Eurotrash fun, I took in Lars Damoiseaux's *Yummy*--a slick, violent comedy (of sorts) set in an Eastern European plastic surgery center, and Michael Venus' *Sleep*--a dreamy thriller that explores the seamy underbelly of a seemingly innocent spa town. *Yummy* is a tasty slice of not-so-weird gore; *Sleep* is a kind-of-weird excursion into nightmares, Nazis, bad drugs, with a demoniacal wild boar snuffling its nose at the edges of reality. Both fine additions to the festival, and both would have made great midnight screenings had the audience been alive to see them. (That is, had the audience been able to see them live.)

Fantasia's unlikely stabs at mainstream attractions consisted of *Minor Premise* and *Dinner in America*. As Eric Shultz's debut feature, *Minor Premise* adds to the slender catalogue of "thoughtful science fiction". It never gets as dark as Cronenberg (this is not a criticism), and isn't quite as clockwork-clever as Nolan (a criticism, perhaps, albeit a minor one), but it demonstrates that a new and exciting talent has entered this woefully underpopulated scene.

Minor Premise would hold its own in a high-minded, smarty-pants narrative marathon.

Dinner in America (brought to us by Adam Rehmeier) is about as quirky a movie as I'd ever dare to recommend to a 366 fan. It's a romantic comedy at heart, with strangely sweet romance and often savage comedy. At times the simmering rage in *Dinner in America* is hard to process: every character we encounter comes from a comfortable suburban background. However, as the story progresses, we learn that life's edges are only smoothed over by money, ranch homes, and pre-fab gourmet dinners. There's more than a hint of *Teorema* to be found, as Victor enters the lives of several strangers and immediately takes an axe to their civilized pretenses.

But on to the weird-worth-whiles before I run out of space. Unlike my esteemed colleague, I believe *Fried Barry* shines as a gloriously weird outing. Our main man Barry (Gary Green, hopped up and zonked out under the direction of Ryan Kruger) goes on a wild dream quest like a latter-day Cesare from *The Cabinet of Doctor Caligari*. Cruising through the South African nightlife, Barry takes all drugs given him and gamely grunts his path through countless adversaries to achieve the status of hero. All before being drawn back up into the stars by the aliens that thoroughly (thoroughly) probed and addled him at the start.

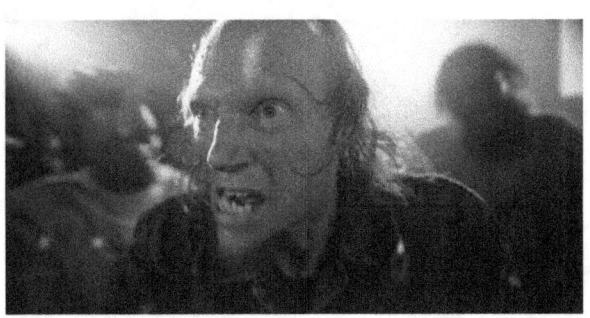

Fried Barry

Two calmer films also caught my eye: Sabrina Mertenss *Time of Moulting* and Chino

Moya's *Undergods*. The former is an episodic, 50-or-so-part series of oppressively shot, still-camera snippets of a young girl from '70s West Germany as she grows up under the excessively watchful eye of her ever-ailing mother and the never watchful eye of her present-but-absent father. Imagine a piece of twine wrapping around your heart that is slowly twisted tauter and tauter until suddenly given a good yank. Twinge-y stuff, but very satisfying--as satisfying, somehow, as it is oblique.

Undergods is episodic in the more traditional sense, being something of an anthology film all linked together through some happenstance and the presence of two affable corpse collectors. Set in the near future, society hasn't quite collapsed, but is well on its way to crumbling apart. The particulars of the individual stories are all thematically intertwined: angst, paranoia, decay, and all the other dystopian goodies we could want are present and accounted for-- suffused with a striking color palette, idiosyncratic performances, and streaks of Gilliam-esque drollery.

There was more to watch, and I dutifully did so, but I failed to get even half of the screenings I usually get up to. I blame the pandemic, Canada, the US government; hopefully next year we'll be able to provide a more thorough coverage. But to undercut that complaint, I am glad that *something* akin to a festival took place at all. Being able to catch the twenty movies I did, while tucked away in my study, was no small relief: even though Fantasia's festival trappings were canceled this year along with countless others, the stories continued.—Giles Edwards

SUPPLEMENTAL 2020 FESTIVAL, THEATRICAL, AND ONLINE DEBUT RELEASES

Air Conditioner – Described as a "pleasantly surreal" trip through the streets of Luanda, Angola, occasioned by the search for a replacement air conditioner after the city's units all spontaneously and simultaneously fail; it played YouTube's "We Are One" online festival and has not been seen since.

Anonymous Animals [*Les Animaux Anonymes*] – Animal-headed creatures hunt humans in this dialogue-free French experiment that played at the Sitges Film Festival.

Bad Men from a Melting Moon – The plot description says simply "a man believes he has been hit by a train." The trailer was no help, either, but it has a magnificent title, a few awards from obscure experimental film festivals, and a director with a pretty odd biography, as the author of a series of vanity press books (later turned into vanity animated feature films) about a cat named Bubble Meows.

Corona Zombies – Full Moon Pictures becomes the first studio to shamelessly exploit the pandemic, mixing humorously redubbed footage from *Hell of the Living Dead* and *Zombies vs. Strippers* with newly shot sequences to create a topical satire. They followed *Zombies* up with two equally rushed sequels in the same vein, *Barbie & Kendra Save the Tiger King* and *Barbie & Kendra Storm Area 51*.

I Was at Home, But... -- A boy mysteriously disappears, then reappears. A challenging, minimalist German art movie that appeared on home video too late for us to get to in 2020.

Jiu Jitsu -- Nicolas Cage shows up as a mystical jiu jitsu teacher who lectures five jiu jitsu chosen ones about how to defeat an alien jiu jitsu master. Without Cage, this would just be a joke; with him, it just might be a funny one.

Light Years – A 30-year old man goes on an annual "cosmic vision quest" to honor his dead friend. A low-budget psychedelic comedy that appeared out of nowhere in November 2020 on DVD, Blu-ray, and VOD.

Mandibles – Quentin Dupieux's latest (yes, he already has a new one out after *Deerskin*, reviewed earlier in this volume) is about two friends who try to exploit a giant fly they find in their car's trunk. *Mandibles* debuted at the scaled-back Venice Film Festival in September 2020, and has not been seen much since; we'll try to track it down in 2021.

Nine Days – A man pits spirits in a competition: the winner will be born into our world. This debuted at Sundance to generally good, if puzzled, reviews; plans for a wider release fell victim to the pandemic, but don't be surprised to see it turn up in 2021.

The Nowhere Inn – Singer St. Vincent collaborated with Carrie Brownstein to create a fictional documentary described as "distorted and bizarre." It played the Midnight category at Sundance, but future festivals were canceled due to Covid-19, and it disappeared off the radar.

Omniboat: A Fast Boat Fantasia – Portmanteau feature centered around a Miami speedboat; it counts *Swiss Army Man* directing team Daniels among the contributors. A Sundance offering that has not been sighted since.

Saint-Narcisse – Bruce LaBruce blasphemy about a man's erotic longing for his long-lost identical twin. Played at Sitges.

Sister Tempest –Influenced by everything from *Alice in Wonderland* to *Zardoz*, Joe Badon's tale of two sisters is truly bizarre low-budget offering.

It played some small festivals in late 2020 but look for more coverage from us when it gets a home video release in 2021.

Sky Sharks – Another absurdist shark B-comedy, this time featuring flying sharks piloted by Nazi zombies. Played at a few film festivals late in 2020, and scheduled for a March 2021 U.S. home video debut.

Ten Minutes to Midnight – An aging punk radio host (*Texas Chainsaw Massacre II*'s Caroline Williams) is bitten by a bat, and may be turning into a vampire. Apparently it gets wild and gory, as it's earned some comparisons to *Evil Dead II* and *Dead Alive*. Debuted in theaters in 2020, but the release was so limited we were unable to see it; look for us to catch up with *Midnight* in 2021.

Wendy – Benh Zeitlin's second feature film comes 8 years after *Beasts of the Southern Wild* is a retelling of Peter Pan set in Neverland and told from Wendy's perspective. Its short theatrical run was cut short by the pandemic.

The Wolf Hour – An agoraphobic writer (Naomi Watts) suffers in her apartment while the Son of Sam terrorizes NYC outside. Received mixed reviews, but the *New York Times*' Jeannette Catsoulis did call it a "punishingly theatrical experiment that teeters on the verge of surreality."

SUPPLEMENTAL 2020 HOME VIDEO RELEASES

"12 Monkeys: The Complete Series" (2015-2018) – A four season TV series adapted from Terry Gilliam's canonically weird time travel fantasia. Individual seasons had been previously released, but 2020 collected the complete run (including webisodes) on DVD or Blu-ray.

Aenigma (1987) – An Eighties occult slasher set in a girls' boarding school. While not regarded as one of Lucio Fulci's "better" movies, the synopsis references a "grisly surrealism," and Video Vacuum said it contains "some of the most bonkers imagery Fulci ever put on film." On Blu-ray from Severin with a commentary track by Troy Howarth and Nathaniel Thompson (who later teamed up to commentate *Death Laid an Egg*, supra) and other special features.

"Al Adamson: The Masterpiece Collection" – Ah, Al. This set contains all 31 "masterpieces" from schlockmesiter Al Adamson spread across 14 Blu-rays and including, most notably for us, *Dracula vs. Frankenstein* and *Carnival Magic*, along with the doc *Blood & Flesh – The Reel Life and Grisly Death of Al Adamson* and a 126-page booklet. We never dreamed this day would come.

Alice in Wonderland (1933) – Kino Lorber got the rights and issued Hollywood's all-star (Cary Grant, Gray Cooper, and W.C. Fields as a grotesque Humpty Dumpty) *Alice* on Blu-ray for the first time. With a bonus commentary track from film historian Lee Gambin.

Amazon Women on the Moon (1987) – Kino Lorber's 2020 Special Edition release of the all-star sketch comedy B-movie spoof includes a new featurette and new outtakes, and marks the first time the film has appeared on Region A Blu-ray.

Beyond the Door (1974) – A pregnant woman gets possessed by Old Nick. Starring Hayley Mills' sister, it's an Italian *Exorcist* rip-off with a small cult following. From Arrow, it debuted on Blu-ray in 2020 as a two disc limited edition with the uncut version, theatrical version, the feature-length documentary *Italy Possessed*, and more.

"Barry J. Gillis Triple Threat Collection": This set from the very underground Gillis starts off with the surreally bad *Things* (1989, Gillis produces, writes and acts) and adds previously unknown-to-us title *The Killing Games* (2012) and the new release *House of Many Sorrows* (Gillis acts, writes, produces and directs the latter two). Independently released in 2020 on DVD or BD-R (we recommend DVD, as you may experience difficulties playing the BD-R format).

"Blood Hunger: The Films of Jose Larraz": 3-disc Arrow set including *Whirlpool* (1970), *Vampyres* (1974), and *The Coming of Sin* (1978). *Vampyres* is a popular and sexy lesbian vampire shocker, but we were more curious about the rare *Sin* [AKA *Sodomia*], about a girl who dreams of a naked man on horseback who then appears to her and is described as "dreamlike." This "Special Edition" Blu-ray set contains lots of extras, but is pricey; 2019's "Limited Edition" set was much cheaper and probably sufficient, though lacking a couple of interviews unique to this 2020 release.

Brain Damage (1988) – The Aylmer, a phallic creature who inserts a euphoric psychedelic directly into its host's brain stem, made his debut on Blu-ray for the first time in 2020, courtesy of Arrow.

Caniba (2017): There was no guarantee this ultra-disturbing experimental documentary about real-life cannibal Issei Sagawa was ever going to be released on home video, but Grasshopper made it happen in 2020 on DVD and Blu-ray.

Come and See (1985) – What may be the most intense war movie ever made joined the Criterion Collection in 2020 in a new restoration, on 2 DVDs or a single Blu-ray. Criterion extras include an appreciation by ace cinematographer Roger Deakins, a vintage interview with late director Elem Klimov and a more recent one with his brother, a Soviet-era documentary on the Belorussian atrocities depicted in the film, 2001 interviews with actor Alexei Kravchenko and production designer Viktor Petrov, a short "making of" featurette, the theatrical trailer, and of course a supplementary booklet.

The Comic (1985): Set in a future dystopia, the storyline involves an orange-haired comedian who kills a rival to get a gig. Another oddity uncovered in 2020 by Arrow Video, who promote it with the suspect claim, "From the annals of bizarre cinema comes perhaps the most bizarre one of them all!"

"The Complete Lenzi/Baker Giallo Collection": This year saw the release of a major set containing four gialli directed by Umberto Lenzi and starring Carol Baker: *Orgasmo* [AKA *Paranoia*] (1969), *So Sweet So Perverse* (1969), *A Quiet Place to Kill* (1970), and *Knife of Ice* (1972). Of the four, *Orgasmo*, with Baker as a rich widow seduced and gaslighted by a pair of men for her money, is the most famous and probably the weirdest. This elaborate box set from giallo specialists Severin Films comes with two CDs containing the soundtracks for the first three films and a single track from *Knife of Ice*.

The Cremator (1969) – 2020 saw Criterion inaugurate this character study of a very odd mortician/Nazi collaborator into their Collection, with director Juraj Herz's short film debut, "The Junk Shop," among the numerous extras.

Danger: Diabolik (1968) – Shout! Factory brought Mario Bava's "groovy '60s cult classic" to Blu-ray for the first time in 2020, with a new audio commentary from the very busy Troy Howarth and Nathaniel Thompson.

Daughters of Darkness (1971): A newlywed couple meet a mysterious Countess (named "Bathory," which should have set off alarm bells) at a deserted resort on their honeymoon. This odd lesbian vampire feature starring Delphine Seyrig was enough of a hit for director Harry Kümel that he convinced United Artists to back the even stranger *Malpertuis* (1972). Now in a 4K restoration on DVD or in a Ultra-HD/Blu-ray/soundtrack CD multipack.

"The Essential Fellini" – A Criterion collection Blu-ray box set release of fourteen Fellini films, including all four of his canonically weird titles: *8 1/2*, *Fellini Satyricon*, *Roma*, and *Amarcord*. Eleven of the movies are newly restored and the box includes "Toby Dammit" along with hours of documentaries and interviews. Released in late November, positioned as an X-mas gift for the cinephile in your life.

The Final Programme (1973) – An international man of mystery searches for a computer programme written by his recently deceased father which will create a new Messiah. Long unavailable in the U.S., Shout! Factory released it on Blu-ray and VOD in early 2020.

"Gamera: The Complete Collection": The complete run of the Japanese flying turtle series (popularized by Mystery Science Theater 3000). As a kid-friendly, cheapo competitor to Godzilla, the Gamera films are a special breed—and this set is pretty expensive. That said, *Gamera vs. Guiron* (1969), which mixes brain-eating aliens, a Hansel and Gretel storyline, and battles between a giant turtle a giant Ginsu knife monster is, in particular, a weird film. Arrow's 8-disc Blu-ray set also includes the three higher-budgeted films from the 1990s reboot.

The Horrors of Spider Island (1960): Canonically Weird or not, did we really need 1960's grimy public domain jiggler *The Horrors of Spider Island* on Blu-ray? Only for the bonus features, which include the complete "spicy" version, *It's Hot in Paradise* (with naughty nudie-cutie skinny dipping); alternate scenes; a mini-doc; and a vintage audio interview with "star" Alexander D'Arcy. From Severin Entertainment, this 2020 special edition release is limited to 3000 units.

Je t'aime moi non plus (1976) – A truck stop waitress (Jane Birkin) falls in love with a gay garbage truck driver (Joe Dallesandro) and convinces him to sleep with her—but there's a catch. Directed by musician Serge Gainsbourg, who put out an album of the same title. It came out for the first time (in North America) on Blu-ray or DVD from Kino Classics, with a commentary track and interviews.

The Lady Kills (1971)/*Pervertissima* (1972) – In the first flick of this Jean-Louis van Belle double feature, a lady kills; Mondo Macabro describes the curious and rare *Pervertissima* as "a bizarre – and possible unique – combination of mondo movie and mad scientist flick." Two films, one Blu-ray.

Let's Scare Jessica to Death (1971) – A woman recovering from a nervous breakdown at a lake finds herself haunted by the undead. This surreal-ish, atmospheric budget horror with a misleading title and a small cult following got a Blu-ray release from Shout! Factory with special features, including a director's commentary.

The Limits of Control (2009) – Arrow Academy gathered new and archival material for this Blu-ray Special Edition of Jim Jarmusch's odd, inconclusive anti-thriller, released in late 2019.

Lord Love a Duck (1966) – Kino Lorber released a remastered version of this cult high school satire on Blu-ray for the first time in 2020.

"The Maya Deren Collection" – Kino's 2020 box set contains essentially all of the avant-garde filmmaker's output, including the Canonically Weird *Meshes of the Afternoon*. It includes commentary tracks for Deren's six major shorts, outtakes, and a 53-minute documentary.

Millennium Actress (2001) – This late 2019 DVD/Blu-ray combo pack from Shout! Factory—newly restored—surprisingly marked Satoshi Kon's retrospective of Japanese cinema, as seen through the eyes of a dying actress, on Blu-ray.

"Monty Python's Flying Circus: The Complete Series" (1969-1974) – The complete original run of the breakthrough surreal comedy series that launched the career of 366 fave Terry Gilliam and eventually led to *Monty Python's The Meaning of Life* (1983). Restored and on Region A Blu-ray for the first time, with tons of outtakes and featurettes.

Morgan: A Suitable Case for Treatment (1966) – An insane man is obsessed with Karl Marx, gorillas, and his ex-wife's love life. Some call this British ode to nonconformity a cult comedy. Kino Lorber debuted it on Blu-ray or DVD for the first time (in the U.S.).

Never Give a Sucker an Even Break (1941): Finally, a break for us suckers: W.C. Fields' crazy final film had not been available (outside of box sets) in the U.S. before this 2020 Kino Lorber Blu-ray release. Includes a commentary track by film historian Eddy Von Mueller and a contemporary Fields documentary originally broadcast on Canadian TV.

The Passion of Darkly Noon (1995): An orphaned fundamentalist develops an erotic obsession for the married woman who nurses him back to health. Philip Ridley's follow-up to the Canonically Weird *The Reflecting Skin* (1990) had been out of print and hard to find for a while; Arrow to the rescue, with a Blu-ray debut featuring a new commentary track from Ridley, and all the usual bells and whistles.

The Peanut Butter Solution (1985) – This bizarro Canadian kiddie flick about a boy who loses his hair after being frightened by ghosts finally made it to DVD, Blu-ray and VOD for the first time in late 2019, thanks to the good folks at Severin Films.

The Point (1971) – An oblong-headed boy is ostracized in a community where everyone has pointed heads. Singer-songwriter Harry Nilsson supposedly came up with the idea for this televised children's special while tripping on acid; it finally appeared on Blu-ray in 2020.

Reflections in a Golden Eye (1967) – In 2020 Warner Archives released a 2-disc Blu-ray of John Huston's story of repressed sexuality at an army base; it included the full-color version released to theaters, along with the gold-tinted cut Huston preferred.

"Rob Zombie Trilogy"—This Blu-ray release of the serial-killing Firefly family saga features the weird (but annoying) *House of 1,000 Corpses*, the popular (but not weird) *The Devil's Rejects*, and the few-bothered-to-watch late sequel, *3 from Hell*. A bare-bones 2020 Blu release that may be of interest to Zombiephiles.

"The Scare Film Archives Volume 1: Drug Stories!" – A 2020 compilation of a collection of drug scare films curated by American Film Genre Archives from the Something Weird vaults. The hysterical, moralizing atmospheres combined with low-budget attempts to replicate bad LSD trips tend to make these artifacts both campy and strange. Blu-ray only.

Secret Ceremony (1968) – A prostitute (Elizabeth Taylor) who's lost her daughter and an orphan girl (Mia Farrow) start a strange relationship that's complicated by the arrival of the girl's stepfather (Robert Mitchum). Joseph Losey's eerie psychological thriller had been previously unavailable on U.S. home video; it's now on DVD or Blu-ray courtesy of Kino Lorber.

She (1984) – Goofy post-*Conan* post-apocalyptic B-movie starring Sandahl Bergman as leader of a band of wasteland Amazons. Features a giant in a tutu and other vintage '80s nuttiness. Released in a special edition DVD or Blu-ray from Kino Lorber.

She Mob (1968)/*The Girl from Pussycat* (1969): In *She Mob*, a gang of lesbians (including a leader in the most outrageously impractical steel cone bra you've ever seen) kidnap a gigolo; *The Girl from Pussycat*, meanwhile, plans a bank robbery between lesbian orgies. AFGA cites Russ Meyer, John Waters, Jean-Luc Godard (!), and Doris Wishman as points of reference; we suspect that last listed director is the most appropriate comparison, by a wide margin. A Blu-ray double feature, released in late November.

Shining Sex [*La Fille au Sexe Brillant*] (1977): A Jess Franco joint about an alien and an android who turn a stripper into a sex slave who kills with her genitals. A weird, though typically slow, softcore sci-fi offering from Severin Films that fell just beneath our review priority deadline.

Slaughterhouse Five (1972) – Billy Pilgrim has come unstuck in time... Film adaptations of Kurt Vonnegut novels have seldom fared well either with critics or audiences, but this may be the exception. Released in late 2019 in a typically packed Blu-ray from Arrow Video.

The Sore Losers (1997) – An alien sent to the American south to complete a killing spree hooks up with some delinquents and inadvertently messes up his kill count. Unclassifiable punk/rockablilly/trash/surrealism feature from Memphis' own Mike McCarthy, in a 3-disc Blu-ray/DVD/soundtrack CD set. Although these sets were only available directly from the director, and appear to have been sold out, the film did show up for rental on Amazon Prime in 2020.

Spookies (1986) – A sorcerer seeks to sacrifice the lives of some unfortunates who turn up on his doorstep. An 80s cult item, released for the first time in a two Blu-ray set (!) from Vinegar Syndrome (who proclaim, "Of all of the bizarre horror films made in the 1980s, SPOOKIES easily ranks among the weirdest.")

"Stanley Kubrick 3-Film 4K Collection": This 2020 release included the Canonically Weird *2001: A Space Odyssey* (1968), *The Shining* (1980), and *Full Metal Jacket* (1987), all restored in 4K for Blu-ray and Ultra HD disc.

Sukiyaki Western Django (2007) – A nameless gunman rides into a town where two rival gangs of samurai scheme to find and seize a hidden cache of gold. In 2020, MVD visual released *Sukiyaki Western Django* on Blu-ray for the first time (in the North American market). All extras were the same as on the previous DVD release, but the one thing that made this release special was the inclusion of the extended cut that played at the Venice Film Festival and in Japanese theaters. There are no significant differences between the two versions, however; Miike simply snipped away insignificant bits from many once-longer scenes, resulting in a shorter, faster-paced, and improved film.

Tammy and the T-Rex (1994) — A mad scientist implants Tammy's dead boyfriend's brain into a Tyrannosaurus rex. This new release restores the gore that was cut from the original to qualify it for a PG-13 rating.

The Tenant (1976): 2020 saw Shout! Factory put out the third part of Roman Polanski's "apartment trilogy" on Blu-ray for the first time, with a heavy dose of bonus features including new interviews with the director and crew members, a commentary track by the busy duo of Troy Howarth and Nathaniel Thompson, an archival audio interview with Roland Topor (who wrote the original novel), and more. Considering the shabby state of older releases, this is the one *Tenant* fans have been waiting on.

Teorema (1968) – Pier Paolo Pasolini's chilly, ambiguous fable about a mysterious stranger who sleeps with, and destroys, a bourgeois family joined the Criterion Collection in 2020.

Toto the Hero (1991): At long last, Jaco Van Dormael's canonically weird debut—about a deluded man who convinces himself he was switched at birth with a neighbor in order to justify his erotic attachment to his sister—made it to home video in North America. Arrow Academy is *our* hero. Blu-ray only.

"Twin Peaks: From Z to A" – There have been a lot of repackagings of "Twin Peaks" over the years, but this late 2019 release may be the ultimate set. The original series, *Fire Walk with Me* (1992) (with deleted scenes), "The Return," and new behind-the-scenes featurettes, are all spread across twenty-one Blu-rays, in an innovative box that turns into a "red room display."

Valhalla Rising (2009) – IFC released Nicolas Winding Refn's hallucinatory Viking tale on Blu-ray for the first time (in North America) this past year.

"The Vincent Price Collection"— Includes the horrors *The Pit and the Pendulum*, *The Haunted Palace*, *The Fall of the House of Usher*, *The Masque of the Red Death*, *Witchfinder General*, and, most notably, the canonically weird *The Abominable Dr. Phibes* (1971). This in-time-for-Halloween 2020 release is a reissue of an almost-identical 2013 set; it lost the Price introductions from the original set, but adds an extra minute of footage to the *Red Death* disc.

Viy (1967) – The masterpiece of Soviet horror, from a Gogol story about a seminarian who must pray over a witch's corpse, finally gets a decent North American DVD and Blu-ray release, courtesy of Severin.

Waxworks (1924) – Waxworks (1924): Silent specialists Flicker Alley released a newly restored DVD/Blu-ray version of the Expressionist classic about a poet who imagines backstories for wax figures in late 2020.

"Wild Palms" (1993): Mysterious corporations scheme to take over America in the "near future" using virtual reality tricks. This Oliver Stone-produced miniseries was greenlit due to the popularity of "Twin Peaks" during the 90s brief "weird is cool" phase; released on Blu-ray in 2020, with multiple commentary tracks.

The Wild, Wild World of Jayne Mansfield (1968): A totally tasteless and defamatory mondo-exploitation "documentary" about the busty actress who died tragically young. Severin's Blu-ray release included an interview about Jayne with celebrity Satanist Anton LaVey and a little-seen mondo film called *The Wild Weird Wonderful Italians* (1963) as bonus features.

366 WEIRD MOVIES CANON

After 10 years of reviews, in 2019 we finally completed our list of the 366 Best Weird Movies of All Time. Realizing that the list is not exhaustive and new weird movies will continue to be released through the years, we also have inaugurated a separate list of Apocryphal Movies, which you can check out after the Canon proper. Apocryphal movies either debuted after we completed the list in 2019, or were runners-up for canonization. Tracking all these titles down will provide a lifetime's worth of weird enjoyment. Should 366weirdmovies.com ever go offline, you'll be glad to have this handy print version.

3-Iron [*Bin-jip*] (2004) – A homeless young Korean man trains himself to be invisible so he can romance another man's wife

3 Women (1977) – Identities merge and personalities shift when ingénue Pinky becomes obsessed with delusional Millie

8 1/2 (1963) – Memories and dreams collide with reality in Fellini's self-reflexive, stream-of-consciousness classic about a director trying to make a movie

200 Motels (1971) – Frank Zappa's psychedelic review includes Ringo Starr as Larry the Dwarf, Keith Moon as a nun groupie, and an oratorio devoted to the penis

2001: A Space Odyssey (1968) – Space monoliths turn apes into men and men into star children

The 5,000 Fingers of Dr. T (1953) – A mad doctor enslaves 500 boys to play his giant piano in this surreal musical fantasy courtesy of Dr. Seuss

The Abominable Dr. Phibes (1971) – Art-deco B-movie with fascinating production design and campy acting from star Vincent Price

Adaptation. (2002) – Charlie Kaufman can't get started on an adaptation of "The Orchid Thief," so he writes himself (and his twin brother) into the screenplay

The Adventures of Buckaroo Banzai Across the Eighth Dimension (1984) – Buckaroo's a neurosurgeon/particle physicist/secret agent/rock star with a backing band of soldier-of-fortune scientists opposed by transdimensional aliens and… it just goes on from there

After Hours (1985) – A word processor stranded in SoHo overnight is bedeviled by a series of odd women and odder coincidences

After Last Season (2009) – An amateurish embarrassment about two med students, a killer on the loose, and a ghost, so full of misguided directorial choices and failed attempts at cinematic poetry that it takes on a dreamlike character

Akira (1988) – A telekinetic maniac wrecks Neo-Tokyo in this trendsetting cult anime

Akira Kurosawa's Dreams [*Yume*; AKA *Dreams*] (1990) – The master filmmaker relates eight "dreams," including one where he wanders through Vincent Van Gogh's paintings

Alice [*Neco Z Alenky*] (1988) – Ultra-creepy Czech stop-motion animated version of the Lewis Carroll classic, shot in eerie stop-animation in a decaying house

Alice in Wonderland (1966) – Surreal and dreamlike adaptation of the nonsense classic depicts the main characters as Victorian ladies and gentlemen rather than talking animals

Allegro non Troppo (1976) – "The Italian *Fantasia*" has some mildly surreal animated sequences, with black and white sequences of an orchestra of old ladies that may be even stranger

Altered States (1980) – Ken Russell's visionary tale of genetic regression under the influence of magic mushrooms may be the greatest "trip" movie ever made

Amarcord (1973) – A year in the life of an Italian town under Fascist rule, as Federico Fellini (mis)remembers his youth in comic vignettes that range from strange to surreal

The American Astronaut (2001) – An absurdist indie sci-fi/western/musical/comedy co-starring the Boy Who Actually Saw a Woman's Breast

Antichrist (2009) – Controversial, extremely graphic allegory about a man and woman lose their child and retreat to a cabin in the woods where they go crazy

The Apple (1980) – Nutty, campy musical flop that is simultaneously an allegory for the Garden of Eden and the rise of disco

Archangel (1990) – Surreal, nearly silent meditation on forgetfulness set in an icy Russian city just after World War I

Arise! The SubGenius Movie (1992) – "Bob" just might save abnormals from the flying saucers on X-day; learn how in this bizarrely edited fake cult recruitment video

Arizona Dream (1993) – A dream fish swims through the desert and Johnny Depp is romantically trapped between a cougar who dreams of flying and her suicidal daughter

Audition (1999) – A widower holds a fake audition to select a new wife, and makes the absolute worst pick possible

Bad Boy Bubby (1993) – Relentlessly offbeat character study of a man who was locked in a basement until age 35, then unleashed on modern Australia

Barbarella (1968) – Slinky Barbarella flies through the sinful galaxy finding herself in sexy psychedelic situations

Barton Fink (1991) – A leftist Hollywood screenwriter endures a case of writer's block that turns into a living nightmare on the eve of WWII

Batman Returns (1992) – The Caped Crusader faces off against a capitalist, an S&M themed feline feminist, and a deformed survivor of an infanticide attempt with an army of missile-equipped penguins in the weirdest summer blockbuster ever

The Beast [La Bête] (1975) – A drawing room nuptial drama, only with scenes of explicit (simulated) bestiality

The Beast of Yucca Flats (1961) – Dadaist narration courtesy of the eccentric Coleman Francis makes this tale of a nuclear blast turning Tor Johnson into a ravaging desert "beast" weird indeed

Beasts of the Southern Wild (2012) – Six-year old Hushpuppy lives in "the Bathtub" with her dying daddy, and imagines aurochs coming to get her

Beauty and the Beast [*La Belle et la Bête*] (1946) – One of the greatest fairy tale films ever made, with Surrealist-inspired set design including living candelabras

The Bed Sitting Room (1969) – Ralph Richardson mutates into a bed sitting room in this absurd post-apocalyptic comedy

Begotten (1991) – Legendary experimental film, featuring God disemboweling himself and other metaphysical atrocities

Being John Malkovich (1999) – You can enter the head of the titular actor through this weird metaphysical comedy, the screenwriting debut of bizarre movie titan Charlie Kaufman

Belladonna of Sadness [*Kanashimi no Beradonna*] (1973) – A medieval beauty is raped on her wedding night and makes a revenge pact with Satan in this violent, erotic, psychedelic anime

Belle de Jour (1967) – A young French housewife has bondage fantasies that gradually merge with her everyday reality in this once-salacious arthouse hit

Beyond the Black Rainbow (2010) – Modern recreation of a circa 1983 midnight movie, about a telepath imprisoned in the mysterious New Age Arboria Institute

Birdboy: The Forgotten Children (2015) – Cute teenage animals are wracked with despair, delinquency and drug-abuse on a post-apocalyptic island

The Black Cat (1934) – The first and best of the Boris Karloff/Bela Lugosi team-ups is an Expressionist horror masterpiece about Satanism and vengeance

Black Moon (1975) – Louis Malle's unexpected venture in surrealism features gender genocide, breastfeeding, and a unicorn

Black Swan (2010) – A ballerina goes mad as she encounters her lustful double while preparing to dance the lead in "Swan Lake"

Blancanieves (2012) – A modern silent retelling of the legend of Snow White set in the bullfighting culture of 1920s Spain

Blood Diner (1987) – Severely out-of-whack horror-comedy with (possibly unconscious) fascist undertones

Blood Freak (1972) – Pot + experimental turkey meat turns Herschell into a turkey-headed killing machine in the world's only Christian anti-drug gore movie

The Blood of a Poet [*Le sang d'un poète*] (1930) – Early Surrealist work where a poet gets a mouth stuck on his hand, visits a strange hotel, and commits suicide after losing a card game on a snowy Parisian street

Blood Tea and Red String (2006) – The Dwellers Under the Oak seek to recover their stolen doll from depraved white mice in this surreal stop-motion animated fairy tale for adults

Blue Velvet (1986) – Jeffrey finds a severed ear and it leads him to a melancholy nightclub singer, a deranged drug-huffing pervert, and a suave karaoke version of Roy Orbison

The Boxer's Omen [*Mo*] (1983) – Surreal black magic battles featuring an evil wizard with a detachable head and a nude she-demon birthed from crocodile carcass

A Boy and His Dog (1975) – Post-apocalyptic tale of a wasteland rapist and his far more intelligent telepathic dog companion

Branded to Kill [*Koroshi No Rakuin*] (1967) – Seijun Suzuki's surreal, scrambled yakuza thriller about a rice-sniffing hitman famously got him fired by the studio who financed it

Brand Upon the Brain! (2006) – "Guy Maddin" "remembers" his childhood growing up with a domineering mother and a mad scientist father in a lighthouse/orphanage

Brazil (1985) – Terry Gilliam's must-see dystopian black comedy mixes expressionism, surrealism, fantasy, and film noir to create a keen satire of bureaucracy

Bronson (2008) – Overwhelmingly stylized biopic of Charlie Bronson (born Michael Peterson), the self-mythologizing celebrity who prides himself on being Britain's most violent prisoner

Bubba Ho-Tep (2002) – Elvis and black JFK team up to fight a mummy terrorizing their rest home

The Butcher Boy (1997) – Neglected and largely left to his own devices, the incredible Francie Brady goes insane before our very eyes

The Cabinet of Dr. Caligari [*Das Cabinet des Dr. Caligari*] (1920) – The titular Dr. engages a somnambulist to commit murders in a strangely slanted Expressionist town

Careful (1992) – Residents of an Alpine village fear avalanches and their own incestuous desires in this comic surrealist melodrama shot in "two-strip" Technicolor

Carnival of Souls (1962) – Low-budget creepfest is a minor miracle on film

Catch-22 (1970) – Mike Nichols' underappreciated adaptation of the classic novel is star-studded absurdism

Cat Soup [*Nekojiru-so*] (2001) – The surreal adventures of an anthropomorphic cartoon cat and his half-dead sister

Cemetery Man [*Dellamorte Dellamore*] (1994) – Surrealist arthouse zombie gore film about the caretaker of a graveyard where the dead refuse to stay down

Un Chien Andalou (1929) – A razor through an eyeball announces the Surrealist revolution

Christmas on Mars (2008) – The Flaming Lips bring us the most vaginal imagery ever seen in a psychedelic science fiction Christmas movie

The City of Lost Children [*La cité des enfants perdus*] (1995) – Visionary steampunk fairytale from Jeunet & Caro

City of Women [*La città delle donne*] (1980) – An aging Lothario finds himself lost in a province populated and ruled by females, until he finds refuge at the citadel of the world's last macho man

Clean, Shaven (1993) – A deinstitutionalized man seeks his lost daughter in what may be the most clinically accurate depiction of schizophrenia ever filmed

A Clockwork Orange (1971) – Kubrick weirds it up in this disturbing moral fable

The Color of Pomegranates [*Sayat Nova*] (1969) – Impressionistic, poetic retelling of the life of Armenian bard Sayat Nova in a series of surreal tableaux

Come and See [*Idi i Smotri*] (1985) – Bleak and intense Soviet WWII classic about a boy solider, with dreamlike passages

The Company of Wolves (1984) – "Little Red Riding Hood" told as the werewolf nightmare of a pubescent girl

Conspirators of Pleasure [*Spiklenci Slasti*] (1996) – A man with a chicken complex and a woman who snorts dough are two of the six characters whose bizarre fetishes intersect in this intricate Surrealist joke

The Cook the Thief His Wife & Her Lover (1989) – Peter Greenaway's lavish Jacobean revenge fable is set in a French restaurant where a boorish Thief terrorizes the staff and customers

Cowards Bend the Knee, or, the Blue Hands (2003) – Typically surreal modern silent from the inimitable Guy Maddin mixing melodrama, Greek tragedy, psychosexual guilt, and hockey highlights

The Cremator [*Spalovac Mrtvol*] (1969) – An oddball Czech cremator harmonizes his homegrown Buddhism with Nazi ideology

Crime Wave (1985) – A silent screenwriter who can only complete beginnings and endings struggles to create the great Canadian "colour crime movie"

Cube (1997) – Five strangers wake up in a hi-tech booby-trapped cube, with no idea who built it or why

Daisies [*Sedmikrásky*] (1966) – Sexy Czech hippie chicks wreaking havoc in this banned satire of something or other

The Dance of Reality [*La Danza de Realidad*] (2013) – Alejandro Jodorowsky's surrealistic autobiography is one of his most accessible films, although it still features a woman who can only sing opera and who cures plague with her urine

The Dark Backward (1991) – The world's worst comic nearly becomes an overnight success when he grows a third arm out of his back in this grotesque show business satire

Dark City (1998) – Mysterious bald Strangers manipulate events and geometries in a city of endless night for their own purposes

Dead Alive [AKA *Brain Dead*] (1992) – A rabid monkey incites the most absurdly gory zombie movie ever made

Dead Leaves (2004) – Hyperactive anime about a guy with a television head and a girl with mismatched eyes breaking out of a mutant clone prison on the moon

Dead Man (1995) – Hypnotic, dreamlike Western about a man bearing the name of a dead poet and an Indian named Nobody

Dead Ringers (1988) – Twin gynecologists (!) go crazy in this odd psychodrama from horror maestro David Cronenberg

Death Bed: The Bed That Eats (1977) – Rediscovered oddity about a man-eating bed is a surreal horror/art film/black comedy, or something?

Death by Hanging [*Koshikei*] (1968) – A Korean killer survives his execution, and puzzled police bureaucrats try to recreate the capital crimes to cure the condemned's amnesia

Death Laid an Egg [*La morte ha fatto l'uovo*] (1968) – A Surrealist giallo set at an experimental poultry farm that's breeding headless chickens

Delicatessen (1991) – Jeunet & Caro's first film is a bizarre but oddly sweet black comedy involving cannibalism in post-apocalyptic Paris

Dementia [*Daughter of Horror*] (1955) – Silent, experimental, and noirish horror about a woman soon to be involved in a "mysterious stabbing"

Der Samurai (2014) – A man with a katana in an evening dress terrorizes a rural German town

Desperate Living (1977) – This grunge fairy tale includes cross-dressing, cannibalism, necrophilia, bat rabies, and gap-toothed queen Edith Massey serviced by leather-bound Nazis

Destino (2003) – Reconstruction of an abandoned 1946 collaboration between Salvador Dalí and Walt Disney; it's a five minute moving Dalí canvas

The Devils (1971) – Ken Russell's most violently deranged film is the true-ish story of a convent of nuns who accuse a priest of being an incubus in league with the Devil

Dillinger is Dead [*Dillinger e Morto*] (1969) – Nearly forgotten late 1960s avant-garde alienation piece about a gas-mask designer who spends an evening puttering about his apartment

The Discreet Charm of the Bourgeoisie [*Le charme discret de la bourgeoisie*] (1972) – Six upper-class twits (and a bishop) attempt to have dinner together, but they are always interrupted

Django Kill... If You Live, Shoot! [*Se sei Vivo Spara*] (1967) – An ambiguously dead antihero who shoots golden bullets fights Mr. Sorrow and his gang of gay fascist cowboys

Doggiewogiez! Poochiewoochiez! (2012) – A remake of The Holy Mountain composed entirely of found footage of dogs

Dog Star Man (1964) – A man climbs up a mountain, a star explodes, a baby suckles, and probably more things happen, although you can hardly tell through the four layers of superimposed images

Dogtooth [*Kynodontas*] (2009) – Three children are raised to adulthood in a bizarre estate where words mean just what the tyrannical father wants them to in this shocking Greek art film

Dogville (2003) – This misanthropic fable is like de Sade's "Justine" played out on the set of Wilder's "Our Town"

Donnie Darko (2001) – Angsty, apocalyptic, fantastical drama about a screwed-up, possibly time-traveling teen is an irresistibly lovable mess

Don't Look Now (1973) – Classic psychological horror with a weird twist

The Double (2013) – In a comically nightmarish nowhere, meek clerk Simon James is bedeviled by James Simon, his exact double and his exact opposite

Dr. Caligari (1989) – This pop-surrealist work by a hardcore porn director suffers from bad acting, but it is weird as hell

Eden and After [*L'éden et après*] (1970) – Bored college students steal a painting and end up in Tunisia, although it could just be the drugs in this surreal sadomasochistic story that could be described as *Alice in Wonderland* meets *Justine* meets *The Trip*

Eisenstein in Guanajuato (2015) – Delirious biopic postulating that Soviet director Sergei Eisenstein lost his virginity to his guide while in Mexico to film a movie that never got made

Elevator Movie (2004) – Surreal and minimalist independent feature about two people trapped in an elevator for months; well-scripted and weird as hell but very amateur

El Topo (1970) – Mystical and surreal Spaghetti Western from Alejandro Jodorowsky

Enemy (2013) – A history professor is obsessed with tracking down a man who appears to be his exact double; spiders appear

Enter the Void (2009) – Provocative and pretentious, Gaspar Noé's "psychedelic melodrama" is nonetheless the best trip film of the young millennium

Eraserhead (1977) – The ultimate nightmare experience, about horror at procreation and loathing for one's own offspring

Escape from Tomorrow (2013) – Surrealist satire secretly shot in Disney World, with mad scientists, evil witches, French jailbait, and a cat flu plague

Eternal Sunshine of the Spotless Mind (2004) – Jim Carrey unexpectedly shines as he fights against a memory-erasing procedure he impulsively undertook; a weird crowd-pleaser

Even Dwarfs Started Small [*Auch Zwerge haben klein angefangen*] (1970) – Dwarf inmates revolt against their dwarf oppressors at an unnamed institution; they burn flowerpots, crucify monkeys, and laugh at defecating camels

Evil Dead II (1987) – The frenetic, fantastic and crowd-pleasing movie about a man trapped in a cabin menaced by evil spirits, mixing equal parts horror and absurd slapstick comedy

The Exterminating Angel [*El àngel exterminador*] (1962) – Attendees at a fancy soiree find they cannot leave the premises–for no reason whatsoever

Eyes Without a Face [*Les Yeux sans Visage*] (1965) – Georges Franjou's influential, poetic horror film

The Face of Another [*Tanin no kao*] (1966) – A man whose face has been burned in an accident gets a synthetic mask based on a stranger's face and sets out to seduce his own wife

The Falls (1980) – Absurdist mockumentary about the 92 survivors of the Violent Unexplained Event whose names begin with "Fall"

Fantasia (1940) – Dinos, demons and hippos illustrate the classical music canon in Walt Disney's weirdest classic

Fantastic Planet [*La Planète Sauvage*] (1973) – Tale of humans kept as pets by giant blue aliens, told in a Terry-Gilliam-meets-Salvador-Dalí-in-space animation style

Fantasy Mission Force [*Mi ni te gong dui*; AKA *Dragon Attack*] (1983) – An anachronistic team of misfits (including Jackie Chan and guys in kilts) fight Amazons and stay at a haunted house while on a quest to rescue Allied generals captured by Japanese Nazis in Canada

Fear and Loathing in Las Vegas (1998) – Terry Gilliam's adaptation of Hunter S. Thompson's cult novel about two burnouts taking insane quantities of drugs in the City of Sin

Fellini Satyricon (1969) – Bizarre androgynous costuming and mythological leaps of logic gird a great director's decadent extravaganza

Female Trouble (1974) – Juvenile delinquent Dawn Davenport (Divine) proves that "crime is beauty" on her way to the electric chair

A Field in England (2013) – Deserters from the English Civil War eat psychedelic mushrooms and hunt for buried treasure at an alchemist's command

Fight Club (1999) – Manhood finds itself tested at the millennium when an actuary and an eccentric soap-maker found an underground "fight club" and find it taking on cult proportions

Final Flesh (2009) – Four separate porn-troupes-for-hire enact an absurdist prank script about the apocalypse

The Forbidden Room (2015) – Guy Maddin's collection of reimagined lost films, with tales curled inside each other like Russian nesting dolls

Forbidden Zone (1982) – Frenchie is lost in the 6th Dimension and her family and friends must save her from the king and queen in this surreal musical that often looks like a Fleischer Brothers cartoon

Freaks (1932) – A trapeze artist marries a dwarf for his money, leading to gruesome revenge in this infamous film populated by real carnival freaks

Funeral Parade of Roses [*Bara no sôretsu*] (1969) – Basically, a psychedelic Japanese drag adaptation of "Oedipus Rex"

Funky Forest: The First Contact (2005) – Selection of surreal, interwoven sketches from three Japanese directors is uneven, as you would expect, but contains some of the weirdest sequences you're likely to come across

Glen or Glenda (1953) – Ed Wood's pro-transvestite documentary, with Bela Lugosi as an omniscient one-man Greek chorus and a dream sequence featuring bondage

The Godmonster of Indian Flats (1973) – A mutant sheep embryo develops into a monster that threatens an old-West themed town involved in a sticky real estate deal

Goke, Body Snatcher from Hell [*Kyuketsuki Gokemidoro*] (1968) – Survivors of an airline crash squabble among each other while psychedelic space vampires pick them off

Goodbye Uncle Tom (1971) – A fake shockumentary about slavery in the American south, with nudity and depravity on an epic scale

Gothic (1986) – Hallucinatory excess from Ken Russell, about the night Mary Shelley conceived "Frankenstein"

Gozu [*Gokudô kyôfu dai-gekijô: Gozu*] (2003) – Erotically charged, grotesquely surreal Takashi Miike horror/yakuza mashup

La Grande Bouffe (1973) – Four successful men lock themselves inside a chateau and eat themselves to death

Greaser's Palace (1972) – A zoot-suited Jesus visits a Western town to enact a series of absurd parables

The Greasy Strangler (2016) – Lard-loving Big Ronnie (who doubles as the Greasy Strangler) and his son live together and conduct scam walking tours, until a "disco cutie" comes between them

Gummo (1997) – Indisputably weird but ceaselessly unpleasant portrait of hopeless white trash

Häxan [*Witchcraft Through the Ages*] (1922) – Silent documentary about witchcraft containing the most diabolically visionary horror images of all time

Head (1968) – Prefab pop band the Monkees commit career suicide with this psychedelic spit in the eye of their young fans

Heavenly Creatures (1994) – Peter Jackson brings the fantasy world of two teenaged murderesses to life in this crime drama based on a real-life case

Hedwig and the Angry Inch (2001) – Hedwig, a punk band leader and victim of a botched sex change operation, chases the rock star who stole her songs across the U.S.

Hellzapoppin' (1941) – Anarchic musical comedy from vaudevillians Chick Johnson and Ole Olsen is probably the weirdest Hollywood musical of all time

Help! Help! The Globolinks [*Hilfe! Hilfe! Die Globolinks*] (1969) – The world's only psychedelic children's opera about an alien invasion

Holy Motors (2012) – "Mr. Oscar" drives around Paris taking on "assignments" that require him to become a hit man, accordionist, and a fashion-model abducting leprechaun

The Holy Mountain (1973) – An extravagant, psychedelic tour of world mysticism has a guru lead a Christ-figure and companions on a quest to storm the Holy Mountain

The Horrors of Spider Island [*Ein Toter hing im Netz*] (1960) – A bad misogynist fever dream involving poorly dubbed buxom women, and some spiders, on an island

The Hourglass Sanatorium (1973) – A man meets strange characters at a dreamy sanatorium where the rules of time and logic do not apply

Hour of the Wolf [*Vargtimmen*] (1968) – An artist is invited to visit the castle of—demons? ghosts? hallucinations?—in Ingmar Bergman's Gothic horror

House [*Hausu*] (1977) – The weirdest haunted house movie ever made; no one forgets the scene where the piano eats the girl

Howl's Moving Castle [*Hauru no ugoku shiro*] (2004) – An 18-year old girl is turned into an old woman and goes to work for a wizard in a steampunk castle

How to Get Ahead in Advertising (1989) – A hotshot ad exec grows a pimple that turns into a head in this bizarre, biting satire

Hugo the Hippo (1975) – Hugo's family is brutally slaughtered by Paul Lynde, who later subjects the hippo and his human pal to horrifying hallucinations in this delightful children's fare

The Hypothesis of the Stolen Painting (1978) – A Collector poses actors into tableaux vivants in an attempt to divine the esoteric message in a series of 19th century paintings

I Can See You (2008) – This "psychedelic campfire tale" is slow to start, but climaxes in a 20-minute freakout

Idiots and Angels (2008) – A loathsome man grows wings in this occasionally surreal animated black comedy that expertly mixes cynicism with romanticism

If.... (1968) – Malcolm McDowell debuts as a rebellious youth in a British boarding school who fights a (largely imaginary) battle with the authorities

I'm A Cyborg, But That's OK [*Saibogujiman Kwenchana*] (2006) – Romantic comedy set in a mental asylum is likely to remain the weirdest example of its genre

The Immaculate Conception of Little Dizzle (2009) – Experimental cookies cause hallucinations and pregnancy in male janitors in this indie comedy sleeper

Indecent Desires (1968) – This roughie about the symbiotic sexual relationship between a transient, a magic ring, a doll, and a blonde secretary is our choice to represent the oeuvre of Doris Wishman

Inherent Vice (2014) – Pot-smoking detective "Doc" Sportello investigates kidnappings, fake murders, a sinister consortium of dentists, and more in this baffling adaptation of Thomas Pynchon's novel

Ink (2009) – Visually impressive low-budget fantasy about a mysterious figure who snatches a sleeping girl into a world of dreams

INLAND EMPIRE (2006) – This story of Laura Dern trapped in a nightmare while filming a cursed script is perhaps David Lynch's weirdest movie

Innocence (2004) – A girl arrives, in a coffin, for her first day at a strange all-female boarding school

Institute Benjamenta, or This Dream People Call Human Life (1995) – An ambitionless man enrolls in a school for servants and enters into ambiguous relationships with the brother and sister who run the institute

It's Such a Beautiful Day (2011) – Psychedelic animation about the life and death of a terminally ill, terminally confused stick figure in a hat

I Will Walk Like a Crazy Horse [*J'irai Comme un Cheval Fou*] (1973) – Accused of murdering his mother, a man flees to the desert where he meets—and falls for—a mystical dwarf

Jacob's Ladder (1990) – Big-budget cult mindtrip movie with unforgettable demonic hallucinations

Japanese Summer: Double Suicide [*Muri shinjû: Nihon no natsu*] (1967) – A nympho who can't get laid meets a suicidal man who can't get killed in the surreal Sixties satire

John Dies at the End (2012) – A psychedelic drug called "Soy Sauce" gives two slackers the psychic powers necessary to sense an incoming extra-dimensional invasion

Johnny Got His Gun (1971) – Antiwar classic about a limbless, blind, and deaf casualty of the First World War, trapped inside his own head where he lives out a mixture of dreams and fantasies

Keyhole (2011) – A gangster journeys through a haunted house unlocking forgotten family memories

Kin-Dza-Dza (1986) – Russian junkyard sci-fi satire about a planet with bizarre customs and an absurdly arbitrary class structure. Also, koo!

Kontroll (2003) – A kontroller living in the Budapest subway chases after a mysterious killer pushing people onto the train tracks in this mythic thriller

Kung Fu Hustle [*Kung Fu*] (2004) – Totally off-it's-rocker kung fu comedy/fantasy that became a smash international hit

Kwaidan (1964) – Old Japanese ghost stories turned into Expressionist art

L'Age d'Or (1930) – A documentary about scorpions turns into the story of a man and woman's frustrated love, then into Jesus' Sadean orgy

The Lair of the White Worm (1988) – Ken Russell's ultra-fun, tongue-in-cheek horror movie filled with phallic symbols and impaled nuns

Last Year at Marienbad [*L'Année Dernière à Marienb*ad] (1961) – Trapped in a ghostly hotel, a man insists he met a woman last year; the woman denies it; things get strange

The Legend of Suram Fortress [*Ambavi Suramis Tsikhitsa*] (1984) – The fortress of Suram is doomed to crumble eternally until a youth entombs himself in its walls

Lemonade Joe [*Limonádový Joe aneb Konská Opera*] (1964) – Anarchic Czech Communist musical Western spoof about a lemonade-drinking cowboy who challenges the whiskey monopoly in a frontier town

Léolo (1992) – A French Canadian boy who believes he was conceived from an Italian tomato contaminated with semen uses imagination to escape from his dysfunctional family

L'Immortelle (1963) – A professor in Istanbul finds and loses a mysterious woman in novelist Alain Robbe-Grillet's directorial debut

L'Inhumaine [*The Inhuman Woman*] (1924) – Arty avant-garde sci-fi melodrama about a stuck-up diva and the men she drives to madness

Liquid Sky (1982) – Tiny aliens harvest endorphins from New Wave punks at the point of orgasm, killing them in the process

Lisztomania (1975) – Composer Franz Liszt battles composer/vampire Richard Wagner in this crazy classical music comedy

Little Otik [*Otesánek*] (2000) – A barren woman adopts a log as a child, and it comes to life and begins eating the neighbors in this black comedy adaptation of an Eastern European folktale

The Lobster (2015) – Find a mate in 45 days or be turned into an animal of your choice

Lost Highway (1997) – A jazzman allegedly kills his wife, then one day disappears and a totally different man wakes up in his death row cell

Love Exposure (2008) – A virginal Catholic who makes his living as a pornographer with ninja skills at upskirt photography tries to save his unrequited love from a religious cult in this bizarrely plotted four hour comedy epic

The Love Witch (2016) – A mix of witchcraft, campy romantic melodrama, and bubbling feminist subtext, presented as a tribute to 1960s Technicolor spectacles

Lucifer Rising (1981) – Egyptian gods and goddess conjure Lucifer and flying saucers in this short (30 minutes), occult, avant-garde masterpiece

Lunacy [*Sileni*] (2005) – Jan Svankmajer directs the Marquis de Sade in a pair of tales by Edgar Allan Poe

The Lure [*Córki Dancingu*] (2015) -Poland's disco-musical about killer mermaids

Maelstrom (2000) – This tale of a pretty young socialite's guilt is narrated by a talking fish

Malpertuis (1972) – Harry Kümel's big weird dark house tale was confusing and a flop despite the presence of Orson Welles, but drips with surreal atmosphere nonetheless

Mandy (2018) – When a hippy cult leader kills lumberjack Nicolas Cage's girl, Nic goes on a psychedelic revenge rampage

Maniac (1934) – Resurrection of the dead, an orangutan-man rapist and edible cat eyeballs all feature heavily in this deranged exploitation movie that seems to have been directed by an actual maniac

'Manos': The Hands of Fate (1966) – Could have been the worst movie ever made, if not for the redemptive presence of the great oddball character Torgo, the spastic satyr

The Man Who Fell to Earth (1976) – David Bowie is the alien who falls to Earth and corrupted in this nonlinear, experimental sci-fi movie

Marquis (1989) – The story of the Marquis de Sade's imprisonment in the Bastille, performed by characters in animal masks and featuring Sade's penis in a speaking role

Meet the Feebles (1989) – Fragile egos, double-dealings, accidental killings, pornographic sidelines, rohypnol-aided assault, and drug and sex addictions plague puppets at a variety show

Meshes of the Afternoon (1943) – This fifteen minute afternoon nightmare with cloaked figures with mirrored faces gave birth to the American avant-garde

Metropolis (1927) – Fritz Lang's futurist fantasia, a political allegory with Biblical imagery, undercover robots and Bauhaus designs

The Milky Way [*La Voie Lactee*] (1969) – A dry and cerebral, but very weird, story by surrealist master Luis Buñuel about two tramps meeting various Biblical characters and embodiments of Catholic heresies while traveling on a pilgrimage

Millennium Actress [*Sennen joyû*; AKA *Chiyoko: Millennium Actress*] (2001) – A retired actress recounts her life, with her interviewers entering a story that mixes up reality with scenes from her movies

Mind Game (2004) – Nishi goes on a psychedelic journey after being killed by a yakuza, returns to Earth, and lives in the belly of a whale with an old hermit in this anime with rapidly shifting art styles

Monty Python's The Meaning of Life (1983) – Monty Python discusses life in a series of (frequently weird) sketches

Mood Indigo (2013) – A wealthy inventor's wife grows ill from a water lily growing in her lung in this whimsical and surreal adaptation of Boris Vian's novel

mother! (2017) – Jennifer Lawrence finds hordes of boorish guests descending on, and wrecking, the tranquil home she is refurbishing with her celebrity poet husband

Mr. Nobody (2009) – The last mortal man in the world remembers dozens of parallel reality variations of his life

Mulholland Drive (2001) – Radical identity shifts and surrealistic nightclub acts ignite this dreamlike noir fable about love, guilt, and Hollywood

My Winnipeg (2007) – In Guy Maddin's Winnipeg, sleepwalkers roam the streets at night, horses freeze in the river, and mother is everywhere

Naked Lunch (1991) – David Cronenberg's adaptation of the unadaptable William S. Burroughs novel features film's scariest typewriters

Natural Born Killers (1994) – A pair of serial killers become celebrities as they slay their way across a hallucinogenic America

Neon Genesis Evangelion: The End of Evangelion (1997) – This apocalyptic anime feature, serving as an alternate ending to Hideaki Anno's popular TV series, is basically Jungian psychoanalysis acted out by giant robots

Never Give a Sucker an Even Break (1941) – The "Great Man" (W.C. Fields) tries to sell a studio an absurd script that begins when he falls out of an airplane chasing his plummeting whiskey flask

Night of the Hunter (1955) – A homicidal Preacher with "LOVE" and "HATE" tattooed on his hands hunts children carrying treasure in this Southern Gothic Expressionist fable

Night Train to Terror (1985) – God and Satan watch badly edited horror films on a train while a New Wave band practices one compartment down

Ninja Champion (1985) – Rose seeks revenge against her diamond-smuggling rapist, while in another movie clumsily pasted on to that one, an Interpol ninja assassinates evil ninjas while they practice circus tricks

The Ninth Configuration (1980) – A psychiatrist argues for the existence of God in an experimental military mental hospital, but is he as crazy as his patients?

Nosferatu [*Nosferatu, eine Symphonie des Grauens*; AKA *Nosferatu, a Symphony of Horror*] (1922) – F.W. Murnau's unauthorized Expressionist adaptation of "Dracula" is a mélange of sex and disease

No Smoking (2007) – Quit smoking, the Bollywood way, in one of India's few intentionally weird films

Nostalghia (1983) – Andrei Tarkovsky's slow, beautiful, dreamlike spiritual parable about a homesick Russian poet in Italy

Nothing but Trouble (1991) – Dan Akroyd's grotesque Hollywood misfire about a weird old "reeve" ruling from a junkyard in a backwoods New Jersey "shire"

November (2017) – A tragic romance set in a world where our forefathers' craziest superstitions are literally true

Nuit Noire [*Black Night*] (2005) – In a world where the sun only shines fifteen seconds a day, a strange African woman crawls into a solitary entomologist's bed to die

O Lucky Man! (1973) – Sprawling satire with Malcolm McDowell, Kafkaesque interrogations, a half-man half-hog, and breastfeeding

Orpheus [*Orphée*] (1950) – When Jean Cocteau refashions the Greek myth for postwar France, Orpheus and Death fall in love, and Death's chauffeur gets the hots for Eurydice

A Page of Madness (1926) [*Kurutta ippêji*] – A janitor takes a job in an asylum where his wife is held in this silent Japanese film heavily influenced by the European avant-garde

Pan's Labyrinth (2006) – Guillermo del Toro's beautiful fairytale; a girl completes quests at a faun's behest, while her real world Fascist stepfather is a monster beyond all fantasy

Paprika (2006) – Stunning Satoshi Kon animation; scenario involves terrorists invading dreams, then turning them loose on the streets of Tokyo

Perfect Blue [*Pafekuto buru*] (1997) – A Japanese pop idol tries her hand as an actress, and the pressure of unhappy fans and selling out leads her to a psychotic break with reality

Performance (1970) – Gangster James Fox is fed magic mushrooms and turned into a hippie by Mick Jagger and groupies in this psychedelic stunner

Persona (1966) – A mute actress and her nurse switch personalities at a vacation home – maybe?

Phantasm (1979) – Crazy, nightmarish, obstinately illogical drive-in horror flick about a kid and a sinister funeral home, featuring the terrifying "Tall Man"

The Phantom of Liberty (1974) – A series of Surrealist sketches by the great Luis Buñuel

Phantom of the Paradise (1974) – A rock n' rollin' mix of Phantom of the Opera and "Faust," with just the right amount of crazy

Pi (1998) – Amazing black and white photography and a pulsing electronica soundtrack drive this intellectual thriller about a mad math genius seeking a mystical number

Pierrot le Fou (1965) – A television personality goes on the lam with his babysitter in this playfully fractured, classic Nouvelle Vague road movie

The Pillow Book (1996) – Gorgeous experimental video, full of layered images, illustrates this story of a woman obsessed with creating living books by drawing on nude bodies

Pink Flamingos (1972) – Divine goes to excessive lengths to prove she is the filthiest person in the world

Pink Floyd the Wall (1982) – Bombastic, unfocused, overwrought and often brilliant rock opera, with knockout animation from British political cartoonist Gerald Scarfe

Playtime (1967) – A plotless "day in the life" of modernist Paris that ends with chaotic revelry in a crumbling restaurant

The Pornographers [*"Erogotoshitachi" yori Jinruigaku nyūmon*] (1966) – Ogata makes pornographic movies while sleeping with his landlady and lusting after her teenage daughter, under the watchful eye of a carp the widow believes is her reincarnated husband

Possession (1981) – Anna leaves her husband, but not for another man... or even another human

Prospero's Books (1991) – Shakespeare's "The Tempest" as an avant-garde video version of Renaissance painting come to life, with plentiful nudity and all parts voiced by Sir John Gielgud

Reality [*Réalité*] (2014) – An aspiring filmmaker gets lost in nightmares inside of nightmares when he is tasked with finding an award-winning scream as a prerequisite to funding his movie

The Red Squirrel [*La Ardilla Roja*] (1993) – A suicidal man pretends to be the boyfriend of a beautiful amnesia victim, but how long can he keep up the charade?

The Reflecting Skin (1990) – Uneven but sometimes powerful flick teeming with symbolism about a kid who thinks his widow neighbor is a vampire, among other strangenesses

Reflections of Evil (2002) – A bizarrely edited piece of avant-outsider art about an angry, obese street peddler who is watched over by the ghost of his dead junkie sister in a purgatorial L.A.

Repo Man (1984) – A punk kid takes a job as a repo man and searches for a car with a mysterious glowing cargo in the trunk

A Report on the Party and Guests [*O slavnosti a hostech*] (1966) – Picnickers are kidnapped and taken to a party in this Kafkaesque allegory on totalitarianism made (and banned) in Communist Czechoslovakia

Repulsion (1965) – Disturbing Roman Polanski peek inside Catherine Deneuve's disintegrating mind

Robot Monster (1953) – A gorilla alien in a diving helmet and his bubble machine invade Bronson Canyon

The Rocky Horror Picture Show (1975) – Even without its bizarre cult following, this naughty musical b-movie spoof would have earned a place on the list

Roma (1972) [AKA *Fellini's Roma*] – An infamous ecclesiastical fashion show with roller-skating cardinals highlights this Felliniesque sequence of vignettes set in the Eternal City

Rosencrantz & Guildenstern Are Dead (1990) – The two minor characters from "Hamlet" wander around the castle of Elsinore, unaware that they are actually characters in a play

Rubber (2010) – The best animated tire serial killer movie ever made gets bonus points for including an audience that comments on the absurdly comic proceedings

Rubin & Ed (1991) – Antisocial weirdo Rubin agrees to attend a real estate seminar with sad sack salesman Ed, if Ed will help him bury his dead pet cat first

The Ruling Class (1972) – The 14th Earl of Gurney is unfit to serve in the House of Lords because he believes he is God, but he becomes even worse after he is "cured"

Run Lola Run (1998) – Lola has twenty minutes to raise 100,000 Deutschmarks and get it to her desperate boyfriend; fortunately, she gets a do-over

The Saddest Music in the World (2003) – A legless Winnipeg beer baroness holds a contest to discover the titular music in this typically retro comic outing by Guy Maddin

Sans Soleil (1983) – Remarkable, meandering mondo-style arthouse documentary that mixes a trip to a cat shrine and a monkey porn museum with cinematic poetry

Santa and the Ice Cream Bunny (1972) – Insanely bad holiday cheer about Santa's sleigh stuck on a Florida beach, and Thumbelina, and the sad-sack Pirates World amusement park...

Santa Claus (1959) – With the assistance of his henchman Merlin, Santa fights the Devil while delivering presents on Christmas Eve in this culturally confused Mexican take on Kris Kringle

Santa Sangre (1989) – Psychedelic slasher film about a man raised in a circus who acts as the hands for his armless mother

The Saragossa Manuscript [*Rekopis Znaleziony w Saragossie*] (1965) – A Napoleonic soldier listens to stories inside of stories, all of which may be related to two women claiming to be his Muslim cousins who want to seduce him

Save the Green Planet [*Jigureul jikyeora!*] (2003) – A man kidnaps and tortures a pharmaceutical executive, believing him to be an alien spy from the Andromeda galaxy

A Scanner Darkly (2006) – An undercover cop addicted to a powerful future narcotic is assigned to investigate himself in this rotoscoped adaptation of the paranoid Philip K. Dick novel

Schizopolis (1996) – Fletcher Munson struggles to write a speech for a Scientology-like leader while his doppelgänger is having an affair with his wife

The Science of Sleep (2006) – The melancholy love life of a man who can't distinguish dreams from reality

Scott Pilgrim vs. the World (2010) – A Toronto slacker must defeat his new girlfriend's seven evil exes in this video game styled cult pic

The Secret Adventures of Tom Thumb (1993) – The fairy tale retold in stop-motion animation and pixilation, set in a dystopian city full of bugs and monstrosities

A Serious Man (2009) – The Coen brothers' retelling of the Book of Job as an absurdist comedy is mystifying and brilliant in equal parts

Seven Servants (1996) – A dying Anthony Quinn hires shirtless young men to stick their fingers up his nostrils

Shadows of Forgotten Ancestors [*Tini zabutykh predkiv*] (1964) – An old Ukrainian folk tale told as an elliptical experimental film by incomparable stylist Sergei Parajanov

Shanks (1974) – A mute puppeteer (played by Marcel Marceau) learns to operate dead bodies like marionettes, and ends up fighting bikers

Shock Corridor (1963) – Eccentric auteur Sam Fuller imagines Cold War America as a mental asylum in this campy melodrama with remarkable expressionist visuals

Silent Hill (2006) – Sloppy scripting and apocalyptic imagery combine to create a truly weird experience

Sin City (2005) – Visually stunning, ultraviolent postmodern noir

The Singing Ringing Tree [*Das Singende, Klingende Bäumchen*] (1957) – This magical fairytale featuring an evil dwarf, a prince in a bear suit, and a nightmarish mechanical goldfish terrified a generation of British children

Sita Sings the Blues (2008) – An animated retelling of the Indian epic "Ramayana," with music video interludes featuring a Betty Boop-like demigoddess singing the torch songs of Annette Hanshaw

Skidoo (1968) – Carol Channing strips, Jackie Gleason drops acid and Groucho Marx is "God" in this all-star psychedelic misfire

Skins [*Pieles*] (2017) – The lives of a butt-faced woman, a reluctant pedophile, an eyeless prostitute, and other internally and externally deformed people intersect in unexpected ways

Society (1989) – This horror satire about a teen who doesn't fit in with his high society family is famous for its wild, surrealist makeup effects

Solaris [*Solyaris*] (1972) – Minimalist, mystical science fiction about a conscious planet that recreates a cosmonaut's dead wife

Songs from the Second Floor (2000) – Millennial and existential panic in a nameless Swedish city, told in a spare, absurd style

Sorry to Bother You (2018) – Far-left-field absurdist agitprop satire about a black telemarketer who shoots up the corporate ladder when he learns to use his "white voice"

Spider Baby, or the Maddest Story Ever Told (1967) – The Merrye family reverts to savagery as they age in this horror/comedy with an utterly unique tone

Spirited Away [*Sen to Chihiro no Kamikakushi*] (2001) – Hayao Miyazaki's masterpiece about a girl trapped in a bathhouse of spirits is Japan's answer to "Alice in Wonderland"

Stalker (1979) – Andrei Tarkovsky's slow, mystifying, beautiful science fiction parable about three men's journey to a room which can grant their innermost wishes

Steppenwolf (1974) – The psychedelic effects in this faithful adaptation of Herman Hesse's novel have dated badly

Strange Frame: Love & Sax (2012) – Romance and intrigue on the moons of Jupiter in this psychedelic animated lesbian science fiction musical

Street of Crocodiles (1986) – Eerie reminiscences unfold when a gaunt man is brought to life after a globule of spittle activates a machine

Survive Style 5+ (2004) – Five fantastical interlocking stories about a revenant wife, a hypnotized salaryman, three teenage burglars, an ad exec, and an assassin with a translator

Suspiria (1977) – Bizarre, unreal color schemes and a pounding score surrealize this horror fairy tale about a coven of witches operating a ballet academy

Sweet Movie (1974) – A beauty contest winner's prize is to marry a billionaire, while in a second plotline a socialist sea captain sails down an Amsterdam canal with a hold full of sugar in this scatological political satire

Sweet Sweetback's Baadasssss Song (1971) – The first blaxploitation movie was actually an experimental art film with explicit sex and a cop-beating hero who spends the movie evading the Man

The Swimmer (1968) – Cheerful go-getter Ned decides to swim home through his neighbor's pools, but has he forgotten something important?

Swiss Army Man (2016) – A suicidal, shipwrecked man uses a flatulent, talking corpse to find his way home

Synecdoche, New York (2008) – Charlie Kaufman working without a net in this absurdist, recursive, and dreamlike story of a depressed heater director who builds a replica of New York City inside a warehouse

Tales from the Quadead Zone (1987) – We chose this ultra-low-budget anthology of horror stories to represent the work of outsider VHS shlockmeister Chester N. Turner

The Taste of Tea (2004) – The quaintly surreal adventures of a rural Japanese family include a girl plagued by a giant doppelganger only she can see

Taxidermia (2006) – A penis ejaculating fire is the take-home image from this surreal and twisted Hungarian generational epic; barf bags recommended

Tekkonkinkreet (2006) – Orphans White and Black scrape out an existence on the surreal streets of Treasure Town

The Telephone Book (1971) – A nymphomaniac falls in love with the world's greatest obscene phone caller in this arty underground sexploitationer that climaxes with a surreally obscene animation

The Tenant (1976) – A new roomer in an odd apartment complex takes on the personality of the previous tenant, who committed suicide

Teorema (1968) – A handsome stranger sleeps with each member of a bourgeois family, and their lives self-destruct when he disappears

The Testament of Orpheus [*Le testament d'Orphée*] (1960) – The conclusion of Jean Cocteau's "Orphic" trilogy casts the poet as a time-traveler interrogated by his own fictional characters

Tetsuo: The Iron Man [*Tetsuo*] (1989) – A man inexplicably transforms into metal, set to an industrial soundtrack in grainy 16mm black and white

That Obscure Object of Desire [*Cet obscur objet du désir*] (1977) – A wealthy French businessman romances a young Spanish girl over the years, but she will never submit to him

Thundercrack! (1975) – An absurdist underground spoof of Old Dark House movies, with hardcore sex scenes and an amorous gorilla

Tideland (2005) – Terry Gilliam's dark and controversial riff on "Alice in Wonderland"

Time Bandits (1981) – Time-traveling, thieving dwarfs feature heavily in this weird kiddie film mixing fantasy, comedy, and theology

The Tin Drum [*Die Blechtrommel*] (1979) – A three-year old German boy refuses to grow up, then witnesses the rise of Nazism

The Tingler (1959) – A creature that lives in your spine and causes you to die if you don't scream gets loose in this very theater

Titus (1999) – Anachronistic avant-garde adaptation of Shakespeare's most exploitative play, with gang rape, body parts cut off, and cannibalism

Tokyo Gore Police [*Tôkyô Zankoku Keisatsu*] (2008) – A female cop hunts spontaneously mutating serial killers in this very weird, often imitated splatterpunk classic

Toto the Hero [*Toto le Heros*] (1991) – A man nurses a lifelong grudge against the neighbor he believes stole his life (and maybe the love of his sister)

Trash Humpers (2009) – Geriatric miscreants vandalize a trash-strewn Nashville and force Siamese twins to eat soap-soaked pancakes in this non-narrative celebration of VHS aesthetics. A "reader's choice" poll winner.

The Tree of Life (2011) – Terrence Malick wonders how best to tell the tale of a Texas boy's strained relationship with his demanding father, and concludes the answer is to include dinosaurs

The Trial (1962) – Josef K. finds he's accused of a crime, but no one will tell him what it is in Orson Welles' adaptation of Franz Kafka's absurdist/existentialist classic

The Triplets of Belleville [*Les Triplettes de Belleville*, AKA *Belleville Rendez-vous*] (2003) – Three retired jazz singers help a nearsighted grandma and her overweight dog save a bicyclist from art deco gangsters in this dialogue-free animation set in a surrealistic 1940s milieu

Tromeo & Juliet (1996) – The creators of *The Toxic Avenger* remake the Bard's tale as an obscene punk epic, with predictably bizarre results

True Stories (1986) – A deadpan narrator in a cowboy hat observes the lives of the strange residents of fictional Virgil, Texas

Tuvalu (1999) – Can Anton get his family's Turkish bathhouse to pass inspection while winning the heart of the girl who blames him for her father's death?

Twelve Monkeys (1995) – A time-traveler from a dystopian future trying to investigate a cult called "12 monkeys" is mistaken for a madman

Twin Peaks: Fire Walk with Me (1992) – David Lynch took an on-the-edge TV series over the cliff with this divisive prequel exploring Laura Palmer's last days

Uncle Boonmee Who Can Recall His Past Lives [*Loong Boonmee raleuk chat*] (2010) – Meditative Thai movie where the border between this world and the next is as thin as a strip of film

Underground (1995) – A Yugoslavian gangster tricks his partner into hiding out in a cellar for decades, making him believe WWII is still raging outside

Under the Skin (2013) – An alien dissolves single men in black goo

Upstream Color (2013) – An examination of what happens when a woman is infected with a will-sapping worm that is then implanted in a pig to create a psychic link

Urusei Yatsura 2: Beautiful Dreamer (1984) – The characters of an anime sitcom about an amorous flying alien find themselves trapped in one of the cast's dreams

Valerie and Her Week of Wonders [*Valerie a Týden Divu*] (1970) – The onset of menses turns 13-year old Valerie's innocent world of childhood into a dream of rapist priests, lesbians, incest, and vampires

Vampire's Kiss (1988) – Nicolas Cage's weirdest role features him overacting brilliantly as a literary agent who believes he's turning into a vampire

Vampyr (1932) – Dreamlike early talkie about a student of the occult who wanders into a French village suffering a vampiric infestation

Vertigo (1958) – An acrophobic detective falls for a mysterious woman in Alfred Hitchcock's obsessive exploration of sexual desire

Videodrome (1983) – Discovery of a pirate snuff film broadcast leads to a hallucinatory melding of man and media

Visitor Q [*Bijitâ Q*] (2001) – Takashi Miike's story about a mysterious visitor who disrupts dysfunctional family dynamics breaks the lactation taboo

Viva la Muerte [*Long Live Death*] (1971) – Fernando Arrabal's surreal, semi-autobiographical story about a boy who discovers his mother turned his father in to the Spanish Fascists

Waking Life (2001) – The story of a young man who finds he's dreaming and can't wake up, with serious philosophical monologues and dialogues interspersed, painstakingly animated by over thirty artists in differing styles

Waltz with Bashir (2008) – Dreamlike animated documentary about the director's loss of memories related to his time as a conscripted Israeli soldier during the 1982 war in Lebanon

Wax, or the Discovery of Television Among the Bees (1991) – An experimental mock documentary about a computer programmer who begins communing with Mesopotamian bees, who set him to a strange task

Weekend (1967) – A money-grubbing couple travel through a surreal French countryside full of burning wrecks, fictional characters, and feral hippies as they try to secure an inheritance from the wife's dying father

Werckmeister Harmonies [*Werckmeister harmóniák*] (2000) – A Whale and a Prince bring a local apocalypse to a poor but peaceful Hungarian town

Why Don't You Play in Hell? [*Jigoku de naze warui*] (2013) – A team of amateur filmmakers luck out when a real-life yakuza asks them to film a bloody raid

The Wicker Man (1973) – Horrifying and intelligent tale of a devout detective's search for a missing girl on a Scottish island where the residents have adopted an ancient pagan religion

Wild at Heart (1990) – Sailor and Lulu flee mother's assassins as they tool down the yellow brick road that leads to madness

Willy Wonka and the Chocolate Factory (1971) – A laborer race of orange and green dwarfs and the bad acid boat trip from hell tip this kiddie musical into the weird column

The Woman in the Dunes [*Suna no onna*] (1964) – Existential allegory where an amateur entomologist is trapped in a sand pit with a widow, forced to shovel sand to survive

Wool 100% (2006) – Our only weird movie revolving around knitting is the tale of a strange girl who appears in the lives of two reclusive old pack-rat sisters

WR: Mysteries of the Organism (1971) – A celebration of the sexual revolution that begins as a straightforward documentary on controversial psychologist William Reich and ends with a decapitated head declaring she's not ashamed of her Communist past

Yellow Submarine (1968) – Animated film inspired by Beatles songs is a psychedelic trip through surreal seas in a quest to defeat the music-hating Blue Meanies

You, the Living [*Du Levande*] (2007) – 50 bittersweet, absurdist sketches on the crushing mundanity of everyday life

Zardoz (1974) – John Boorman's pretentious, campy sci-fi epic full of floating stone heads, psychedelic effects, and Sean Connery in a red diaper

Zazie dans le Metro (1960) – 10-year old Zazie explores a Paris filled with transvestites, dirty old men, desperate widows, and polar bears in this absurdist tribute to slapstick comedy

A Zed and Two Noughts (1985) – Two zoologist brothers enter a strange ménage à trois with the legless woman who survived an accident that killed their wives

Zéro de conduite (1933) – Boys in a French boarding school rebel in this anarchist/surrealist anti-establishment classic

APOCRYPHA (alternates that just missed the cut-off for canonical status)

Big Man Japan (2007) – Mockumentary about Japan's last giant monster fighter, featuring kooky kaiju

Celine and Julie Go Boating [*Céline et Julie vont en bateau*] (1974) – The whimsical, magical title characters take memory candies to solve an old mystery

Electric Dragon 80000V (2001) – B&W Japanese punk superhero musical with ample industrial noise guitar solos

The Fabulous Baron Munchausen [*Baron Prásil*] (1962) – An astronaut finds he's been beaten to the Moon by Baron Munchausen, who returns him to Earth to teach him the ways of earthlings

Gemini (1999) – Shinya Tsukamoto adapts an eerie Edogawa Rampo story about a successful doctor's discovery of the evil twin who was separated at birth

The Happiness of the Katakuris (2001) – A musical about a Japanese family who keep discovering corpses in their bed and breakfast—partly done in Claymation

The Lighthouse (2019) – Against his superior's warning, an apprentice lighthouse tender harms a seabird; madness follows

She's Allergic to Cats (2016) – A would-be director makes "weird video art that no one watches," while pursuing a beautiful woman and his dream project: a remake of *Carrie* featuring a cast of cats

Singapore Sling (1990) – While searching for his lost love, a detective is kidnapped by two psychotic women who use them in their S&M roleplaying games in this bizarre cross between film noir and torture porn

Under the Silver Lake (2018) – A California slacker becomes embroiled in perhaps the biggest cover-up that has ever bamboozled the Golden State

AVAILABILITY GRID (accurate as of Dec. 1, 2020)

MOVIE	DVD	Blu-Ray	VOD	Amazon Prime (Free)	Netflix	Tubi	Other
"Alejandro Jodorowsky 4K Collection"		Y					
Antenna, The			Y				
Assassin 33 A.D.	Y			Y		Y	Roku Channel
Bacurau	Y	Y	Y				Criterion Channel, Kanopy
"Boogiepop and Others"		Y	Y				Funimation, Crunchyroll
"Boogiepop Phantom"		Y					Funimation
Butt Boy	Y	Y	Y	Y		Y	Vudu
Can't Kill This	Y	Y	Y	Y		Y	Hoopla, Epix
Capone	Y	Y	Y	Y			Kanopy
Cats	Y	Y	Y				HBO
Chained for Life	Y	Y	Y				
Color Out of Space	Y	Y	Y				Hoopla, Shudder
Coma	Y	Y	Y				
Come to Daddy	Y	Y	Y	Y			
Dead Dicks	Y	Y	Y				
Dead Ones, The	Y	Y	Y				
Death of Dick Long, The	Y	Y	Y				Hoopla, Kanopy
Deerskin	Y	Y	Y				HBO
Disappearance at Clifton Hill	Y		Y				Hulu
Dreamland	Y			Y			

MOVIE	DVD	Blu-Ray	VOD	Amazon Prime (Free)	Netflix	Tubi	Other
Fabulous Baron Munchausen, The	Y	Y	Y	Y			Criterion Channel
Gretel & Hansel	Y	Y	Y				Epix
Horse Girl					Y		
I Lost My Body					Y		
I'm Thinking of Ending Things					Y		
Impossible Monsters	Y	Y	Y	Y		Y	
In Fabric	Y	Y	Y				Kanopy
Jesus Shows You the Way to the Highway		Y	Y				
Kinetta	Y	Y	Y				Criterion Channel, Kanopy
Knives and Skin		Y	Y				Hulu
Lake Michigan Monster		Y	Y				
Love Express: The Disappearance of Walerian Borowczyk	Y	Y	Y				
Mad Fox, The		Y					
"Midnight Gospel, The"					Y		
Monos	Y	Y	Y				Hulu
Murder Death Koreatown	Y	Y	Y	Y			
My Hindu Friend	Y	Y		Y		Y	Vudu
Platform, The					Y		
Possessor	Scheduled 12/8	Scheduled 12/8	Y				

MOVIE	DVD	Blu-Ray	VOD	Amazon Prime (Free)	Netflix	Tubi	Other
Psychomagic: A Healing Art	Solo disc scheduled 12/11	Solo disc scheduled 12/11	y				
Queen of Paradis				Y			
Redoubt							Museum screenings only
Scorsese Shorts	Y	Y					Criterion Channel
Seven Stages to Achieve Eternal Bliss			Y	Y			Hulu
Shadowplay	Y		Y			Y	
Shasta Triangle, The			Y				
She Dies Tomorrow	Scheduled 12/8		Y				
She's Allergic to Cats			Y			Y	Vudu
Ship of Human Skin, A	Y	Y	Y	Y			Roku Channel, Hoopla
Sleepless Beauty		Y	Y				
Small Talk							Vimeo (free)
"Solid Metal Nightmares"		Y					
Spindrift's Haunted West	Y		Y				
Suburban Birds	Y	Y	Y				
Synchronic							In theaters at press time
"Third Day, The"							HBO

MOVIE	DVD	Blu-Ray	VOD	Amazon Prime (Free)	Netflix	Tubi	Other
"Three Fantastic Journeys by Karel Zeman"	Y	Y					
Time Warp: The Greatest Cult Films of All Time, Vols. 1-3			Y				
Tommaso	Y	Y	Y				Kanopy
Twentieth Century, The							In theaters at press time
Until the End of the World	Y	Y					Criterion Channel
Vampire Burt's Serenade	Y	Y		Y		Y	
Verotika		Y	Y				Shudder
VHYEs	Y	Y	Y				Hulu
Vivarium	Y	Y	Y	Y			
Wave, The			Y				
We Are Little Zombies	Y	Y	Y				
Welcome to the Circle	Y	Y	Y				
"What Did Jack Do?"					Y		
Wolf House, The	Y		Y				
Why Don't You Just Die!		Y	Y				
"World of Tomorrow Ep. 3"							Vimeo (rental)

www.ingramcontent.com/pod-product-compliance
Lightning Source LLC
Chambersburg PA
CBHW080548220526
45466CB00010B/3076